etry : medieval
861·1

The making of the
Poema de mio Cid

The making of the
Poema de mio Cid

COLIN SMITH

Cambridge University Press

Cambridge

London   New York   New Rochelle
Melbourne   Sydney

Published by the Press Syndicate of the University of Cambridge
The Pitt Building, Trumpington Street, Cambridge CB2 1RP
32 East 57th Street, New York, NY 10022, USA
296 Beaconsfield Parade, Middle Park, Melbourne 3206, Australia

© Cambridge University Press 1983

First published 1983

Printed in Great Britain at the University Press, Cambridge

Library of Congress catalogue card number: 82-14663

British Library cataloguing in publication data
Smith, Colin
The making of the Poema de mio Cid.
1. Cid (Poem) – Authorship
I. Title
861'.1   PQ6373
ISBN 0 521 24992 9

for Jennie, Rebecca, and Jocelyn

(a las sus fijas   en braço' las prendia,
legolas al coraçon   ca mucho las queria)

Contents

Introduction

This is a somewhat bold book. It is the first in which the following proposition is argued: that the *Poema de mio Cid*, composed in or shortly before 1207, was the first epic to be composed in Castilian; that it was in consequence an innovatory and experimental work, in ways apparent in the surviving text; and that it did not depend on any precedents or existing tradition of epic verse in Castilian or other Peninsular language or dialect. This proposition would not have commended itself to most of those of older generations who laboured in the study of the *Poema* and related matters, and it may not commend itself to many today, although I think it may be said that in the past decade opinion among scholars has been moving in a positivist spirit towards at least the tolerance of such a possibility. My own views have moved in the same way. Whereas in 1970, when preparing my edition of the poem for the Clarendon Press (published in 1972; Spanish version, 1976), I made a good many concessions to long-established 'traditional-ist' theory, and some to then recent studies by the 'oralists', it has seemed to me since that a perfectly coherent view could be developed of the *Poema* as a wholly new work of the early thirteenth century, by a single learned author who was not dependent either on an existing epic tradition in Castilian or on earlier vernacular poems about the Cid. In a fragmentary way this view has been adumbrated in articles published since 1972, some of them gathered in translation in my *Estudios cidianos* (Madrid, 1977); these, with still more recent work, form the basis of some chapters of the present book. I hope in it to draw strands together and give a coherent account of how the poet went about his business, with conjectures also about why he wrote as he did.

My approach is simple, based on the text and on comparisons with other texts, and on what we know about the literary culture of the times. It does not depend upon, nor – as is customary – pay tribute to, those theories of epic production which need to

1

postulate long periods of a development which is unrecorded for us. It does not accept the relevance of poetic creation by oral improvisation, which is incapable of proof with respect to medieval epic verse in the Romance languages. In case such statements should seem arrogant, or too dismissive and unfair, I should add that neither traditionalism (now 'neotraditionalism') nor oralism is inherently capable of disproof, and that neither is wrong-headed or grotesque. I accept the traditionality of the Spanish ballad in its evolution from the fourteenth century to the present day, just as I accept the findings of colleagues about oral improvisation in modern Serbo-Croat. Whether the traditionalism of the ballads – involving, certainly, much material which had originated in epic – can be applied to the creation and development of epic in the early medieval centuries, and whether the findings of the oralists in modern Yugoslavia can properly be applied to epic production in early Romance, I take leave to doubt. On the one hand, such theories partake still (despite the ultra-modernity of the methods of the oralists) of a view of the medieval past and of the creative process which is fundamentally Romantic and, in the pejorative sense of the word, *decimonónico*. On the other hand, such theories tax one's credulity and give way before an approach which is both positivist and simpler. That much medieval verse is formulaic, none can deny, but that this proves its orally-improvised nature does not follow. Lively passages and episodes in direct speech in chronicles by no means give proof, for Spanish and for French, as was at one time thought, of their dependence upon numerous lost epic texts. Variations between chronicle accounts of the same heroic story do not necessarily mean that in each case the chronicler was adopting material from the latest reworking of a poem. I repeat: traditionalist and oralist accounts, detailed, scientifically argued and often brilliantly written, may amply convince those disposed to be convinced; but they assume too much; they often complicate what are quite simple matters; and they are, in the last analysis, superfluous. I intend no disrespect to their distinguished exponents, but suggest the need for a clear-sighted view of the small amount of evidence we have.

Lest there should still seem to be some arrogance in this, I must now stress my total humility in the presence of the poet. He was the maker, and all critics, researchers, and literary historians stand very small in his shadow. For reasons given in this book, I call him Per Abad, and regard him as the first major author in Spanish literature. Although I think his work experimental, I mean this in the sense of 'nobly adventurous' rather than that of 'tentative'. His lines have never palled in my many years of working with them. I turn to them constantly with intense pleasure, delight to find each year that new students are excited by them. I find that they spring to mind and are highly quotable, and I feel moved when hearing or reading some new point which has been made about the poet's art. To me Per Abad is one of the great narrative and dramatic poets, and if his work has oddities and even defects inherent in the experimental process, it may be the more approachably human for that. A just appreciation of the poet's art – which, by the way, does not go back much more than some forty years – gives further strength to the approach I have outlined. I do not believe that the haphazard operation of an ancient part-memorised tradition, still less a perpetually renewed improvisation by illiterates, could have produced a work of the fine qualities that we find in the *Poema*. This was, I assert, a *literary* production, conceived in accord with the ideology of a feeling and educated individual, planned and well-rounded, drawing upon sources which the author loved and re-created imaginative-ly, obedient to a special and personal conception of the hero, and made with words carefully chosen and sensitively placed. This poet did not create – no artist does – out of the void. He had his exemplars, for form and style and much detail, in the massively established epic tradition of France, just as, precisely at the same time, Spanish builders of cathedrals and churches and monas-teries were adopting architectural styles from France.

There are, I think, no nationalistic concerns here, and in any case, such concerns would be a backward projection of a modern vice. The often admirable internationalism of the Middle Ages is a healthy training-ground for moderns. However, as will be seen, the question cannot be altogether avoided in even the briefest remarks about how the theory of epic origins evolved in Spain at the end of the nineteenth century and the start of ours. The remarks will concern a noble, if misguided, effort. Nor is there any danger of national passions being provoked by my present approach. Spaniards have, during the 1970s, been oddly muted on the subject. Their regard for D. Ramón Menéndez Pidal (d. 1968) remains of the highest, but they have welcomed open-mindedly the work of non-Spaniards which has rectified and even overturned long-cherished beliefs. The political and social stance of Spain has been, after all, since 1970, one of change and futurity rather than of total conservatism. There is, however, a curious division within the English-speaking world. Hispanic studies in the United States are powerful and, in some aspects of the discipline, outstanding. Not only are some of the best present-day representatives of traditionalism there, but oralist theory was born there and commands the allegiance of many. As a result, Americans have labelled the approach of the present study 'neo-individualist' and have tried to identify it as the expression of a collectivity, presumably subversive, which they call the 'British school'. Such labelling strikes the pragmatic British as an American foible, and is not helpful. I certainly do not write as a member of a school, and cannot cite others in Britain or elsewhere as predisposed to applaud my arguments. So much is this the case that, having enjoyed and benefited from the collaboration of others, I have preferred this time to trouble none of them with a request. There is, finally, the label 'bédiériste' which some have attached to earlier work of mine, again using this in a pejorative sense for one who would subvert the great edifice of traditionalist thought which has stood so long in the main street of Spanish literary history. Perhaps; I have read Bédier and profited from him; but, although admiring him greatly, I retain reservations about some aspects of his work, and remind readers that (although much that is said about France is relevant to Spain) he had – so far as I recall – nothing to say specifically about the origins and development of epic in Spain.

The adherents of traditionalism and oralism can speak for themselves. I am not going to rehearse their views in order to refute them, and this is not a polemical book. The following note provides, in brief form, a guide to the present state of criticism.

Bibliographical note

A balanced survey of trends in scholarly opinion and research on the *Poema* is provided by A. D. Deyermond in the introductory essay 'Tendencies in *Mio Cid* Scholarship, 1943–1973', in the volume which Deyermond edited, '*Mio Cid' Studies* (London, 1977), 13–47. An admirable complement, written from a traditionalist–oralist point of view but concerned to take into account the recent work of scholars of other persuasions, is provided by C. B. Faulhaber in *Romance Philology*, 30 (1976–7), 83–101. A full catalogue and survey of the history of critical opinion is provided by M. Magnotta, *Historia y bibliografía de la crítica sobre el 'Poema de mio Cid' (1750–1971)* (Chapel Hill, 1976); Magnotta, in each section, allows the opinions to speak for themselves but concludes in terms of a simple reassertion of Menéndez Pidal's views, so that the book has to be used with caution and after reading a mildly hostile review such as that of R. M. Walker in *Modern Language Review*, 73 (1978), 666–8. New developments may be studied in the annual volume *The Year's Work in Modern Language Studies* published by the Modern Humanities Research Association.

The classic exposition of traditionalist theory in relation to epic studies is that of Ramón Menéndez Pidal, in numerous works. His great book on the *Poema* is his *Cantar de mio Cid*, 3 volumes (Madrid, 1908–11), containing studies of the MS, the geography, historical and chronistic relations of the poem, its metrics, grammar, and vocabulary, together with indispensable diplomatic and critical texts. It has been republished several times, with 'Adiciones' first added in 1944–6. For texts other than the *Poema* and more on the chronicles, see Pidal's *Reliquias de la poesía épica española* (Madrid, 1951; reprinted in 1980, with an important introductory essay by D. Catalán). Essential essays are gathered in volumes of the Colección Austral: *Castilla, la tradición, el idioma*; *Los godos y la epopeya española*; *De primitiva lírica española y antigua épica*. His most mature and best-documented statement is that to be found in *'La Chanson de Roland' y el neotradicionalismo* (Madrid, 1959; French translation, Paris, 1960). Carmen Conde published a survey of Menéndez Pidal's work (Madrid, 1969), and others appeared after the death of 'the Master' in 1968; of these, the best for our purposes is probably that by Dámaso Alonso, most readily consulted in his *Obras completas*, volume IV (Madrid, 1975). A brief restatement of traditionalist principles is that of S. G. Armistead, 'The *Mocedades de Rodrigo* and Neo-individualist Theory', *Hispanic Review*, 46 (1978), 313–27, with much bibliography (and an odd lapse in condemning moderns for reviving aspects of Bédier's ideas, described as 'aged', even though traditionalist thought is rooted in much older times). I reply in an essay kindly accepted by the same journal.

For the oralist approach one should turn, in addition to the standard expositions of A. B. Lord and others, to the work in the Hispanic field of E. de Chasca, *El arte juglaresco en el 'Cantar de mio Cid'* (2nd edn, Madrid, 1972), and *The Poem of the Cid* (Boston, 1976). The comparative and statistical approach is illustrated by J. J. Duggan, 'Formulaic Diction in the *Cantar de mio Cid* and the Old French Epic', *Forum for Modern Language Studies*, 10 (1974), 260–9, a volume (also published in book form) to which Lord contributed an important restatement. Menéndez Pidal made clear the points on which he differed from oralist theory in respect of Spanish epic: 'Los cantores épicos yugoeslavos y los occidentales. El *Mio Cid* y dos refundidores primitivos', *Boletín de la Real Academia de Buenas Letras de Barcelona*, 31 (1965–6), 195–225. The differences are argued the other way round by de Chasca in his 1976 book.

This said, it is proper to pay tribute to the high quality of the work of British colleagues in recent times. This work retains its independent criterion and is not, I repeat, a contribution to any notional 'British school'. Two studies by Peter Russell in the 1950s have come to be regarded as fundamental, and are gathered, with new work, in his book *Temas de 'La Celestina' y otros estudios (del 'Cid' al 'Quijote')* (Barcelona, 1978). Alan Deyermond's *Epic Poetry and the Clergy: Studies on the 'Mocedades de Rodrigo'* (London, 1969) is a reasoned and documented inquiry into the nature of the poem, with grave implications for our view of the genre as a whole. Several Britons contributed essays to Deyermond's *'Mio Cid' Studies* of 1977. Ian Michael published his edition of the *Poema* at Manchester in 1975, with a fine prose translation by Rita Hamilton and Janet Perry; Michael's text was republished at Madrid in 1976 (2nd edn, 1978), with full introduction, notes, and critical apparatus. His editorial principles are, like mine, strongly conservative, and his contributions to the study of the geography of the poem most valuable. Kenneth Adams (of Dublin) studied the metrics of the poem in 1972, and an aspect of tense-usage which depends on French models, and other important matters, more recently. In 1977 Roger Walker identified a French source for aspects of the Corpes episode. Brian Powell's Ph.D. dissertation 'The *Poema de mio Cid* from the twelfth to the fourteenth century with particular reference to its prose redaction in the *Crónica de veinte reyes*' (1977), is about to be published; I refer to it here, with the author's kind permission. Other excellent work by John Cummins, David Hook, David Pattison, Geoffrey

West, Roger Wright, and recent publications by Deyermond, Russell, etc., will be mentioned in their places. In Spain itself the decade has been relatively unproductive, but three books published there merit mention. A. Ubieto Arteta refashioned older work and added much that was new in *El 'Cantar de mio Cid' y algunos problemas históricos* (Valencia, 1973). Some portions of M. Garci-Gómez's *'Mio Cid': estudios de endocrítica* (Barcelona, 1975) are most valuable, but others are highly idiosyncratic. The same may be said of his edition of the poem (Madrid, 1977), in which dubious things are done to the text. The original and exciting book of M. E. Lacarra (1980a) will occupy me greatly in Chapter 3.

Note on names and texts

The poem bears no title in the MS (the first folio is lost, but it is not sure that this would have stated a title), and there are no references to it in the Middle Ages. The poet calls the second division of his work a *gesta* (l. 1085) and a *cantar* (l. 2276), and might have used either of these words to describe the complete poem. At the end of the MS, after the author's explicit, a presenter of the work added a few lines in which the text is described as a *romanz*, evidently the word which later came to mean 'ballad' (*romance*), but here akin in sense to French *romanz* as in *Florence de Rome* ('Voires de voire estoire issuz est li romanz', l. 20; 'con vos orrez après en cest romanz chanter', l. 3312) or to the usage of the copyist of 'V⁴' of the *Roland*, 'Explicit liber tocius Romani ronciualis ...' The Spanish *Apolonio* poem announces itself as 'hun romance de nueua maestria' (stanza 1c), Berceo calls his *Loores* a 'romance' (232b), and the *Primera Crónica General* mentions 'la estoria del Romanz dell inffant Garçia' (431.a.33). From this it seems that in its time the epic of the Cid might equally well have been known as a *romanz*, this signifying 'long narrative poem'. My impression is that a majority of critics from the eighteenth century to the present day have called the work *Poema de mio Cid*, regardless of the fact that *poema*, a learned word, is not recorded in Spanish until very late, and *poeta* in the *Conde Lucanor* of about 1330, so that an anachronism (with respect to the poet's own day) is certainly being committed. What is perhaps significant is that traditionalists and oralists mostly seem to have settled for *Cantar* as a title, though Menéndez Pidal at different times used both *Cantar* and *Poema* for it. The point is discussed by von Richthofen, Garci-Gómez, and others. I have no strong feelings about it (on a related question, see note 6 to Chapter 1), but have adopted *Poema* consistently because it seems to have majority support, has international cognates, and seems to represent the dignity of the work in the best way.

I quote from my 1972 edition of the poem, recognising that there are things in it I would now wish to do differently. The *Primera Crónica General* is cited from the edition of Menéndez Pidal (2 volumes, Madrid, 1955). I have dispensed with abbreviations which sometimes make for difficult reading, and with asterisks which many use to indicate texts assumed to have existed but no longer extant, since their use can be tendentious.

1   The twelfth-century background

It is plainly not satisfactory simply to assert that the *Poema* was the first Castilian epic or the first long poem of any kind in Spanish. Some argument can be expected in support. Traditionalists and oralists assume that the epic genre was very ancient, though it had doubtless evolved in form and nature from shorter poems up to the lengthy and highly-wrought texts which survive for us. They assume that the historical event which is at the core of the poem and the surviving form of the poem are related as cause and effect, and that the earliest surviving versions – in France, of the twelfth century, and in Spain of the thirteenth – are but late representatives of works which in their earlier stages were not written down at all (the oralist view) or were orally transmitted but may have been written also in texts which are lost (the traditionalist view, which has never wholly excluded writing from the processes of composition and transmission). Traditionalists try to fill the void left by the lack of early texts by reference to non-historical episodes and picturesque details in Latin and, later, vernacular chronicle accounts, assuming these to point not only to the growth of a legend (as many do) but also to the existence of a vernacular poetic text. The most notable example of this effort to fill the void is Menéndez Pidal's brilliant book on the *Roland* (1959), preceded by the corpus of reconstructed Spanish materials in his *Reliquias* of 1951.

There is, however, no firm evidence for France or for Spain which compels us to believe in the existence of full vernacular epics in those countries much before the date which can reasonably be assigned to the earliest surviving texts. These are, in France, the *Chanson de Roland* in its 'Oxford' version of about 1100,[1] and in Spain, the *Poema de mio Cid* of 1207 or a short time before. Since much of this book proceeds by comparison of Spanish with French affairs, we may begin the argument by taking this difference of roughly a century between the dates at

9

which epic established itself in the two countries as a significant one. The cultural time-lag of Spain in comparison with France has been discussed by several scholars (e.g. Curtius, 1953: 541–3; Deyermond, 1971: 55–8). The facts are recognised and the underlying reasons not hard to ascertain. They are in no way discreditable to Spaniards and have nothing to do with shortcomings or indifference on their part.

Visigothic Spain had a literary, legal, and ecclesiastical culture superior to any other in the West, but this was shattered by the Moslem invasion of 711. Visigothic churchmen and court officials took refuge, with their books, in the impoverished circumstances of Asturias and the Pyrenean region, where mere survival was for long the object, or in France, whence they never returned. The author of the *Historia Seminensis* in the twelfth century is clear about the loss. He begins his work by remarking that 'Cum olim Yspania omni liberali doctrina ubertim floreret, ac in ea studio literarum fontem sapientie sitientes passim operam darent, inundata barbarorum fortitudine, studium cum doctrina funditus evanuit.' In Al-Andalus a brilliant culture developed, reaching its zenith in the tenth century and by this time so powerful that literature and writing in Arabic overbore the latinity of the still-strong communities of Mozarab Christians. The fruits of this Arabic culture began to benefit Europe in general when scientific and what one may call high intellectual texts were translated into Latin at Toledo and elsewhere in the twelfth century by the collaborative effort of Moslems, Jews, and Christians, under ecclesiastical patronage; but, as has often been noted, these benefits flowed on from centres of diffusion in France, and the Christian states of the Peninsula were not, in that twelfth century, greatly stimulated by them to scientific or intellectual endeavour. They simply lacked the cultural preparedness which would allow them to respond. In the middle years of the thirteenth century, now under royal patronage, translation of scientific and high intellectual works from Arabic was resumed, and there began the adaptation from Arabic into Castilian of literary works of wisdom and entertainment; from these there did indeed begin to flow a tradition of Castilian prose-writing. Efforts to demonstrate the influence of heroic narrative in Arabic upon emergent Castilian epic have been made but are unconvincing, and the only written evidence for the former in Spain is late (Marcos Marín, 1971; Galmés de Fuentes, 1978).

Culturally and economically impoverished, and perpetually threatened by Moslem incursions, the early Christian states of northern and eastern Spain produced for the literary record no more than a few sparse chronicles in Latin. A Bede or an Alfred is not conceivable there, and although Alfonso II of Asturias had contacts with Charlemagne, any species of 'Carolingian renaissance' could not have happened in his realm.[2] In the tenth and eleventh centuries the story of these states is of endemic warfare, not only against the might of Al-Andalus but also between Christian kingdoms. In the last years of the tenth century Almanzor in regular expeditions devastated León, Galicia, and parts of Castile, not sparing religious centres. It was no time for men to indulge the luxury of sitting with pens or books in their hands. Even in the few monasteries which had some kind of literary life, such as San Millán, Silos, and Cardeña in the tenth century, achievements were fitful rather than great and continuous. After the death of Almanzor in 1002 and the collapse of the Caliphate in 1031 the balance of military power shifted quite rapidly to the Christian side, and good progress was made, above all by the capture of Toledo in 1085. But the resulting threat to the whole of Al-Andalus led the rulers of its petty kingdoms to call in the Almoravids of Africa, who not only checked the Christian advance by inflicting severe defeats on the arms of Alfonso VI but also recovered lost territory (including, eventually, Valencia, earlier taken by the Cid). The rule of Alfonso's daughter Urraca (1109–26) was beset by inter-Christian anarchy and invasion by the Aragonese. The early years of her son, Alfonso VII (1126–57) were spent putting down rebellions by the nobles, and later, expeditions into the south ended with the irruption of the Almohads into the Peninsula (1146). Their stiffening of Moslem resistance was so effective that as late as 1195 they were able to inflict a crushing defeat on Alfonso VIII at Alarcos. Nor were internal Christian affairs in a happier state. Castile and León, united under Alfonso VI from 1072, were again divided on the death of Alfonso VII, and at the time of Alarcos, Leonese troops were fighting on the side of the Moslems and immediately afterwards were raiding deep into Castilian lands adjoining León. In 1212 Alfonso VIII was able to avenge Alarcos. He then had the aid of contingents from other Peninsular kingdoms and of a crusading army from beyond the Pyrenees (in part a rabble, and of doubtful military efficacy), and his victory at Las Navas de

Tolosa laid open the way for the conquest of much of Andalusia in the 1230s and 1240s. The year 1230 brought the final union with León.

After Las Navas, the accession of Fernando III in 1217, and the definitive union with León, Castile entered upon a new and happier phase. But it can be readily appreciated that throughout the twelfth century, that great period of 'renaissance' in France and other countries, military matters had inevitably filled men's minds in much of Spain. The arts of peace, the steady endeavour which is needed for any artistic, intellectual, or literary achievement, the resources which permit literary patronage, the leisure of a public able to encourage and appreciate what artists and intellectuals produce, were simply not allowable over long periods in many areas. Although notable churches were built, military architecture and engineering had the priority. The Church, which in other circumstances would have provided the schooling and would have set spiritual and intellectual goals before its members, was important to the State as a source of finance for campaigns, and for militant leadership in warlike enterprises. The southern French Cluniac Jerónimo, brought to Toledo by its French archbishop in 1096, was sent to become bishop of newly-won Valencia at the side of the Cid; Per Abad in his *Poema* introduces him with the approving comment that 'bien entendido es de letras e mucho acordado' (l. 1290), and indeed one would expect no less of a distinguished Cluniac, but the poet's chief interest was to portray Jerónimo as a fighting bishop on the analogy of Turpin in the Roland story, that is, 'de pie e de cavallo mucho era areziado' (l. 1291). As a plain-spoken Christian of the muscular variety, Jerónimo is, surely, in the poet's creation, an exemplar for priests in the years leading up to the great campaign that culminated at Las Navas in 1212. (It is in almost direct consequence of this portrayal that we find Rodrigo Jiménez de Rada, the young Archbishop of Toledo, who was Navarrese and had trained at the Sorbonne, carrying the Virgin's banner at Las Navas; later in life, in quieter times, he went on to become a distinguished historian.) The *Chronica Adefonsi Imperatoris* of 1147–9 portrays the monarch waging God's battles in a thoroughly Old Testament spirit and involves a lively adaptation of biblical parallels, motifs, and language, but has nothing to say of any artistic or intellectual achievements. Such was the mood of the time. Alfonso VIII was much praised by Provençal poets who visited his court and was famed for his generosity, and his Plantagenet wife Leonor would certainly have had literary and musical tastes; but for every *maravedí* spent in these ways one feels that thousands must have gone to military equipment, stores, and the costs of campaigning. There can have been little surplus wealth for cultural pursuits.

Had the needs of warfare not conditioned life in this way, the Christian kingdoms in the twelfth century could well have shared in the benefits of the cultural influences flowing strongly from France. Spain had not received that vigorous injection of Norman blood which transformed France and eventually England, and it did not have a region like Provence in which, in noble courts and in settled conditions, a brilliant aristocratic culture could flourish. Yet northern Spain did receive a huge influx of pilgrims along the road which led from the Pyrenees to Compostela, the *via francigena* or *camino francés* to the supposed tomb of St James, and in the twelfth century, after the road had been put in order in the eleventh with staging-posts and bridges and hospitals (and even, in the mid-twelfth, its guide-book), that pilgrimage was at its height. The stimulation to literary and musical activity in Compostela and elsewhere in Galicia and in the young kingdom of Portugal was considerable. Diego Gelmírez, Bishop and eventually Archbishop of Compostela from 1100 to 1140, included literary enterprises as part of his unscrupulous but brilliantly successful campaign to make his see – and this is no mere metaphor – the Rome of the West, and probably not the least of his claims to be remembered is that he brought from France a master to teach the *trivium* and maintain a cathedral school. In Castile, León, and Navarre, any loss of population caused by war, or by the movement of people to the frontier areas as settlers, was balanced by the establishment, in towns all along the pilgrim road, of whole streets and quarters of *francos* (that is, 'foreigners in general', but mostly French). The benefits to Spain in terms of new blood and new skills must have been great. Still visible today at many points along the road and near it are the cathedrals, churches, and monastic buildings in Romanesque and later styles which were built by French craftsmen for Spanish patrons, or by native craftsmen who had learned from the French. These, one could say, were the admirable consequences in stone of the pilgrimage and its accompanying spirituality. Of literature in the vernacular there is, during the twelfth century, no corresponding consequence visible or to be hypothesised, though one may suppose that French priests, lawyers, and other literate people travelled with a certain literary culture, and even though it is sure that literate people from France made both their Latin and their vernacular texts known in Spain during the century. It is likely too that French *jongleurs*, travelling with their compatriots along the road and settling among the *francos*, would have made the *chansons de geste* known, together with other materials such as lyrics and saints' lives. I shall return to these matters. For the moment, it may be concluded that despite stimulation from beyond the Pyrenees, Spain during most of the twelfth century was not ready to begin a serious vernacular literary culture.[3]

It is hard to know what to make of the abundant evidence for the presence of Provençal troubadours at the courts of Peninsular rulers throughout the twelfth century and, of course, the thirteenth. One would expect to find them in Catalonia and Aragón, but their assiduity in attending upon Alfonso VIII is more remarkable; according to the evidence summarised by Alvar (1977: 75–133), eighteen poets had some relation with him, and of these at least eight visited his court. Certain nobles of his entourage were patrons too, and the Languedoc poets were known in the court of Alfonso IX of León at the same time. Yet there seems to have been no encouragement in this for the composition of lyric and other forms in Castilian or Leonese. The courts appreciated Provençal song and verse in their original language, just as the later lyric production of Castile was to be dominated by the conventional use of Galician dialect. The only vernacular poet of twelfth-century Castile known to us by name, Gonzalo Ruiz, presumably wrote in Provençal (Alvar, 1977: 151–3).

Another powerful cultural influence from France was ecclesiastical, that of the reformed Benedictines from the Abbey of Cluny and other centres, who began to figure prominently in Spain in the closing decades of the eleventh century. This penetration depended on the energetic support of the monarchs, from Fernando I (d. 1065) onward. Cluniac influence was paramount under Alfonso VI. Under Cluniac guidance and in accordance with the royal wish for a measure of europeanisation, the standard Roman liturgy replaced the ancient Mozarabic one (1080), and in the royal chancery and in many of the monastic scriptoria, the Carolingian hand displaced the Visigothic one. The Cluniacs were educated to a standard then uncommon among other orders, joining administrative skills and legal expertise to good latinity and, perhaps, a higher sense of spiritual mission. On conquering Toledo in 1085, Alfonso VI appointed as its first archbishop the French Cluniac Bernard de Sédirac; there were other French clergy in his train, and on returning from Rome in 1096 through France, Bernard recruited others, including Jerónimo, Bishop of Valencia and later of Salamanca and Zamora. From about 1100 one finds numerous other Cluniacs ruling Spanish sees and in other positions of power. Already the Cluniac take-over of important monasteries had begun, sometimes against the fierce resistance of native Benedictines, as at Sahagún in 1078 and Cardeña in 1144. There is no question but that as a result of Cluniac activities the quality of Latin written in the Peninsula, in both legal and literary texts, improved greatly, but there is no hint that this stimulated any imitation in the vernacular. It is also notable that the stylistic resources of the historians, in Latin, were enriched under Cluniac education and by new library resources, for writers borrowed much not only from the Bible and from patristic texts, but also from the classics known to them in the standard *curriculum*. The Pope (Gregory VII) had after all advised Alfonso VI that in his choice of a man for the see of Toledo he should seek someone with 'litteralis scientiae peritia' in addition to 'religio et doctrina', and of the men that Bernard brought to Spain, Jiménez de Rada wrote 'Hos inquam praedictos viros litteratos, providos, et honestos Primas Bernardus per Gallias transiens, in Hispaniam secum duxit' (*De rebus Hispaniae*, VI.27), the adjective *litteratos* having pride of place. Several of the twelfth-century Latin products of Spain are the work of French Cluniacs. The *Chronica Adefonsi Imperatoris* with the *Poema de Almeria* is probably the work of Arnault, Bishop of Astorga, who was French. The *Chronica Najerensis* was produced at the Cluniac house of Santa María de Nájera by a Frenchman. The *Historia Compostelana*, which terminates in 1139, was in part the work of its inspirer, Diego Gelmírez, but he had five collaborators of whom two were French, two Spanish, and one might have been either.

Anything that the Cluniacs achieved in their own monasteries or in an already very learned Toledo did not necessarily find a response in other orders or among secular clergy, still less among laymen. We know of cathedral schools in Toledo, Santiago, Salamanca, León, Palencia, and Sigüenza, but not with certainty of any others. The general impression is one of isolated Cluniac achievements and of a rare product by a native (e.g. the *Historia Seminensis*), but also of general and great cultural poverty. Not until the middle years of Alfonso VIII of Castile can one begin to note signs of improvement, with *magistri* (educated abroad, since no Peninsular body awarded the title) being attested frequently, some in teaching capacities, and Spaniards going to study in France and northern Italy, their main objective being training in new-found Roman law and in canon law. In about 1210 the foundation of the schools of Palencia, the teaching staff for which was largely brought from France (although theology had been taught in Palencia from at least 1184), brought immediate consequences for both standards of learning and vernacular literature, since the verse genre known as the *mester de clerecía* seems to have been invented there, perhaps about 1220. An important stimulus to church learning and to the provision of improving literature in the vernacular came with the dispositions of the Fourth Lateran Council of 1215, even though other of the dispositions for long had little effect in Castile–León because so much effort was put by the Church into organising and settling the large area of Andalusia conquered by the Christian armies after 1212.[4]

Even Latin literary culture in most parts of twelfth-century Spain was sporadic and undistinguished when compared with the products of France, Britain, and even Germany. There is nothing from Spain to equal in scope and quality such works as William of Malmesbury's *Historia* or Ordericus Vitalis's *Historia ecclesiastica*, nothing of a verve and influence comparable with Geoffrey of Monmouth's *Historia regum Britanniae* (even if this, as recently proposed, was part-parodic and ironic in intention), nothing to set beside the rich crusading literature in prose and verse. Only the *Codex Calixtinus*, including the *Liber Sancti Jacobi*, was to have vast international repercussions, but in this the canons of Compostela seem to have been no more than contributors to what was largely an enterprise of French Cluniacs. Even the tradition of saints' lives, already so rich in other countries in both Latin and the vernacular, was weaker in Spain, and the same is true of all manner of theological and ecclesiastical writing. Nor do we find in Spain outside Catalonia any trace of the Latin lyric of the kind that was flourishing elsewhere.[5] One may suppose the loss of some texts, but the impression hardly changes. What thin tradition of historiography existed seems to have been known to and exploited by the monastic authors of the *Historia Seminensis* and *Chronica Najerensis*.[6] The former uses Isidore, the *Chronica* of Alfonso III, the *Chronica Albeldensis*, Sampiro, some annals, possibly one or two Arabic histories, and for stylistic adornment the Bible, certain of the classics (notably Sallust), and Einhard. The *Najerensis* uses most of existing historiography, by then including the *Seminensis*, and one or two minor lost texts. Clearly a good monastic library of the period provided resources which enabled reasonably complete surveys of Spanish affairs, beginning in the Gothic period, to be composed, although the coverage was patchy; and the training of monks, especially in France among the Cluniacs but also in Spain (the author of the *Seminensis* seems to have trained in a monastery of León[7]), enabled a few to write in fair, lively, and at times quite ambitious Latin. Both works were copied and circulated, and were used by later historians; but neither is a masterpiece and neither had any influence outside its country of origin. I reserve for separate consideration the twelfth-century writings about the Cid.

Linguistic considerations might at first glance seem to have favoured the early emergence of a vernacular literature in Castile-León. The quality of Latin written in legal documents of the tenth and eleventh centuries is often appalling, even the standard formulae degenerating towards Romance forms. During this time we know virtually nothing about the operations of lawyers working for the crown or for nobles, nor about the issue and keeping of records by the monasteries, but it is plain that native standards of education were extremely low. Throughout this time, however, Latin of a sort continued to be the sole language of literacy, and the rare attempts to write words and phrases in the vernacular show how hard it was to escape from the tradition of even a defective latinity (e.g. 'Facanos Deus omnipotes tal serbitio fere ...' in the *Glosas Emilianenses*). Although in the twelfth century the Cluniacs established better standards for use in literary works, the notaries and scribes who wrote legal diplomas went on cheerfully, for the most part, in the old ways. When legal documents did begin to be redacted in Romance, one reason was evidently to avoid the embarrassment of writing bad Latin. The other, more positive, was naturally to give all concerned the opportunity of understanding what was being enacted (see further below, p. 81). The town charters (*fueros*) were at first in Latin, but bilingual versions including Latin and vernacular texts seem to have been produced quite early, as at Avilés perhaps soon after 1155,[8] in part because judges could not read Latin in all cases (and in some instances could not read at all[9]); eventually Romance became the norm for all such charters. Royal and national codes adopted Romance during the thirteenth century. The Visigothic *Forum Judicum* of León was translated into Castilian by royal order in about 1220, and the great reforming codes of Alfonso X were written in Castilian from the start in a wholly new spirit of being addressed to all the people. In more ordinary usage one finds Romance used in the record of a 'Pesquisa sobre los términos de Ledigos' drawn up at Carrión in 1194, and in another record of an inquiry about the estates of Oña in about 1202; this was natural enough, because the record consisted of the direct testimony of those concerned, though similar documents earlier had been set down in Latin after the local people had presumably testified in the vernacular. Castilian seems to have been used for the first time at top level for the peace-treaty of Cabreros, 26 March 1206, between Castile and León. Official encouragement for the use of Romance in all legal documents came with the change of personnel in the royal chancery of Castile in 1217, when Fernando III came to the throne and the old chancellor, Diego García, was replaced.

The factors discussed – the military situation, the relative poverty of the Latin tradition in both literary and other writings, the dearth of educational facilities – appear to unite to make of the twelfth century something of a cultural desert in Castile and León, with notable but infrequent green oases such as Toledo and Compostela. In contrast, the middle years of Alfonso VIII and the early decades of the thirteenth century brought the beginnings of cultural renewal, of which literary and juridical writing in the vernacular were a part. Literature is on the whole made from other literature; models feed the imagination and create a wish to imitate and perhaps outdo. When the literature has come from outside – from another country, France, or in another language, French or Latin – the challenge to the imitator calls forth exceptional powers. Spain seems to have been fortunate in the individuals who responded to the challenge, for their work is in several instances excellent and in no way merely a muted echo of what they found in their models. We find the native spirit already strongly present in such early writing. There is no reason to place the earliest vernacular texts of Castile and adjoining regions much, or indeed at all, before 1200. The *Auto de los reyes magos* is of that time. Its modest 147 lines made available in the vernacular what had presumably been spoken earlier in Latin, and 'It is probable that the author was a Gascon priest who settled in Toledo, like so many Frenchmen of that period, and wrote the *Auto* for the Epiphany services there' (Deyermond, 1971: 208–9). The *Disputa del alma y el cuerpo* seems to have been composed in the early years of the thirteenth century on a French model, initiating the genre of the 'debate' poem; the text is copied in an Oña manuscript. Partly in the same tradition is the delightful love-narrative known as the *Razón d'amor*, probably of the middle years of the thirteenth century, which draws upon the tradition of Galician–Portuguese lyric and leads into a second (though perhaps primary) part, the *Denuestos del agua y el vino*, another debate formed on some text in the *Denudata veritate* category. The *mester de clerecía* genre of non-epic narrative verse was begun by Gonzalo de Berceo, priest and notary of La Rioja, who in addition to his recognised corpus of religious verse was possibly – now in the view of some – the author of the *Libro de Alexandre*. His first work may date from about 1220. The *Alexandre* has important sources in Latin and French, most notably the *Alexandreis* of Walter of Châtillon (about 1180), which was widely used as a school text for instruction in Latin and rhetoric. The verse-form of *cuaderna vía* in which all these works are written was adapted from the French alexandrine with influence also from a medieval Latin model. The best reasoning about the origin of both form and matter is that they were devised together at the young university of Palencia by Berceo or the author of the *Alexandre* (who may be the same person), under the guidance of the *magistri* who had come, with their books and their Latin and their rhetoric, from France. The classically-minded *Alexandre* was then a direct product of the schools, and the religious poems of Berceo were both that and also a response to the directives of the Fourth Lateran Council, doubtless under the patronage of ecclesiastical superiors in monastery or diocese. The study, within an organised course, of the Latin *auctoritates* as models, and of Latin rhetoric both within itself and as a system which could be adapted to the vernacular, is a fact of high importance in the creation of the new verse literature.[10]

The lyric is in a special class. Unquestionably, people have always sung, with varying emphasis and competence, about love, spring, absence, homeland, work, drink, death, and much else. The concern of the medievalist is in part to determine when and how a tradition of popular song achieved literary status by leading professional musicians and literate poets to take an interest in it to the extent of adapting its modes and sentiments in new, more polished compositions, and by leading courtly patrons and public to form an appreciative audience. In Castile and much of León, apparently, that moment did not come until very late, in part because the literate adopted the modes of Galician lyric as their own for this purpose (much as conventional mid-Atlantic English is internationally the language of the modern pop-song), and in part because any native tradition of lyric was not such as to command the attention of musicians and scribes for a long time; also, perhaps, because royal and noble courts were not inclined to adopt such fashions until (so far as we know) the late fifteenth century. In Aragón and Catalonia in the later twelfth and thirteenth centuries the lyric of Provence, and its purveyors in person, held sway. Only in Galicia and in what became (after 1139) the kingdom of Portugal was a popular tradition of lyric and perhaps of dance taken up by literate poets and musicians, who produced, from the late twelfth into the fourteenth century, a very splendid school of poetry. Within it, strong native habits such as the distinctive parallelistic structures of the *cantigas d'amigo* can be recognised as prime features. Whether such intensive cultivation, eventually by royalty itself (Don Dinis of Portugal, 1261–1325), would have occurred without stimulation from Provence, is doubtful. The exceptional importance of foreign pilgrims and visitors to Compostela in the twelfth century, and elsewhere along the pilgrim road, has been mentioned above. Clearly there and in other parts of Galicia and Portugal, but not in Navarre or Castile or eastern parts of León, the native tradition of lyric (with its music, and possibly dance) was apt for a singularly productive marriage with the courtly sensibilities of Provence, or at least patrons were forthcoming to act as sponsors at such a marriage. The Galician and Portuguese poems of the three great fifteenth-century *cancioneiros* are for the

most part attributed to named authors, the earliest of them being
João Soares de Paiva who was born in 1141, so that a date towards
the end of the twelfth century for the emergence of the new
school seems appropriate. Uncertainty about the status of the
Mozarabic *kharjas* makes it wise to exclude them from discussion
for the moment.[11]

Much has been written on the mingling of courtly or learned
and popular elements in lyric, and the question is important for
our study of epic. In recent years the tendency has been, rightly,
to blur the once-rigid lines of demarcation and to recognise that
many kinds of verse and other writing draw elements from both
learned and popular sources, or better, from sources that we can
ultimately (perhaps rather remotely) define by such terms. One
man is a blend of all that he has seen and heard and felt: if priests
and notaries and other literate persons hum pop-songs to
themselves and eventually write them down, or compose new
songs partly in conformity with others, then part-literate or
illiterate minstrels will adopt elements from renditions of learned
material offered to them by public reading or performance, and
will learn new musical modes imported from abroad. Folk-motifs
belong not to the 'folk' in a restricted sense, but to all people both
literate and illiterate, just as patterns of myth are present in all
minds. A good recent study of the *Razón d'amor* develops this
middle view: 'With its complex architecture and subtle echoes of
popular verse, the *Razón* confirms the inseparability of the
popular and *culto* traditions in poetry and points significantly to
the popular origins of all cultured verse' (Van Antwerp, 1978–9:
4). This is amply demonstrated in detail. One must add,
however, that the *Razón* is joined to the indisputably learned
debate between Water and Wine (which here have allegorical
extensions, perhaps even Cathar significance), and that one must
not neglect the way in which the poet–protagonist of the *Razón*
introduces himself, as 'un escolar' who has lived long in
Germany, France, and Lombardy, 'pora aprender cortesia',
surely an insistence not only on his apprenticeship in courtly
varieties of love but also on his serious poetic standing. Whatever
features have been drawn from the tradition of popular song –
and they are numerous, as can be documented from later records
of 'poesía de tipo tradicional' – they have all been moulded by the
superior sensibility of an educated poet and set down in a written
composition; and writing, in the twelfth and thirteenth centuries

and for long after, was a learned act performed by a small minority of the cultured.

In vernacular prose of any pretensions, nothing is found before 1200. The *Fazienda de ultramar* combines historical information of the guide-book type with Old Testament materials (drawn not from the Vulgate but from a twelfth-century Latin version of the Hebrew text) for the use of pilgrims to the Holy Land in crusading days, and seems to be a translation of a work originally produced in Latin for 'Remont ... arçobispo de Toledo', the Frenchman who held the see from 1126 to 1152. The translation is probably of early thirteenth-century date; it is not a question of an original composition in the vernacular of the years before 1152, as its first editor thought when publishing the newly-discovered text in 1965. This *Fazienda* is the forerunner of other ambitious translations of the Bible in the thirteenth century. In about 1223 there was composed a *Semejança del mundo*, a vernacular version of materials largely derived from Isidore which, in the same way as the *Fazienda*, looks ahead to more ambitious scientific compilations and translations in the vernacular undertaken by and for Alfonso X (1252–84). Castilian prose thus began, naturally enough, by translating and adapting materials from great authorities, and Alfonso X powerfully continued this, adding many other sources, including Arabic ones.

In historical writing the vernacular may have made a slightly earlier start. The model here was not the full histories of the eleventh and twelfth centuries such as the *Chronica* of Pelayo of Oviedo or the *Historia Seminensis*, but annals of the kind common in Carolingian France and the middle years of Anglo-Saxon England, in which important events – including the failure of crops and the appearance of comets – were recorded in brief form. Some of the monasteries and episcopal centres kept these, in Latin, later in the vernacular (the *Cronicón* of Cardeña, known to us in its redaction of 1327, has this form). At the end of some MSS of the *Fuero general de Navarra* is copied a group of annals in Navarrese dialect concerned with the ancient world and another related to the *Anales toledanos primeros*, on Toledan and Navarro–Aragonese affairs, together with a set of Latin annals entirely about Navarre. There is also a genealogical work in Navarrese, the *Linaje de los reyes de España*, and a *Linaje de Rodrigo Díaz el Campeador*, which I shall discuss later. Of this group of annals and genealogies the earliest in redaction is that on the Cid, for in it

King Sancho of Navarre is referred to as still living, and the text must therefore have been written before 1194, when he died. As a collection, these texts seem to have been written in a MS of the *Fuero* between 1205 and 1209. The Aragonese *Liber regum* or (better) *Cronicón villarense* is something more than a set of annals but less than a full history; it is to be dated between 1194 and 1211, and a Castilian version was made of it about 1200. Use of Navarrese dialect, of Aragonese, and of Castilian in the *Anales toledanos*, also in the early years of the thirteenth century, did not immediately lead to the use of the vernaculars for what one may call mainstream historical writing, since the use of Latin was continued by Lucas de Tuy in his *Chronicon mundi* of 1236 and by Rodrigo Jiménez de Rada in all his historical works; but these were, of course, highly-trained churchmen, and in the scope of their works they went far beyond the annals written for a local purpose.

These arguments will not impress traditionalists and oralists with regard to epic. To them, statements about *literary*, that is *written* texts, their precise dates, the cultured Latin tradition, and so on, are irrelevant, since according to their ideas epic as we know it in French and Spanish was the product of illiterate minstrels (although, as noted earlier, traditionalists have reservations about the need to suppose absolute illiteracy throughout), and had already had, by the twelfth century, a long period of cultivation in forms unrecorded for us, its stories and materials stemming, ever-evolving, from the time of the historical events on which it was based. Traditionalists could, indeed, reason that the very weakness of the Latin tradition in most of Spain, and the inadequacy of the Latin used for all purposes, would *per contra* have stimulated literary production in the vernaculars at an early date. Yet, just as I have argued that no vernacular literature in other genres can be dated to much before 1200, in Spain, so I argue the same for epic, in proceeding towards my proposition that the *Poema de mio Cid* of 1207 was the first work of its kind in Castilian. By 'of its kind' I mean an extensive, highly-wrought and well-rounded product, a *cantar de gesta* of the same species as the *chansons de geste*. Whether there existed earlier more modest poems of a heroic tone, out of which the full *cantar de gesta* in some fashion grew, will be seen in due course.

A prime text for those who believe that the Castilian epic genre existed in, and perhaps long before, the twelfth century is the

Chronica Najerensis, which they think contains materials drawn from a number of vernacular epics. Before we can consider the nature of these materials, some discussion of the date of the work is needed. Ubieto's conclusion (1966) that the chronicle is the work of a monk of the Abbey of Santa María de Nájera, in La Rioja, a region ruled in the twelfth century variously by Castile and Navarre, and by Castile definitively from 1176, is fully acceptable. The monk used certain phrases from an *Epitome vitae Sancti Hugonis* well-known in Cluniac circles, and the monastery had been Cluniac since 1079. The author has details of French history not likely to be known to a Spaniard, and in contrast is inaccurate in some details of the Spanish kingdoms; he was therefore in all likelihood French. Nájera was on the *camino francés* and an important centre. Its monastery was a distinguished one with a good library, and the author of the chronicle supplemented his information quite widely by making inquiries of, or visiting, other monasteries. As for the date of his work, the chronicle formally concludes with the death of Alfonso VI in 1109, but has references of a later kind, for example to the death of Princess Sancha, daughter of Queen Urraca of Castile–León, who according to the chronicle died in 1152 but in view of an inscription really died in 1159. That the chronicler mentions the Emperor Alfonso VII without recording his death (1157) is hardly significant, since his reign does not figure in the formal structure of the work and the only mention of him (III.56) is brief and in a purely genealogical context. Cirot, the first editor of the text, thought it of about 1160, and Menéndez Pidal in 1923 adopted this, the dating being widely accepted on his authority. However, the author's error about Princess Sancha may mean that he was writing somewhat later than 1160. More recently, doubt has been cast upon a related dating, that of the *Historia Seminensis*, a major source for the *Najerensis*. The *Seminensis* was put by Menéndez Pidal and others at about 1110, since the last obviously datable reference in it is to the death of Alfonso VI in 1109. The text is placed by the editors of its 1959 edition in the second decade of the twelfth century. However, C. Sánchez-Albornoz thought that it was composed 'avanzado el siglo XII', and in 1976 C. Linaje Conde argued that it belongs to the second half of the century, which would make the *Najerensis* later still, perhaps bringing it to a date not far short of 1200.[12] The *Seminensis* shows no possible use of sources in epic, and even if the *Najerensis* does, its value as testimony to the existence of a full epic genre at an early date is reduced. The basic study of materials in the *Najerensis* which putatively derive from epics is that of Menéndez Pidal (1923: 330–52). Earlier, Cirot marked such passages in his edition with special type. In order, these vernacular poems are: *Fernán González, Condesa traidora, Infante García, Los hijos del rey Sancho de Navarra,* and *Sancho el fuerte.* To these an enthusiastic supporter, Salvador Martínez, has added four further themes present in the chronicle and supposed by some to derive from epics, these preceding in chronology the earliest listed by Pidal: *Covadonga, Abdicación de Alfonso el Magno, Condes de Castilla rebeldes,* and *Los jueces de Castilla,* together, perhaps, with materials derived from a French *Chanson de Roland* or a Spanish *Roncesvalles.*[13] Most of these additions to Pidal's canon can be dismissed as not meriting comment, since the sources of the unhistorical or picturesque details are known to us and are not in vernacular epic. *Covadonga,* which Pidal in another publication (1951: xxxi–ii and 22–6) claimed to have been the theme of an early epic or vernacular poem, nearly contemporary with the date assigned to this pseudohistorical event (718 or 722), is perhaps worth more attention. The spirited narrative of this first successful action against the Moslems was taken by the *Najerensis* (II.7) from the *Chronica* of Alfonso III, and is an inspired tissue of biblical phraseology and ecclesiastical myth whose sources were in part indicated by García Villada in his edition of the *Crónica de Alfonso III* of 1918, more fully by Sánchez-Albornoz (1957; 1967: 172–83), and again by Dr G. R. West.[14] Certainly the Covadonga passage stands out by reason of its style from the generality of materials in these chronicles, both in its details and in its use of dialogue. But the dialogue is plainly biblical in origin, since, for example, the exchange '"Pelagi, Pelagi, ubi es?" Qui ex fenestra respondens ait: "Adsum"' corresponds to 1 Samuel 3.4 and 10, and in a later reply Pelayo directly quotes Matthew 13.31, introducing this by saying 'Non legisti in Scripturis diuinis quia . . . ?' There is a treacherous bishop, Oppa, while Pelayo fights for the Church. David is cited directly. The miracle of the sling-shots of the Moslems being turned back upon the attackers repeats the miracle of the arrows in the legend of Saints Cosme and Damian, well-known in the Mozarabic liturgical cycle. The biblical source of the final cataclysmic miracle is acknowledged in the text: 'Non

istud inane aut fabulosum putetis, sed recordamini quia qui
Rubri maris fluenta ad transitum filiorum Israhel aparuit, ipse
hos arabes, persequentes ecclesiam Domini, immensa montis
mole oppresit.' When the same story appears in the *Seminensis*, it
is further adorned with phrases from Sallust: 'The narration of
incidents that took place in medieval Spain in the language of a
Roman historian is characteristic of a literary, not a historical
endeavour' (West, 1975: 206). Indeed; and the original Covadonga narrative is characteristic of ecclesiastical writing of the
inspirational kind, having little to do with historiography and
nothing to do with vernacular epic or heroic chant. That the
people of Asturias–León in the early centuries needed to be
encouraged in their resolve by such flattering parallels with the
Israelites, by the promise of miraculous aid, and by the dignity of
biblical phraseology, is natural. That good modern scholars
should be so far deceived about the nature of this text is
extraordinary. I have dealt with it at some length because this
self-deception is crucial. Menéndez Pidal used the purely notional
epics about Roderick, last King of the Goths, and Covadonga, to
help him demonstrate the great antiquity of Hispanic vernacular
epic and thence, of course, its links with an even older heroic
poetry in Gothic, thus further confirming his views about the
essential 'germanism' of medieval Romance epic; and there was
more than a hint that by using standard traditionalist theory the
other way round, it could be shown from the existence of such
epics that there was a measure of historical truth at the base of
such literary legends as that of Covadonga. In this instance as in
others, when a text is inspected coolly, all becomes reasonably
clear, and the vast multi-storeyed edifice of traditionalist theory
and supposition recedes into a misty Romantic limbo.

The theme of Fernán González appears at some length in the
Najerensis. Genuinely historical information about him in two
sections, II.52 and II.56, is drawn from the chronicle of Sampiro
(composed about the year 1000). In II.58 there is briefly told the
story of how the Count was captured by the King of Navarre and
imprisoned, with his sons, 'in Cironia, in ecclesia Sancti Andree
apostoli ... et transmissus Pampilonie, inde Clauillum inde
Tubiam' (which may be historical enough); then, 'unde cum
Sanctia eiusdem regis Garsee sorore, que prius Ordonii regis
Legionis, postea comitis Albari Harrameliz de Alaua extiterat
uxor, habens nesciente fratre colloquium liberatus est dato prius

eidem sacramento, quod si eum inde educeret, eam duceret in uxorem. Quod et fecit'. Mention of the church and the genealogical details suggest a learned source, and indeed the chronicler probably had here some source also used a little later by the *Anales compostelanos*. The tale of how the King's sister freed the noble prisoner under promise of marriage is attributed by Ubieto to a Navarrese legend, and one can well believe that it was a matter of established belief in Navarre and hence of the chronicler; for the Navarrese, it may have been important that their King's sister, pseudohistorically, freed and married the Count who (as the chronicler elsewhere records) liberated Castile from the overlordship of León and secured its independence. But the motif of the noble prisoner freed in this fashion, by an enamoured princess who is a relative of the ruler, or the daughter of the jailer, etc., is very ancient and widespread and has analogues going back to classical antiquity, as has been shown (Cotrait, 1977: 64–5), the likeliest source for it in Navarre in the late twelfth century being one of the French epics in which a Saracen princess falls in love with, and frees, a noble Christian captive, fleeing with him and sometimes marrying him (after due conversion).[15] Fernán González later achieved the honours of a full epic, of ecclesiastical inspiration and tone, after 1264, composed in the monastery of Arlanza where he was buried, and there may have been an epic *cantar* about him; but the *Najerensis*'s account is derived from sources other than such a poem.

Elements of the *Condesa traidora* story appear first recorded for us in the *Najerensis* (II.80, II.85, III.4). It concerns Count García Fernández (ruled 970–95), his treacherous wives, and the manner of his death. That there was eventually a substantial legend in literary form cannot be doubted, for it is present in the chronicles of the thirteenth century. However, it may be doubted whether it was even then in the form of epic verse, for as Chalon remarks, 'Creo que la prosificación que de él hace la crónica alfonsina no procede de un poema épico perdido, sino que está mucho más cerca del género novelesco. No se encuentra en él ninguna descripción de combate, tan frecuente en el género épico. No ha dejado ninguna huella en el Romancero. Presenta un aspecto moralizador evidente. Y, por último, no se descubre ninguna huella de asonancias en estos capítulos de la crónica' (1978*a*: 156; with a summary of views of Guerrieri Crocetti on the same question in Chalon, 1976: 529–31). The fact that the Count's first wife is named Argentina, unknown in the Peninsula but present in French romance (*Argentine*), together with the mention of the French shrine of Rocamadour, have suggested to some a source there for parts of the story as it developed in the thirteenth century; but equally, special interests of the monastery of Cardeña may be involved.[16] For the rest, the tale is quite extraordinarily full of folklore motifs and of literary analogues (Deyermond and Chaplin, 1972: 49–51). Several of these are already present in the short account of the *Najerensis*; one of them, for example, the tale of how the 'Condesa traidora' herself tried to poison her son Sancho but was forced by him to drink the potion, probably derives ultimately from a second-century account by Justinus about Cleopatra of Syria, better known to the Middle Ages in Paulus Diaconus's eighth-century history of the Lombards (where it is told about Queen Rosamunda of Ravenna in 573, repeated by Agnellus of Ravenna in his *Liber pontificalis* of about 834, and recorded again by Godfrey of Viterbo in his *Pantheon* of 1187). From the nature of the references given in the *Najerensis*, the account there derives from monastic sources and is directly related to monasteries, Cardeña and Oña. In ii.80, the chronicle records the manner of García Fernández's death, in battle against the Moors after, through his wife's treachery, his horse had been weakened by being fed on bran, and many of his men had been sent off to enjoy the Christmas festivities at home; and it states the place and precise date of that death, to the day. After the Count's body had been taken to Córdoba and buried there, 'deinde translatus est Caradignam', that is to Cardeña. In iii.4 the *Najerensis* adds that the Count's son Sancho 'Cordobam destruxit, et inde corpus patris sui comitis Garsia Ferrandiz transtulit Caradignam.' This is precisely the kind of material that is likely to be recorded in a monastery's list of obits, the day of the year being necessary because it figured in the list of anniversaries to be celebrated by the abbey. Certainly Cardeña had reason to remember the Count, and he really was buried there.[17] The explanation for his defeat by the Moors and subsequent death is a piece of fiction devised, no doubt also in the monastery, to palliate the defeat and death of a noted ruler. But Oña came into it too, in connection with the poisoning part of the story, given by the *Najerensis* at length in ii.83, for in iii.5 the good works of Count Sancho (son of the 'Condesa traidora') are listed, together with the information that he 'Obiit era Mª Lª Vª. Sepultus apud

Onie Monasterium, quod fecerat', and there is no doubt that he was indeed Oña's secular founder in 1011. Again, a somewhat expanded form of an entry in Oña's book of obits seems to be the chronicler's source, and this was to be expanded further in the thirteenth century, since we find in *De rebus Hispaniae* (v. 3) and in the *Primera Crónica General* (Chapter 764, from 454.b.2) that Sancho founded Oña in expiation of the murder of his mother when he forced her to drink the potion; we are also given a charming etymology for Oña ('Mionna' = 'mi señora'). That the *Najerensis* writer received information from Cardeña and Oña, or had personally visited both places and also other ecclesiastical centres, of which he shows special knowledge, cannot be doubted. Oña provided him with a text of the greatest importance, discussed below.

On the theme of the murder of the Infante García, last Count of Castile (1029), there certainly existed in the thirteenth century a *romanz*, for it is so titled by the *Primera Crónica General*. With considerable variations, the story is told also by Lucas de Tuy and Jiménez de Rada. The *Najerensis* (II.90) recounts García's betrothal, the jealousy of the Vela family, and their murder of the young Count and others in León. There is no hint in this very brief account that any literary text is being followed, and what is told is told as sober history. The source of the chronicler's information is not known, but there is no need to suppose a vernacular poem of the twelfth century. Count García was buried either in León or at Oña, for epitaphs (giving different accounts of the murder) existed in both places, and since the *Najerensis* writer was in touch with both, it may be safely assumed that his source(s) came from there. The Oña epitaph has literary pretensions, calling the Count, within its four hexameters, both 'Absalon alter' and 'Mars alter', so that, on the analogy of the Oña epitaph to Sancho II, discussed below, the existence of a short Latin poem in some way related to the epitaph cannot be ruled out.

Evidence that there ever existed a vernacular poem on *Los hijos del rey Sancho de Navarra* (Sancho el Mayor) is thin. The essence of some pseudohistorical text on this theme is certainly present in the *Najerensis* and two later texts, but it is not in the *Primera Crónica General* and is nowhere called a *romanz* or *estoria*. Menéndez Pidal probably realised that in claiming the *Najerensis* used a vernacular poem he had gone beyond any usable evidence, for the further study of the theme which he announced in 1923 was never written. The tale as given in the *Najerensis* (III.10) includes several readily-identified folkloric motifs (a treacherous son, a slandered queen, a bastard as hero, loyalty rewarded), and the brief account ends with the pious note that 'Garsias uero ductus penitentia Romam petit, pro delicto ueniam petiturus.' The purpose of the story was originally, as Menéndez Pidal said, to explain why on the death of Sancho el Mayor in 1035 Castile, taken to be the best part of the kingdom when redivided, went not to the eldest son but to the second, the fictional reasoning being that of a Castilian (in, one might add, the twelfth century rather than the eleventh, for by that time Castile really was the dominant kingdom). Such genealogical interest together with the note about the penitential journey to Rome lead us to an ecclesiastical, not a popular source. Indeed, the *Najerensis*'s paragraph begins with the devil's intervention: 'Instigante namque maligni hostis uersutia ...' We are led yet again to Oña, where Sancho el Mayor was buried; León also claimed his tomb, less probably, and as we have seen, the genealogical argument about the precedence of his sons would have arisen in Castile and not León. The *Najerensis* is firm about Sancho's burial and has a full note derived from Oña: 'Rex autem Santius, in senectute bona, filio eius rege Garsia Romam redeunte, morbo proprio hac vita decessit era Mª LXXª IIIª, quem Ferdinandus apud Oniense monasterium honore debito sepeliuit' (III.11). There can be little doubt that the chronicler received his information, certainly already fictionalised, from that source.

The last case, and the most important, is that of *Sancho el fuerte*. As we find the cycle fully constituted in the *Primera Crónica General*, it is clear that there existed vernacular epics on *El rey don Fernando y la partición de los reinos, Sancho II y el cerco de Zamora*, and the *Jura de Santa Gadea*. The first may have begun its existence as a preliminary section of the work named in second place, and the last may have been an addition to the second, made in order to link it to the *Poema de mio Cid*. All appear as lengthy prose redactions in the *Primera Crónica General* and later chronicles, making a fine connected story which begins with the death of Fernando I in 1065 and his division of the realm, proceeding to the wars of 1072, the death of Sancho II before Zamora, and the accession of his brother Alfonso VI as ruler of reunited Castile–León. The lost epic(s) had high literary qualities, still visible in the prose redaction and in a remarkable series of ballads.

The *Najerensis*'s account of Fernando I's division of his realm in III.25 and of his death, at length, in III.28, are derived from the *Seminensis*. The sources of the short section on the early years of Sancho II, III.29 to III.33, are not known, but were not poetic. The sections from III.34 to III.47 have a strongly literary air. They tell how at a council the night before the battle of Golpejera near Carrión, which was to be fought between Sancho II of Castile and his brother Alfonso of León, the Castilian boasted of his ability to fight against a thousand men but, faced with the Cid's prudently modest comments, progressively reduced his claim; how, in the battle, the Cid rescued his King from fourteen Leonese knights who were taking him away captive (thus answering in practice Sancho's numerical jousting of the night before); how the battle was won and Alfonso captured, and how Alfonso was eventually allowed to leave for exile in Toledo; how an embassy of Sancho's to his sister in Zamora was rejected and how, in the resulting siege, Sancho was treacherously killed by Bellidus Ataulfus who had come out of Zamora and become the King's man; and finally, how the siege was thenceforth raised, and Sancho's body taken to Oña for burial. An equally literary series of sections follows (III.45 to III.47) in which the dealings of Alfonso with his host, Almemon of Toledo, and Alfonso's return to his kingdom, are told at length.

It is certainly the case that the *Najerensis* sections on Sancho II are exceptionally lively and detailed and that a source in a literary text of a non-historiographic kind is to be postulated for them. Two parts must, however, be removed first. III.38 tells how Alfonso, kept in chains by Sancho, who had resisted all appeals from his bishops and magnates to show mercy, succeeded in sending a message to Abbot Hugh of Cluny about his plight; as a result of Hugh's prayers, St Peter appeared to a bishop to assure him that Alfonso would be restored to freedom and power, and a few nights later, St Peter visited Sancho, 'terribiliter apparuit', threatening him with death unless he released his brother – which he instantly did. This spectacular instance of divine intervention is from the *Epitome vitae Sancti Hugonis* of Cluny (where Alfonso was long remembered with affection).[18] The other section is III.44, in part, which gives the date of Sancho's death, the years of his reign, and the statement of his burial at Oña, which is obviously from an Oña source.

The rest, the major part of the *Sancho el fuerte* story, was in the view of Menéndez Pidal in 1923 taken from a vernacular epic, not only in outline, but in parts in much detail too. On the whole this hypothetical early poem as we know it from the *Najerensis* corresponds quite closely to the thirteenth-century poem known to us in the prose redactions of the later chronicles, and this strengthens the hands of those who believe in that early original in vernacular verse: 'Vemos bien establecida así la continuidad de esta poesía tradicional desde el siglo XII al XIV' (Pidal). Yet there is another explanation for the presence of this admittedly heroic material in the *Najerensis*. Already in publishing the text of the chronicle for the first time in 1909, Cirot had drawn attention to the presence in the Sancho II sections of some hexameters and pentameters:

> Le rédacteur de cette chronique a dû avoir sous les yeux quelque poème dans le genre de celui qui est consacré à la prise d'Almería. On pourrait penser que ce sont des lambeaux empruntés à quelque cahier d'expressions comme on pouvait en avoir dans les écoles du temps, . . . Mais les vers en question sont trop adaptés au sujet pour ne pas provenir d'un poème latin où le même sujet était traité. (1909: 263)

In 1923 Pidal could not quite reject the idea of a Latin poem, but he dismissed it as secondary: 'Pudiera haber un poema latino, que sería, en todo caso, inspirado en el vulgar de D. Sancho; pudiera simplemente el tono poético del cantar-romance haber suscitado en el cronista najerense y en el silense [i.e., *Seminensis*], donde también se descubren versos, el deseo de elevar el estilo con recuerdos de Virgilio o de otros poetas' (1923: 347–8, note). The assumption so confidently made in that phrase 'en todo caso' was a large one. In 1928 Entwistle followed Cirot's hint and attempted nothing less than the reconstruction of parts of the lost Latin poem, to which he gave the title *Carmen de morte Sanctii regis*. Taking the licences – indeed, the general metrical roughness – of the *Poema de Almeria* as a guide, Entwistle was able to reconstruct some sixty lines from all sections of the *Najerensis's* account, including continuous passages of twenty-two and twenty-three lines. He did not claim full accuracy for his reconstruction – many words have to be added to the chronicle text, or varied from it, to give even rough hexameters – but was concerned to give the general idea. He was clear, however, that the Latin poem almost certainly concluded with mention of the burial of Sancho at Oña. Rendering the chronicle's phrase 'et ad monasterium Sancti Saluatoris Onnie deferunt tumulandum' by the hexameter '[hoc] que ad coenobium sic defertur tumulandum', he comments that 'Enounced with all the emphasis of its position at the end of the poem, the phrase indicates that the poet's object was to lead up to the mention of the grave and monument at Oña, the most distinguished in the monastery, and one on which important benefactions depended.' This would leave the chronicler to derive only the date from another source in chronicle or annal (and it is in most of them), or from Oña, with which to close his account in III.44, as mentioned above. Entwistle did not attempt to date the *Carmen* precisely, but thought it contemporary with the *Poema de Almeria*, which he knew to be of 1147–9.

Entwistle's text and commentary are very valuable, but he was inevitably so far influenced by the traditionalism universal in Hispanic studies that he deferred to a number of received ideas: that the *Carmen* was 'based on the *Cantar de don Sancho el fuerte o del cerco de Zamora*, but is not a replica of that work', and that the substantial presence of the Cid in the *Najerensis's* account and therefore in the *Carmen* 'is based on the character he gained from his actions in the *Poema de mio Cid*'. Both assumptions were natural when Entwistle wrote, but today can be seen to be unnecessary. Other scholars have continued to believe in the existence of an early *Cantar de Sancho el fuerte* and have added arguments in favour of it: Reig, Fraker, and, perhaps surprisingly, Deyermond.[19] So far as I know, Menéndez Pidal never commented on Entwistle's work; with much else that the latter published in journals, it would be well worth reprinting.

Can the entire content of the *Najerensis* Sancho II account be explained by a putative source in the *Carmen*? By no means; nor is this necessary. Here as in other parts of his work, the chronicler interwove strands drawn from different sources. He did this for the reigns of Fernando I and Alfonso VI, long-lived monarchs great in battle who had so strongly favoured Cluny, and it was natural, since dramatic events and dynastic fortunes were involved, that he should wish to present a detailed and stylish account of Sancho II. Historical works already exploited by the chronicler gave him the outline history of the reign: the division of the realm, Sancho's attack on Alfonso, his victory, the siege of Zamora, the death of Sancho; all this and more is in the *Seminensis* and the *Chronica* of Pelayo. Changes of emphasis, and of more than emphasis, were naturally made. Of Sancho's death the *Seminensis* says merely that he was killed 'dolo', that is 'by a trick' or 'by stealth'. Oña tradition had long since resolved that his death at the hands of Bellido Dolfos was caused not very indirectly by Sancho's sister Urraca, ruler of Zamora, and so recorded it in Sancho's epitaph: 'Femina mente dira, soror, hunc vita expoliavit.' There is no reason to doubt that this epitaph, in four hexameters with further lines of prose, is contemporary with Sancho's death. Leonese reticence about the death, with that vague 'dolo', was naturally maintained by the *Seminensis* writer who resided in León; in Castilian Oña the full burden of guilt could be assigned in the epitaph, maintained in the *Carmen* as reconstructed by Entwistle, and thence adopted with little change by the *Najerensis*. Beyond the chronicle sources known to us and in addition to the partly-reconstructed *Carmen*, the following points about the *Najerensis*'s materials may be noted:

1.   Dramatisation in direct speech in the chronicles, both Latin and vernacular, is often taken to point to a source in vernacular epic (which used direct speech very effectively). This occurs in III.34 (the numerical exchange between Sancho and the Cid), and III.36 (the Cid and the fourteen Leonese knights). But the source is not therefore necessarily in vernacular epic, for as I have said, the technique appears in the Covadonga episode, which is biblical and liturgical in inspiration, and it appears at length in III.24, which concerns the moving of saintly remains and the building of a shrine for them, the church of San Isidoro in León, most of this deriving from the *Seminensis*. Such techniques were well established in miracle stories, saints' lives, and other ecclesiastical writing in Latin.

2.   In III.36 the Cid, in a dramatic encounter, rescues his King from a party of Leonese knights. Several scholars have observed that a similar incident occurs in the *Historia Roderici* (see Chapter 2) where it is told of the Cid in a related context, that of the siege of Zamora: 'Cum uero Santius Zemoram obsederit, tunc fortune casu Rodericus Didaci solus pugnauit cum .XV. militibus ex aduersa parte contra eum pugnantibus: VII. autem ex his erant loricati, quorum unum interfecit, duos uero uulnerauit et in terram prostrauit, omnesque alios robusto animo fugauit' (920.28–921.2). One may suspect that this 'XV' in some other text read 'XIV', since, as Pidal noted in his edition of the *Historia Roderici*, the *Primera Crónica General* in recounting the same Zamoran incident (and here it follows the *Historia Roderici*) says that the Cid 'se fallo con XIIII caualleros' (though the *Crónica de 1344* has 'quinze').[20] A brief version of the same incident, without mention of the number of knights, is found also in the *Linaje de Rodrigo Díaz el Campeador*. Since Entwistle was able to reconstruct twenty-two hexameters forming a continuous section of the *Carmen* about this incident (prose 'post XIIII

Legionenses qui regem Santium captum ducebant' = verse 'regem *ubi* bis septem ducebant legionenses') it appears that this episode which gives the Cid such prominence could derive from Oña materials just as does all that which more properly concerns the Oña hero, King Sancho, alone.

3.   We can now discuss II.34, the numerical exchange between King Sancho and the Cid the night before the battle, in which all have recognised a poetic origin. The numbers in the royal boast involve 1000, 100, 50, 40, 30, 20 and 10 enemy knights, the Cid replying each time that he will be content with a single adversary and that the outcome will be in God's hands. Pidal thought it easy to imagine 'esta gradación desarrollada en coplas, uniformemente terminadas con la fórmula de modestia del Campeador', which is true. But Entwistle, although not venturing to reconstruct hexameters for this passage, comments: 'The chronicler has not preserved the periphrase which are needed to make the Latin numbers metrical, and he has combined in the form of one *oratio obliqua* what were probably about ten lines of stichomythy. One can perceive the form of a hexameter and a half – "nunquam aliud uerbum Roderici extorquere ab ora / [tunc] potuit nisi quod . . . "' Such numerical play is, indeed, not uncommon in medieval Latin texts, with ingenious periphrasis, and there is no need to suppose a source for the *Najerensis*'s episode in vernacular verse. Some link with a source known to us only in an Arabic form may even be suggested in this instance.[21] The prominence of the Cid here and the fact that Sancho appears as a braggart are slightly strange, perhaps, in an Oña poem, but do not lead us to step outside the Oña tradition; the theme that pride comes before a fall may have provided a motive for monkish moralising.

4.   A strong point in Pidal's case for an early vernacular *cantar* was that the sentence in *Najerensis*, III.40, 'Quid mihi faceret extraneus in planis, cum hec mihi frater uterinus faciat in arduis et munitis?', with which Urraca rejects her brother's proposal for an exchange of lands and an end to hostilities, is an echo of a vernacular phrase which appears in the *Crónica de 1344* as ' . . . que quien vos çerca en la peña sacar vos ha de lo llano', a near-proverbial expression plainly taken from a vernacular poem. An echo there certainly is, especially as the *Najerensis*'s text previously mentions the offer of a *concambium* and the vernacular chronicles mention a *cambio*. But why should the Latin of the *Najerensis* (or even of the *Carmen*, though Entwistle remakes no hexameters here) not have the priority? It should be noted that the vernacular version takes only the *peña/llano* contrast from the *in planis/in arduis* phrasing of the Latin, and, moreover, does not really represent the sense of the Latin. It is easier to postulate a vernacular author who did not fully grasp the Latin, than the other way round. Also, even though Entwistle could not make verses here, the *in planis/in arduis*

phrasing strongly suggests the leonine rhyming of a hexameter. I observe in the *Historia Roderici* (943.17) a phrase used in the letter of challenge sent by the Count of Barcelona to the Cid: 'Si autem exieris ad nos in plano et separaberis te a monte tuo ...', which may suggest a standard topic of Latin rhetoric.

5.   It was suggested by von Richthofen that the manner of the killing of King Sancho as recounted in the *Primera Crónica General* and presumably as told in the thirteenth-century epic was an imitation of what appears in the *Nibelungenlied* about the death of Siegfried.[22] This idea, together with other parallels between Hispanic and Germanic stories drawn by this scholar, has not won much acceptance (naturally enough, given traditionalists' belief in the autonomy and early date of Hispanic epic, and in its 'germanism' as a continuation of Gothic ideology within the Peninsula); but the parallel is certainly there, and is even plainer in the story of the *Infantes de Lara*, discussed below. The account of Sancho's death in the *Najerensis* could not be held to show knowledge of the German story. However, as Fradejas showed (1963: 9–24), the *Najerensis* and hence possibly (but not necessarily) the *Carmen* drew details about the killing from Judges 3.15 to 26, the tale of how Ehud murdered Eglon, King of Moab, delivering the Israelites from their oppressor, as Bellido Dolfos by killing Sancho delivered the Zamorans and the Leonese generally from their oppressor. The *Najerensis* says in III.42 that Bellido Dolfos – here named – killed Sancho with a javelin while the King 'de equo descendens, et nature sederet necessaria'.[23] In Judges 3.24, Eglon's servants do not venture for a time into the closed room where he already lies dead, because 'forsitan purgat alvum'. The murderer has already escaped 'per posticum' (3.24), that is 'through the porch' in the Authorised Version and in modern translations, but 'through the back door' (or 'small door, secret door') seems possible too; this may have suggested the *postigo*, the small door in the walls of Zamora, present in other versions of the King Sancho story. When the news of Sancho's death is heard in his camp, 'Nec mora, fit clamor, tolluntur ad ethera uoces' (III.44), a hexameter which Entwistle puts into the text of his *Carmen*, for it is an echo of *Aeneid*, VIII.70. The *Seminensis*'s account of the same incident has one Virgilian echo (*Aeneid*, II.532) and two of Sallust. Oña and then Nájera were not going to be outdone when it came to literary embroidering, and so important an event as the death of Sancho was seen to demand association with both biblical and classical historiography and style. The pattern was already fixed, in brief compass, by the Oña epitaph of Count (Infante) García in 1029.

Finally, in the survey of heroic themes in the *Najerensis*, mention must be made of sections II.16 and 17, concerning Charlemagne's expedition to Pamplona and Saragossa, with the disaster at Roncevaux (four lines) and, in II.17, Charlemagne's vengeance 'sequente uero anno' (two lines). On this, Martínez wrote that:

Cae fuera de nuestro propósito examinar aquí hasta qué punto conoció [el cronista de la *Najerensis*] el discutido tema del antiquísimo *Roncesvalles* español. Mi intención es citar un texto en el que aparece claro que el cronista conoció, si no todos, por lo menos una buena parte de los héroes muertos en Roncesvalles, aunque se limite a citar sólo tres: '. . . Egiardus suae mensae Caroli Regis praepositus, Anselmus sui palatii comes, Rotolanus [MS 'G': Rodolanus] britannicus comes et alii quos longum est numerare'.

But this argument or at least hint ('Cae fuera . . .') that the *Najerensis* writer knew a Spanish *Roncesvalles* poem is an example of traditionalist inattentiveness to standard Latin historiography, neglected simply because it was Latin. The whole passage of the *Najerensis* is based on the *Seminensis*, where the names of the three dead are given in almost exactly the same terms in a sentence rounded off by 'cum aliis conpluribus ceciderunt', of which 'et alii quos longum est numerare' is a formulaic variation. Ultimately these names, and other details of the campaign, came to the *Seminensis* from Einhard's *Vita Karoli* and the Frankish annals; and the *Seminensis*'s famous remark, that Charlemagne withdrew from before Saragossa 'more Francorum auro corruptus', is an answer to the excessive claims made by French chroniclers about the Emperor's conquests in Spain. As for the *Najerensis*'s reference to the place of the battle as 'in Roscidis Vallibus', this was not in the *Seminensis* but reflects a frequent form of the name in Latin texts of the Pyrenean region from the late eleventh century onward. There is not the slightest evidence that the *Najerensis* paid heed to vernacular verse stories of Roncevaux in either French or Spanish (which is not to deny, of course, that the story was known in Spain in the twelfth century, as is shown by allusions to be discussed later). Only the source of *Najerensis*, II.17, about Charlemagne's vengeance the following year, is unknown to us, but again it was not a vernacular one, for the *Roland* tradition told of Charlemagne's return and defeat of Baligant the following day.

The preceding arguments have been negative but essential too, for in the course of them an important text has been reviewed and the origin and nature of several potentially heroic themes have been discussed. The assumption that the *Najerensis* ('of 1160') took its heroic themes from a corpus of already established vernacular epics is shown to be unwarranted. This is not to deny that in the twelfth century, as earlier, a good deal of legendary development of the facts of history had taken place both in the popular mind and in monkish fantasy and in some Latin writing. Use of such material and its further literary embellishment had occurred in earlier historiography in Spain (as elsewhere), and was to increase in volume in the thirteenth century in both Latin and Romance. The intention of the *Najerensis* writer was primarily pious, as may be gauged from the long sections about the transfer of saintly remains and building of S. Isidoro de León (III.24), the piety and aid to the Church of Fernando I (III.26, concluding with mention of the annual tribute paid to Cluny), the Christian death of the same monarch (III.28), the careful mention of the date and place of burial in monastic churches of kings and others, and the concluding miracle of the water which flowed from the stones beneath the altar of S. Isidoro a week before the death of Alfonso VI (III.58). The Reconquest is seen in these terms: 'In hoc enim quod ciuitatem illam artibus paganorum et ad fidem christianorum reuerti flagitabat, profectu in nomine Ihesu' (III.22, concerning Coimbra). However, the chronicler was – like the *Seminensis* author – a man with an eye for a lively episode and for the possibilities of dramatisation, and he had the instinct to adorn his narration with stylish notes. By temperament and by intention, and also as far as his historiographic technique was concerned, he simply did not need the resources which a hypothetically existing vernacular verse epic might have afforded him.

This argument is not novel. Some years ago C. Guerrieri Crocetti, in a study which has received little comment, took a cool look at the *Najerensis* and traditionalist claims about its materials (1969: 378). After an admirable survey of the author's personality and interests, he denied that the chronicler used vernacular verse as a source (though he was apparently disposed to recognise that vernacular epic existed at the time): 'Nell'animo, come nella prosa, di questo scrittore scarse tracce poteva lasciare la poesia giullaresca, per la quale la sua educazione letteraria doveva sentire lo stesso disprezzo, manifestato più tardi dal Toledano e dai cronisti della *General*.' In style, the *Najerensis* writer has 'forti e frequenti risonanze di motivi virgiliani, sallustiani, senechiani', and as to his sources Guerrieri Crocetti concluded:

In quanto al resto, le veri fonti della *Najerense* sono i cronisti leonesi, nel narrare le vicende di quella regione; gli 'Anales y genealogías, única fuente de que Castilla disponía, a falta de crónicas' (osserva Menéndez Pidal), e la tradizione orale, la quale di solito può acquistare consistenza e fascino di leggenda nelle pagine di questo e di altri cronisti.

Guerrieri Crocetti had some reservations about accepting Entwistle's *Carmen* on Sancho II, but concluded with a brilliant denunciation of traditionalism with regard to chronicles and poems, exposing a logical fallacy, and going on to doubt whether even Lucas de Tuy used materials drawn from vernacular epics. A similar denial of the *Najerensis*'s dependence on vernacular poems has come recently from Cotrait (1977: 328–32, 340, and especially 372–462, passim).

That the *Najerensis* writer had, in addition to a wide range of sources in his own monastic library, close contacts with other Castilian houses cannot be doubted. He may have sought information by letter, but, more likely, made visits to them. From Oña, in the eleventh and twelfth centuries the most powerful of all the Castilian monasteries, he took the vital materials I have indicated (and a further note: that after the treachery at Rueda in 1083, 'Comes uero Gundissaluus et alii apud Oniam sunt sepulti', III.53). Oña evidently had a certain literary tradition, though we know little of it.[24] The monk's interest in and contacts with other monasteries can be traced in the index to Ubieto's edition; but some of his information came from literary texts only, since, for example, his sole mention of San Pedro de Arlanza is taken from the *Seminensis*, and the burial there of Fernán González is not mentioned. What the *Najerensis* writer did not know gives indications about the absence of vernacular epic in twelfth-century Spain. He gives no sign of knowing the story of the Infantes de Lara or the Cid story as we know it in the *Poema* (he even credits Alfonso VI with the capture of Valencia – *Ualentia* – when listing conquests of this monarch in III.52). This latter absence naturally causes us no surprise, since it is the thesis of this book that the *Poema* was composed in 1207 or a little before, without vernacular precedents. The Cid materials that the chronicler includes in his work pertain to the story of Sancho II, and III.34 (the Cid prudently answers the boastful Sancho), III.36 (the Cid rescues Sancho from his Leonese captors), and III.43 (the Cid pursues the Zamoran killer of Sancho towards the city), could all derive from the *Carmen*. Entwistle argued this for the first episode, and has long series of remade hexameters which embrace the second and third episodes. The fact that the Cid ('Rodericus' in the *Carmen*, 'Rodericus' and 'Rodericus Campidoctus' in the *Najerensis*) is given such prominence in the Oña poem is a testimony to his growing stature in legend and literature throughout the twelfth century, and the fact that the *Najerensis* reproduced the episodes of the *Carmen* in such detail is both a tribute to the same and a result of the chronicler's feeling for detail and dialogue. The vernacular epic of *Sancho II* in the thirteenth century, known to us from the chronicles, was to expand further the Cid's role in the last days of Fernando I, at Zamora, in leading the party of Castilians which took Sancho's body to Oña, in administering the oath at Santa Gadea, and so on; and it cannot be denied that the thirteenth-century *Sancho II* epic, a fine creation, owes a good deal to the *Poema de mio Cid* and may be directly associated with it in some way (Smith, 1977a: 170–1). Eventually it was Cardeña which took to itself the Cid and all things relating to him, and it was certainly at Cardeña that the Cid and Jimena had their tombs; but we know of no special interest shown by Cardeña in the Cid during the twelfth century, and it could well be that it was at Oña, because of the known historical connections of the hero with Sancho II, that literary prominence was early given to him.

The first evidence that we have for the existence of a poem about the Infantes de Lara comes after the middle of the thirteenth century in the *Primera Crónica General*, which includes a full prose redaction, and possibly in the references to Lara and its heroes in the *Poema de Fernán González*. Yet traditionalists have always claimed, and most of other persuasions have accepted, that there existed an epic on this theme from the late tenth century, for the poem has as its setting the world of Christian–Moslem relations at that time, and it has been shown that one of the Christian personages went on an embassy to Córdoba in a year variously identified as 974 or about 990. The traditionalist thesis was applied in one of Menéndez Pidal's earliest studies, revised at the end of his life, and has been thought unshakeable by most historians of literature. To deny it is therefore a bold task. Even Deyermond, who has a prudent reserve about most traditionalist claims and denies the existence of epics of King Roderick, Covadonga, etc., is firm about this one, believing that a vernacular *cantar* of the Infantes existed in about the year 1000

(1971: 39, and 1974: 462–5). Nobody has cared to guess what metrical and stylistic form such a poem might have had.

One can only reiterate: there is not the faintest trace of such a poem, nor evidence that one existed, until the *Poema de Fernán González* and *Primera Crónica General* (for which materials were gathered in the 1260s). Traditionalists explain this void, and sustain their belief in a very early poem, in one of several ways or in all of them together. They may appeal to the notion of an *estado latente* by which virtually anything may lie concealed, or by which the 'silence of the centuries' may be held to hum meaningfully for critics with properly attuned ears. They may reduce the poem in stature to a *canto noticiero* or 'news-bearing song', exclusively oral; this is a more tenable idea, but one which by its nature is incapable of proof or disproof. They may argue that since the Leonese chronicle-tradition centred its interest upon royalty, this and other early epics were of no concern to chroniclers because the epic theme did not involve royal personages. This last is the most telling of the arguments, one with which one can come rationally to grips. It applies to Leonese historiography down to the *Seminensis*, and also to the *Chronica Adefonsi Imperatoris* in a way, though this gives a good deal of attention to the nobles and to such local leaders as Muño Alfonso, while the accompanying *Poema de Almería* has a lengthy roll-call of noted captains. In Castile and Navarre, less bound by tradition, the net was cast wider by the *Najerensis* in its numerous references to nobles and ecclesiastics and in its acceptance of the Cid episodes from the *Carmen*, though in these, as noted earlier, the Cid is still present only in so far as he is connected with King Sancho. One senses that if the *Najerensis* writer had known an epic on the Infantes de Lara, he would have included a reference to it, because in its early portions it involves Count García Fernández of Castile, already prominent in the chronicle, just as, if he had known of a poem in some fashion resembling the *Poema de mio Cid*, he would have mentioned the Cid's activities in relation to Alfonso VI, which are crucial in the *Poema*. The silence of the *Najerensis*, and of Lucas de Tuy in 1236 and of Jiménez de Rada in 1243 (both of whom took in a good deal of legendary and fictional material), is surely significant.

There is a perfectly good explanation of the origin and sources of much of the *Infantes de Lara* epic as we know it in the *Primera Crónica General*. In 1944 (republished, 1954: 151–91; with a comment by Riquer, 1962: 182–3) von Richthofen drew attention to the close similarity of the plot to that of the *Thidrekssaga* (*Dietrichssaga*) and showed how a knowledge of this text had reached Spain. In 1256–7 a princess of Norway (where the *Thidrekssaga* was composed about 1250) went at the invitation of Alfonso X of Castile–León to marry one of his brothers. This was Kristin, Cristina, and she married Felipe on Ash Wednesday 1257. A good deal is known about the progress of the large party of Norwegians – more than one hundred persons – and accompanying Spaniards through Catalonia to Burgos, Palencia, Valladolid; somewhere there, perhaps at a court entertainment, a Castilian poet heard the story and resolved to imitate it. Alfonso's was, after all, a highly literary court, and the whole expedition of the Nordic princess, so exceptional, was almost in itself an episode out of romance, as von Richthofen's account (based on Norse sources) makes plain. There is a further element. On its way to Spain, Kristin's party stopped for a time at Narbonne, ruled since 1168 by members of the Castilian family of the Counts of Lara; and, as has been noted, there are correspondences between the *Infantes de Lara* story and the epic cycle of Narbonne in French.[25] It may also be significant that, as Professor Michael kindly reminds me, Kristin's tomb is to be seen in the Collegiate Church of Covarrubias, a few kilometres south of Lara. Perhaps, as von Richthofen and Riquer seem to think, there was some form of the Spanish epic in being long before 1257, and elements from French epic and then from Germanic heroic legend were grafted on to it at a late stage. We do not know, and I would not wish to be positivistic *à outrance* by insisting on the few known facts and dates. The notion of heroic legend being developed in a family, for more than purely genealogical reasons, is an attractive one to which I shall return. The great family is in this sense analogous to a monastic community, and both have their *domus* or *casa*. Certainly the Infantes de Lara had no monastic associations or tomb-cult until after the diffusion of literary works (the epic or the *Primera Crónica General*) in the later thirteenth century, though after that there were materialisations of a gruesome kind.[26]

There remains one substantial argument used by traditionalists to support the claim that a first *Infantes de Lara* poem must have been composed in the late tenth century. As Deyermond summarised it:

[Menéndez Pidal] argued that the story as embodied in the *Estoria de España* [= *Primera Crónica General*] reflects assumptions about relations between Christians and Moors that were out of date by the late 970s, and that the original epic could therefore not have been composed much after that date. An article by J. M. Ruiz Asencio, published after Menéndez Pidal's death . . . shows that c. 990 is a more likely date than the 970s, but the argument remains valid.

Earlier, Deyermond had written that:

A learned poet could, of course, have been familiar with the political relationships of c. 990 long after ordinary people had forgotten them, but since they are not essential to the story, he would have had little reason to include them; a poem composed soon after the event might, however, continue to appeal long afterwards, if its plots and the vigour of its narration outweighed the unfamiliarity of its setting. (1971: 39)

Deyermond assumes, then, that this early poem was by one of the 'ordinary people' and was orally composed, and he has ruled out the learned poet. Let us bring him back. If he was a poet at the court of Alfonso X in 1257, he would have had some learning, and access to chronicles which gave plenty of details about the political situation of the late tenth century. Any learned person would have known something of García Fernández, and the name and reputation of his Moslem enemy, the fearsome Almanzor who was virtual ruler of Al-Andalus, were as well-known as those of Napoleon to us. The 'political' content of the early part of the *Infantes de Lara* story is important but could have been composed by someone with no more than a moderate knowledge of the history of the times, for it involves an inadequate royal grant towards the cost of Ruy Velásquez's marriage, and no contribution from Almanzor; the embassy of Gonzalo Gustioz, father of the Infantes, to Córdoba (carrying the letter in which, as in *Hamlet* – and compare 2 Samuel 11.15 – the receiver is asked to kill the bearer), and his imprisonment there; and the general sense of the dependence of the weak Christian kingdoms upon the will of Almanzor as arbiter even in questions of offence and honour between Christians. Certainly the information of a historical kind which the poet of the *Infantes de Lara* could command was better than that of his contemporary, the monk of Arlanza who composed the *Poema de Fernán González* after 1264 (on this date, see Lacarra, 1979: 19–20), for in this Almanzor figures anachronistically as adversary of Fernán González in 970. It seems, despite this, that the Arlanza poet did take account of the *Infantes de Lara* poem probably composed a few years earlier, for he concerned himself greatly with Lara and its region and located an important battle there, even mentioning one 'Gustyo Gonçalez', putative grandfather of the Siete Infantes, together with his sons and two 'sobrinos', with some prominence (stanzas 448–50, 499, 526–7, 536). Possibly the monastery of Arlanza was by then trying to assert itself as custodian of the legend of the Infantes and objects relating to them. At a later stage, the monastery actually claimed to possess the tombs of the Siete Infantes. The relationship of the *Infantes de Lara* poem to other Spanish epic themes has been much discussed, and relations there certainly were, but nothing forces us to believe in the existence of a full epic on the subject before, perhaps, 1257. The rest is, as so often in what the traditionalists tell us, supposition, romantic *espejismo*, and special pleading.

This is not the place in which to discuss the reasons for this *espejismo*, although such an inquiry, for Spain, is to be commended to those qualified to undertake it. However, I cannot resist the temptation of offering a few hints. The generality of traditionalism, common to all Europe, is a matter of record, and need not detain us. It was the creation of the great German Romantics, and may even go back to Vico (Siciliano, 1968: 138–52). It involved an exaltation of the primitive, the popular, the genuine product of 'the folk', which naturally included a good deal of medieval epic, ballad, and lyric, which is much less 'of the folk' than the Romantics thought. The special application of Romantic theory to Spain by Spaniards in the nineteenth century was natural, acquiring an extra force there because of the very large quantity of seemingly popular ballads and lyrics (though not of epics) to be discovered in the Peninsular languages, and because of their often high quality also. The long continuation of Romantic traditionalist theory, a little modified as 'neotraditionalism',[27] by Spaniards and Hispanists, long after it had been given up by many – not all – elsewhere in Europe and America, can be seen most readily as a consequence of the energy, powerful mind, plain style, and preternaturally long working life of Ramón Menéndez Pidal (see, e.g., Smith, 1970). Moreover, D. Ramón formed a powerful school which expanded and continued his work. Even so, neither a single man nor a school can impose its views on a nation and on a discipline unless the views are consonant with what the nation feels and wants. So it was in Spain around 1900.

The cultural penury of Spain in the late nineteenth century became a matter of concern, perhaps, only at the moment when the country's military inadequacy was revealed by the ease with which the United States defeated Spain in the war of 1898. The outcome of the revelation was the emergence of the brilliant and passionate writers of the Generation of 1898 with their sense of reformist mission (oddly lacking in concreteness and political commitment). But the cultural penury had long been apparent in such features as appalling rates of illiteracy, poor schooling, virtually inexistent public libraries, stagnancy of universities, and lack of interest in technology and experimental science, and such things could be quantified and compared with figures in the rapidly-advancing societies of France, Germany, and Britain. On the one hand, reforms were undertaken and the panacea of 'europeanisation' was preached. On the other hand, could not the Spanish past be made to yield something which would enhance Spanish dignity? The great imperial past was there, as were the splendid achievements of the Golden Age in art and literature. Cervantes and Calderón needed no refurbishing, but the medieval epic and chronicles, and in some ways the late medieval ballads, were not only interesting in themselves but relatively ill-known. While earlier scholars, notably Bello in the years from 1810 (but not published until 1881) and Milá (1874, etc.) had been rational enough in their datings of medieval texts and not concerned to minimise the extent of the dependence of epic on French example, Menéndez Pidal in a long series of brilliant studies emphasised the relative (not total) autonomy of Castilian epic and certain other genres, very greatly expanded the hypothetical corpus of epic, and where there did exist texts that could in theory be dated, assigned to them extremely early dates. The essential germanism of French epic having been demonstrated by Pio Rajna in the 1880s and accepted by Gaston Paris, as directly derived from Frankish and Burgundian presence on French soil, the essential germanism of Spanish epic became for Pidal and his followers an equal tenet of faith, being directly derived from the Gothic presence on the soil of Spain. Hypothetical lost poems, early dates, and Germanic continuity, all formed a coherent whole in the confident postulation of a lost epic about King Roderick more or less contemporary with him, another about Covadonga, discussed above, and so on; and the content of such lost works was adumbrated in some detail. Belief in an epic about the Infantes de Lara in the late tenth century, and others composed in the first decades of the eleventh, was hence natural, and became widespread among Hispanists and mandatory in manuals of literary history. In the case of the *Poema de mio Cid*, where a nearly complete text of great power exists, Menéndez Pidal early in his career adopted the date of 'about 1140' and afterwards defended this in detail, eventually perceiving within the unique text the work of two successive minstrels of whom the earlier, 'de San Esteban', composed 'a raíz de la muerte del héroe', perhaps about 1105, while a successor 'poeta de Medinaceli' rewrote the poem in a more fictional spirit about 1140. Menéndez Pidal and others displayed ingenuity and a wealth of argument in separating the strands of the two poets, in what many now think a wholly misconceived operation. The excessively early dating, even that of 1140, has gravely prejudiced inquiry into the nature of the *Poema* and into its sources, as will be shown.

Clearly the unspoken wish of Menéndez Pidal and his followers was to bring the earliest 'San Esteban' version of the *Poema* as close as possible to 1100, considered the likely date of the 'Turoldus' version of the *Chanson de Roland*; that is, to equate as closely as possible (and whatever the length of the oral epic tradition presumed to have existed in both France and Spain) the earliest and most outstanding of the surviving epic texts of the two nations. In terms of hypothesis and reconstruction, the two nations ran neck-and-neck back, as it were, into the misty centuries. If the traditionalist historians of French epic identified poems of the Merovingian period from chronicles of the time, Spain had its epic of King Roderick and – on unspecified themes but presumably in Gothic – those *carmina maiorum* mentioned by Isidore, continuers of songs said by Tacitus to be current in the undivided Germania of his time.

Traditionalism in Spain had a further strength beyond a nationalistic urge to equal France in the antiquity, number, and dignity of its early texts. The following is an undoubted fact and one which has no parallel in France: that Spanish epics of the thirteenth century were (together with much local, genealogical, and ecclesiastical legend) redacted in the prose of the royal chronicles; that ballads were made from the epics and from the chronicle accounts; that the theatre of the late sixteenth century took its *romance* metre from the ballads and much material for plots from both ballads and printed chronicles; and that the *romancero viejo*, with sixteenth-century and later additions, existed and survives in the oral tradition of the Hispanic peoples. This, as rightly claimed by Pidal and others, is a kind of 'traditionalist' tradition, and a powerful one, although even the most romantically-inclined traditionalists have to agree that within it, the intervention of scribes, educated royal chroniclers, printers, and such literate playwrights as Lope de Vega, must be recognised. That the *romancero* lived orally beside, partly associated with and partly dependent upon, the printed texts of the sixteenth and other centuries, is also a fact, and a very splendid one. However, as has been remarked, the modern collection of 500 variants of the *Gerineldo* ballad does not tell us anything necessarily about how epic was created and transmitted in earlier times. As Lecoy observed, 'Du fait qu'après sa grande période d'éclat, l'épopée espagnole ... a continué à vivre d'une vie latente et vigoureuse pratiquement jusqu'à nos jours, on ne saurait conclure qu'elle a également connu et traversé, avant cette période, de longs siècles d'obscurité où elle ne se manifeste pas à nos yeux' (1959: 422). This part of the traditionalist argument – concerning the fifteenth to twentieth centuries – has helped, then, to colour the rest. It stands on solid fact – though capable of strange exaggerations;[28] but it is not germane to the inquiry into early epic. The theme is of some importance, since one critic has seen in the *romancero* the clue to Menéndez Pidal's clinging to Romantic myths about historicity, the poetic genius of 'the folk', and so on: the Master was 'obnubilé par la persistance des *romances* espagnoles dans la tradition orale' (Delbouille, 1972: 206).

In addition to the dignity of the nation, the instinct of the 1898 Generation to emphasise 'lo popular' was also relevant to the establishment of traditionalist thought about epic. This was a noble side of the inevitably élitist products of the Institución Libre de Enseñanza, in harmony with its rucksack-bearing Sunday excursions and its obsession with Castile as the prime force, for good and ill, in the making of the wider Spain. The inherent virtues of the Castilian people and its *intrahistoria* are the themes both of Unamuno's *En torno al casticismo* of 1895 and of Castro's *España en su historia* of 1948, in which the great debate was renewed. It can be no accident that both men were diligent students of the *Poema de mio Cid*. To emphasise the popular and indigenous traditions of Castile in the interest of future regeneration from that source was one thing, doubtless wholly laudable at the turn of the century. To allow medieval studies to be affected by this was unpardonable, for the process led to the neglect of the Latin, ecclesiastical, and cultured traditions which Spain shared with all Christendom, and it enhanced the tendency, outlined above, to reduce to a minimum the influence of France from the eleventh to thirteenth centuries. One consequence, recently documented by Deyermond (1975), was the enthronement of epic, ballad, and chronicle, which often had 'national' themes held to be treated in popular style, and the degrading or exclusion of the prose and verse *roman* (newly named by Deyermond *libro de aventuras*), which was doubly damned by being not only a foreign import originally but courtly too. The relation of Menéndez Pidal to the 1898 Generation has not been determined precisely, but on these matters they seem to have been instinctively at one.[29] Someone will, one day, write a parallel history of the reception of the Mozarabic lyrics in 1948. Their discovery was rapturously greeted by Hispanists not only because of the charm and interest of the little verses, but also because the earliest Romance lyric could now be documented in a Hispanic dialect at a date perhaps a century earlier than the first lyrics in Provençal. Now, as noted above, the corpus may turn out to be yet another all too corruptible body, a handful of dust.

The British have been in the van in introducing a more rational view of aspects of medieval Spanish literature. Known as a chilly and pragmatic people, they are duly cautious and in their post-imperial moment have no *espejismos* or Romantic delusions to cloud their view. Nor are they concerned to defend the Anglo-Saxon culture of their islands as a living part of their present heritage; they cannot read *Beowulf* or *Maldon* as, with a little help, a Spaniard can read the *Poema de mio Cid* or a Frenchman the *Roland*. The British are moreover aware that the Norman invasion and resulting gallicisation could not, in the cultural sphere, be held to be other than beneficial; it causes them no pain to think that just as their cathedrals were built in styles which emanated from France, so the *Poema de mio Cid* could be seen as a sort of cathedral in words patterned in part on French exemplars.

2 The Cid in legend and literature of the twelfth century, and the date and authorship of the *Poema*

To talk of cultural or indeed of any developments by centuries often involves the slightly false periodisations of the academic view, or reflects the need of scholars to organise their materials and of teachers to plan courses. In the case of the Cid, to talk of the development of legend and literature relating to him in the twelfth century has a certain pleasing precision, since he died in 1099 and the *Poema* can confidently be dated to 1207 or a few years earlier. While the writing of the poem at that date as the first vernacular epic of Spain can be amply justified in terms of the reign of Alfonso VIII and the early thirteenth century, as far as artistic impulses and sources go, the poet would not have selected his theme unless there had already been considerable growth of the Cid as a figure of legend and literature, in Latin for the most part, during the century which elapsed since his death. In the same way – since Hispanic affairs are peculiar by their lateness, not by their nature – it seems obvious that the *Roland* did not emerge from a void about 1100 but was preceded by developments of Carolingian legend and of poetic technique, just as Arthur did not spring fully-armed from the brain of Geoffrey of Monmouth but was partly formed by legend over the centuries. *Ex nihilo, nihil fit*: not even by a poet, a 'maker', and especially not by a medieval poet, to whom the concept of labouring in a craft was fundamental. The nature of Per Abad's apprenticeship and labour in that craft will be discussed later. The first question to ask is: what was the reason for his choice of subject?

The Cid of history had a career whose brilliance, authority, and daring would in any age have marked him out as a candidate for the honours of legend and of epic. He lived, moreover, at a time whose display of energy, rapid change, and sudden reversals of fortune both personal and national marked the period also as a potential heroic age. One has only to think of such obvious features as the death (by treachery?) which the young and

49

handsome Sancho II suffered at Zamora, the taking of Toledo by
Alfonso VI in 1085, which radically altered the military map of the
Peninsula, the resultant arrival of the Almoravids, the Cid's
campaigns in the Levante, the great Christian defeats at Sagrajas
and Uclés, together with the quieter changes wrought by the
Cluniac take-over of the Spanish Church, by the influx of
foreigners in large numbers, and so on. If movement and
migration seem a natural ingredient of any heroic age (in
addition, of course, to military action and great leaders), the
advance to and beyond Toledo, and the Cid's astonishing capture
of Valencia, supplied further drama. In Spain, moreover, all was
firmly set in a world of Christian belief, not merely spiritual and
certainly not crusading in the sense of Urban II at Clermont, but
very practical. As the *Seminensis* chronicler wrote of Alfonso VI,
not for nothing styled 'Imperator totius Hispaniae', he was 'ex
illustri Gotorum prosapia ortus' and was leading his people in the
fulfilment of prophecies about the Reconquest and in the
restoration of a realm considered as the Gothic one ruled from
Toledo. In all this the Cid was of a stature to rival those who were
formally the most powerful in the land. Non-royal, he became a
sort of *taifa* ruler of Valencia. Although he had something of the
character of a gentleman adventurer and was, at different times,
nearly a rebel against his monarch and a mercenary in the service
of the Moslem ruler of Saragossa, he was plainly the outstanding
general of the Peninsula both as strategist and tactician, and was
outstanding too in the intelligence with which he handled civil
affairs both Christian and Moslem. Of his capacity for leadership
there can be no doubt. Men will do a good deal for the promise of
booty, but will not give that extra ounce unless it be for love of the
leader and respect for what he represents: in the Cid's case,
perhaps, a sense of justice and a belief in letting men rise if their
capacities warrant it, as they were free to do when exiled or on
hostile territory. Of any sign of special Christian devotion in the
Cid we know nothing (his donations to monasteries being of the
kind usual among magnates), although of course this was to be
the aspect exploited above all others by legendary accretions in
later times. To appoint a bishop, even a reforming Cluniac, in
newly-won Valencia was merely to replace a Mozarabic prelate,
and was a political act as much as anything: a sign of intended
permanence, an association of the Church's authority with the
military and civil one. The rich endowment of the new cathedral

and its bishop was a political assertion too, as some parts of the extraordinary charter show. The Cid was not a crusader, but he would have been more aware than most of the Reconquest as a Christian duty and amply conscious of the strategic importance of his campaigns in the Levante. Valencia may have been his private fief, and he may have taken it from a Moslem ruler of the old decadent kind, but he could see the special importance of holding it against the assaults of the Almoravids, then at the height of their Islamic revolutionary fervour. It was not a wholly crazy thought which led a Cardeña monk to invent, in the *Estoria del Cid*, an embassy from the 'Sultan of Persia' sent to beg the Cid to stay out of the Crusade then (in his last years) overwhelming Syria and Palestine. In the *Poema* the Cid had, after all, considered but rejected the possibility of an attack on Morocco (ll. 2499–504). If the monk perceived thoroughly Norman qualities in his hero, he was not entirely mistaken.

It is not necessarily the great generals or those who take prizes such as Valencia who attract the aureole of legend. Other features of the Cid's career were recalled and embroidered. In early years he fought in single combat against a Navarrese champion and probably against a Saracen too, acts that would have been publicly witnessed and much talked of. He was in an important position at the side of Sancho II, no doubt seeing action at Golpejera and Zamora (if not in the way that legend made out). There may have been rivalries at the court of Sancho's successor, Alfonso VI, but the King made a highly honourable marriage for him with his relative, Jimena, of the Leonese royal line, in 1074. The Cid was sent on some sort of mission to the King of Seville, whether or not this involved the receipt of tribute, the battle at Cabra, and the brief imprisonment of García Ordóñez, as told in later texts. For one of several possible reasons he was banished in 1081, taken back into favour, and banished again in 1089. Out on a limb after 1081 with a few vassals and followers, but eventually the leader of a very effective private army, he took mercenary service in Saragossa, measured his powers successfully against the might of a whole state, Barcelona, by defeating and capturing its Count in 1082, and again in 1090, and gradually, by military and diplomatic means, came to be a real force in the Levante and eventually took Valencia (1094). Further fighting and much diplomacy were needed to keep this secure. Near the end of his life his only son, Diego, was killed when serving with the royal army at Consuegra (1097), but he had the satisfaction of seeing his two daughters marry nobly, one to a member of the royal line of Navarre, the other to the ruling Count of Barcelona. The magnitude of his effort in taking and keeping Valencia was emphasised by the fact that in 1102, three years after the Cid's death, the city and kingdom were abandoned to the Moors, Alfonso VI having resolved that even the royal power could not maintain itself there.

Single combats, action at the side of Sancho II, banishments in which a man rises from nothing (literally, in view of the confiscations which banishment entailed) to great power, the defeats of the Catalans, the splendid marriages of his daughters: these are features around which legend gathers. By what means, by what human instruments? We do not know with any precision. Old soldiers 'remember with advantages', especially as the Cid had kept his word and had generously distributed to them movable booty, and, to those who had served him longest, the houses and estates of Valencia. Priests, too, who had served the Cid as chaplains and secretaries, and formed the entourage of Bishop Jerónimo, had memories, and an interest in spreading word of the hero's Christian spirit, generosity to the Church, and other good works. The soldiers returned to their homes in the Burgos region and perhaps more widely, talking of their deeds and praising their commander. The priests went wherever duty took them, some, perhaps, to Toledo for a time, others accompanying Jerónimo to his new see in Zamora and Salamanca. The bishop was probably among the longest-lived of those who had been with the Cid and had any prominence, for he seems to have died in 1125. In Navarre was the Cid's elder daughter, Cristina, and her presence was to have considerable consequences, especially when her son, García 'el Restaurador', took the crown of newly-independent Navarre in 1134. In Barcelona was María, who seems to have died young and whose issue was less important than the Navarrese; but the Catalans, honoured by the marriage and apparently bearing no resentment for the defeats inflicted on them by the Cid (which had been factional affairs in any case), were among the first to honour the Cid in a literary text.

In addition to what ordinary people remember and embroider in the telling, special motives are readily discerned in particular groups. There is, first, a genealogical motive in those who genuinely had, and in others who claimed to have, the Cid's blood. The special interest of Navarre and Catalonia has been mentioned. An important genealogical consideration in the very making of the *Poema* will occupy us later. A powerful lineage of Palencia claimed at the end of the thirteenth century, spuriously so far as we know, to descend from the Cid's son Diego, and this might explain the localisation in Palencia of aspects of the Cid story as we find it in the fourteenth-century *Mocedades de Rodrigo* (Smith, 1980c: 48–9). As late as the end of the sixteenth century a genealogical interest produced the copying of the unique MS of the *Poema* and, from that, the diffusion of a small amount of knowledge of it among scholars of the time.[1] At Cardeña in the later thirteenth century these genealogical matters, for the most part spurious, were important in the Cid-cult established there, in the pantheon of tombs, and in the literary texts produced in the monastery, as was also the case in other monasteries and churches.

Monastic interests were often inseparable from family ones. As has been shown, Sancho II at Oña was not only a body in a grave but a man who posthumously inspired, not merely out of the bitterness expressed in his epitaph, a great legend, a Latin poem, and a fine vernacular epic, in all of which the Cid figured with a certain prominence because of his historical association with Sancho. The Cid, however, was buried in Cardeña, as was Jimena,[2] and as were, possibly, one or two of the Cid's captains. So far as we know, Cardeña did not pay any special attention to these tombs during the twelfth century, but it secured (or achieved) mention of itself in several scenes of the *Poema* of 1207, and in the course of the following century, after diffusion of the poem, it turned the Cid into an industry, though still only a part of a much larger industry fuelled by fabrication, pseudohistory, and retrospective historicisation.[3] Other monasteries and cults took their lead from Cardeña, but none had much success (Smith, 1980c: 47–57). Much of what was invented about the Cid at Cardeña passed into the chronicles, achieved print in the sixteenth century, and became an essential ingredient of what was believed to be historical about the hero. Although rational Renaissance historians began to dismantle parts of the corpus, it proved extraordinarily durable and is not without credulous adherents in our day. The cult of the Cid at Cardeña is not therefore a side-issue or a brief episode, but fundamental to

developments after the *Poema*. Since even the tombs there seem
not to have had epitaphs until Alfonso X composed them in
(probably) 1272, the situation contrasts at all points with that of
Sancho II at Oña.

Local memories and legend-making could be as important as
anything genealogical or monastic. Although at a late stage
Palencia tried to acquire a foothold, many things about the Cid
were connected with Burgos, capital of Old Castile, a place
already rich in heroic memories. His family seat was at Vivar; he
held property in the city; and he was buried nearby at Cardeña.
His marriage to Jimena was probably solemnised in the city's
cathedral (though later, Palencia claimed this too). In later
centuries a parish of the city claimed that the Cid was born in it,
the site of his town house was preserved – and is still shown
today – and several churches claimed connections with followers
of the Cid whom we know only from literature (Smith, 1980c: 48,
etc.). As is normal, then, we find a locality with pretensions to a
hero which are factual in part (though not recorded till later) but
invented in part also. Some of the invention might have begun in
the century following the Cid's death, while some of it certainly
stems from the propagation of the *Poema* after 1207 and some
from the Cardeña cult. The *Chronicon Burgense* has little to say
about the hero (text: *España sagrada*, XXIII, 305–10).

Embroidering by memory and the growth of legend, together
with motivated pseudohistorical invention, were both a cause of
literary works about the Cid in the twelfth century and, doubtless, a response to those same literary works, in ways which we
cannot now distinguish. What has not been sufficiently emphasised is the altogether exceptional nature of the texts about the
Cid in the twelfth century. Previous Hispano-Latin histories had
centred firmly upon Leonese royalty, and two of the twelfth
century, the *Seminensis* in León (also that of Lucas de Tuy, 1236,
the last in the tradition) and the *Najerensis* in Navarre/Castile,
continued on the whole to be so centred, though the later works
give more place to Castilian and other Peninsular royal lines. The
work of Pelayo of Oviedo is similarly conditioned, while the
Chronica Adefonsi Imperatoris, though dealing with only a part of a
single reign, is also firmly centred upon its imperial subject. A
biography of a non-royal individual, the *Historia Roderici* about
the Cid, was therefore an innovation, the only possible parallel
being with the *Historia Compostelana* written for Archbishop

Gelmírez, which similarly had special features, a nearly co-incidental date, and may have had a modest influence on the *Historia Roderici*. As for verse, we have few texts. One may guess that the poem about the capture of Toledo, of which thirteen lines survive, was chiefly a eulogy of Alfonso VI, and Entwistle's reconstructed *Carmen de morte Sanctii regis* naturally centred upon the monarch though giving some attention to the Cid in relation to him. The incomplete *Poema de Almeria* begins with praise of Alfonso VII, continues with him in a central position while mentioning components of the host, and probably finished with further biblical parallels and Christian sentiments about the Emperor. Hence the appearance of the *Carmen Campidoctoris*, entirely about the Cid, is exceptional too.[4] Secular Latin texts about non-royal individuals are scarce too, proportionately, in other countries at this time. Two poems by churchmen of Pisa about expeditions – in which the whole force rather than any leader is the hero – may be relevant to the writing of the *Poema de Almeria* (Martínez, 1975). The appearance of the Cid within the work of Ben Bassam (1109) and at length in the work of Ben Alcama on the loss of Valencia (about 1110) is noteworthy and the texts furnish essential details to historians, but these Arabic writings had no influence in Christian Spain in the twelfth century and are not relevant to the developments which led up to the creation of the *Poema de mio Cid*; later, Ben Alcama's work was partially translated into Castilian and merged with the general account of the Cid given in the *Primera Crónica General* and later chronicles.

By 1200 the Cid had grown to uncommon heroic stature. One could say that he had even outstripped royalty as a subject of legendary interest, for while the ruling Counts of Castile from Fernán González to the Infante García, and to some extent Sancho el Mayor and Fernando I, had each already gathered at least a modicum of the gloss of legend, and while Sancho II had a goodly amount of it, it was thereafter the Cid who took over. Alfonso VI did not excite the imagination of legend-makers or authors, except for the romantic elements in the story of his Moorish concubine Zaida, and there were to be no honours in vernacular epic or in picturesque chronicle accounts for Urraca, Alfonso VII, or Alfonso VIII (unless the late tale of his affair with the Jewish girl can be counted). From some indications it would seem that the only rival the Cid had in popular affection and legend among non-royal personages was Alvar Fáñez, as Per Abad recognised when giving him a major role in his *Poema* (Martínez, 1975: 375–95; Vàrvaro, 1971).

The texts in which the Cid rose towards heroic stature are diverse in kind and in provenance, and by no means show a steady and coherent progress. *Per contra*, the diversity testifies to the widespread interest in the man and to the independent growth of materials about him. It is usually held that the *Carmen Campidoctoris*[5] was composed well within the hero's lifetime – 1082–3, about 1090, etc. – but there is no wholly infallible internal evidence of this, and the work could be much later, as Curtius thought. The surviving text has 129 lines of rhythmic sapphics in stanzas, but breaks off in mid-line, and it is unsure how much more was originally written. This prevents us knowing whether the poet went on to tell of the conquest of Valencia, the marriage of the Cid's daughter to the Count of Barcelona, and other matters. The MS is part of a codex at the Catalán monastery of Ripoll, and was certainly the work of a monk there; the MS did not leave the house during the Middle Ages and, as far as we know, no copy of it was made for use elsewhere, although the existing Ripoll text is not the original. The poem has economy and energy and elevates the hero's stature not only by its enthusiasm but by mention of Homer, Paris and Hector, etc. It surveys (but not in the manner of a chronicle) the early activities of the Cid, his banishment, his defeat of García Ordóñez at Cabra, and the start of the clash with Berenguer Ramón II; the text breaks off at the point where, following a thoroughly epic description of the arming of the hero, he is about to pray, evidently for victory at Almenar (1082). The problem of the dating cannot be argued fully here, but reasons suggesting a date perhaps quite late in the twelfth century can be briefly given. The poem has, despite the brevity of what survives, a broad perspective of the Cid's life, indicating hindsight. It tells us nothing that we do not meet in other texts, whereas we might expect from a contemporary a good many details known in Catalonia in the Cid's lifetime but then forgotten. In particular, some of the themes selected by the poet for special treatment are precisely those which other texts dwell upon (e.g. the part played by the 'whispering slanderers' – Wright's translation – in securing the Cid's banishment). There are a few errors of historical fact unlikely to have been made by a contemporary of the Cid. Lastly, despite the poet's effort to create an air of vigorous actuality, at times he unconsciously distances himself from events, giving a clue to his true standpoint. As for what one may guess about the extent of the finished work, it seems unlikely that the poem was to end with the Cid's victory at Almenar, which brought him prestige but no territorial power. So much is said about the Cid's greatness in the early lines of the poem that one would expect it to finish showing the Cid as lord of Valencia, and probably also with mention of the marriage(s) of his daughter(s). Whatever the date of the work, it remains important as showing the Cid achieving a fully literary presentation in the noble medium of Latin verse, in a corner of the Peninsula where good learning mixed with admiration for what the hero had achieved there.[6]

The *Historia Roderici*[7] purports to be, and to a large extent is, a straightforward historical account. Its place of origin and date are uncertain. Dozy thought it composed about 1150, Lang put it at about 1170, but Menéndez Pidal, as usual at the opposite extreme, firmly indicated 1110. The best recent discussion is that of Ubieto, who holds that it was written probably between 1144 and 1147. Horrent supports this. Certainly there are features which suggest a late date. The opening genealogy of the Cid is already part-legendary and is so presented by the author: 'Stirpis ergo eius origo hec esse videtur.' Accounts of single combats, the fight with fifteen (fourteen?) Zamoran knights, the battle at Cabra, and particularly the 1081 raid into Toledan lands,[8] seem to show a literary or at least a legendary development. The vivid account of the second victory over the Catalans at Tévar in 1090 shows a strong literary development, and it is here that the relation of this text to the *Carmen Campidoctoris*, or of both to a lost source, becomes important. In view of the precision of some of the information in the *Historia*, Pidal thought that the author had actually accompanied the Cid at intervals from 1082 (although if he had known the hero personally, he would have taken pride in the fact and presumably mentioned it), and defined the writer as a 'clérigo aventurero y soldado, natural de tierras aragonesas o mejor catalanas, poco docto según el mal latín que emplea'. Certainly he shows a special interest in the eastern kingdoms, and could equally well have been Navarrese (though he does not mention the marriage of the Cid's daughter to Prince Ramiro). There is, however, a better hypothesis. Menéndez Pidal emphasised that the author inserts independent documents textually into his work – the Cid's oaths about Aledo, and the letters exchanged with Berenguer Ramón – and alludes to legal documents which he had certainly seen:[9] as Pidal says, 'disponía sin duda de parte del archivo cidiano'. This collection of documents would have returned with the army from Valencia in 1102 and might have been deposited in Burgos or Cardeña, but the author of the *Historia* shows no sign of interest in the region or the monastery (beyond writing in conclusion that the Cid was buried in Cardeña by his wife 'non modicis muneribus pro eius anima', which is formulaic). The other likely repository of the documents was Salamanca, to which Jerónimo went as bishop after the abandonment of Valencia. It was and is at Salamanca, in the archive of the Cathedral, that the imposing original donation of the Cid to his new-founded Cathedral of Valencia exists, together with the original of a further substantial gift by Jimena in 1101, and it could well have been there also that the author saw the other documents to which he alludes but which are no longer extant. He shows in his work an altogether exceptional interest in, and has very detailed information about, the Cid's activities in and around Valencia, and writes a section on the conversion of the great mosque of the city into a cathedral, its dedication, and the donation to it, later mentioning the bishop (though not by name). Authorship of the *Historia Roderici* by a Salamancan priest who became interested in the Cid because of the hero's documents in the archive there, and an awareness of the earlier presence there of Jerónimo, makes good sense in other ways. Residence in Salamanca in the kingdom of León might have given an author access to a text of the *Historia Compostelana* from which he could have learned the style of his exordium and, more important, the advantage of basing parts of his work on legal documents textually cited. The writer knows about Jimena's Leonese origins (921.10). Leonese residence could explain why the writer, having mentioned the Cid's rise to power under Sancho II, and the hero's action against the fifteen knights of Zamora, none the less says nothing about the death of Sancho II, a matter of sore embarrassment. The writer's considerable knowledge of Catalán and Aragonese affairs would then have proceeded not from his birth or residence in those regions, but from the rich details in the Cidian archive at Salamanca, including the full texts of the letters exchanged with the Count of Barcelona. There can be no certainty about the date and origin of this work,

but its often excellent information and level-headed tone show
that in the middle years of the twelfth century the Cid was worth
a full biography, paralleled only by that commissioned by the
most powerful Hispanic cleric of the day, Diego Gelmírez of
Compostela. The element of literary and legendary adornment in
the text is significant too.[10]

The substantial presence of the Cid in the reconstructed *Carmen
de morte Sanctii regis*, and hence in the *Najerensis*, has been
discussed in the previous chapter. As noted there, the story of the
Cid's encounter with the party of Zamoran knights was probably
taken by the Oña poet from the incident in the *Historia Roderici*, or
perhaps both had a common source. The *Historia Roderici* is
somewhat muted on all that concerns Sancho II, but the Oña poet
saw a good opportunity of developing his theme by making
the Cid not only engage the knights but also free Sancho from
them. The rest of what is said about the Cid in the reconstructed
Carmen (and thence in the *Najerensis*) seems to have been
invented independently at Oña, but the invention and resulting
prominence of the Cid in connection with Sancho II are important
indications of how indispensable the Cid had become at quite an
early stage. As Dr Powell puts it: 'It has to be Rodrigo who
happens to meet the King's murderer, who realises why the
villain flees. It has to be Rodrigo who frees the King at Golpejera.
For it is he who is the famous hero, the great and loyal warrior,
whose presence at important moments in the history of his time
is expected.' Just so did later literature make the Cid the guardian
of the nation's stability and conscience in the deathbed division
of the realm by Fernando I, give him a role at the capture of
Coimbra (1064), and so on. Oña did not go on to compete with
Cardeña in the Cid industry, but its early testimony to the power
of the Cid legends is important, and in an area – north-east of
Burgos, towards Navarre – that was not otherwise Cidian
territory.[11]

The last work in the series is indeed Navarrese, the *Linaje de
Rodrigo Díaz el Campeador*, a brief genealogy and general account
set down before 1194 (published by Ubieto Arteta, 1964). The text
has been neglected until recently. It starts with the Cid's
genealogy, either adapted from the *Historia Roderici* or sharing a
source with it, but there is an important addition: the name of
Nuño Rasura. Furthermore, while the Cid descended from Laín
Calvo, 'del linage de Nueno Rasuera vino l'Emperador', that is

the royal line down to Alfonso VII of Castile–León, making the Cid's lineage the equal of that of contemporary royalty. Laín Calvo and Nuño Rasura 'fueron anvos iudices de Castiellya', this being the first record of the legend which created these two wholly imaginary 'judges' of emergent Castile (see also Chalon, 1976: 393–4). The legend seems to have been an invention of Burgos, perhaps among members of its legal profession, in the last years of the twelfth century, and (as we see in this Navarrese text) was plainly designed to enhance the lineage of the Cid. The notion of two early judges became an ingredient of the Castilian national myth, was firmly believed in the sixteenth century, and is maintained by some today. But Per Abad, who with his legal interests might have been expected to adopt it, reacted against it by depicting the Cid as no more than an *infanzón*, for excellent artistic reasons of his own. The *Linaje* continues with jottings about the Cid's early deeds, activities with Sancho II and at Zamora, exile, the battle of Tévar, and the conquest of Valencia. These materials are partly derived from the *Historia Roderici* or a similar source, but numerous details are added. These latter are significant because they are not idiosyncratic but correspond to others present in the later tradition, and – since the writer of the *Linaje* does not give the impression of inventing on his own account – they may be assumed to be part of an existing tradition too. At the end the writer gives the date of the Cid's death ('Era Mª. CªXXXª.IIª, en el mes de mayo', that is A.D. 1094; presumably a *V* had dropped out of the Era date in copying), not in accord with the *Historia Roderici* ('mense iulio'), and mentions the burial at Cardeña. The text concludes with the Cid's descendants in what is, so far as we know, accurate historical form, including the earliest mention we have of the Cid's son Diego and his death at Consuegra. The vital material here is that the Cid's daughter Cristina married 'L'Ifant don Ramiro', and that her grandson was 'el rey don Sancho de Navarra, a qui Dios dé vida et hondra'. The text as a whole could thus be said to have had the purpose of assuring the reigning monarch that he came of most excellent stock. The opening genealogy of the Cid, equal in dignity to royalty, is fabulous, while the account of the Cid's deeds mingles legend and history; the concluding genealogy was true and needed no embellishment. The *Linaje*'s materials are not provincial or marginal, but show that the author – perhaps in Pamplona – knew a good deal about the Cid-legends fostered elsewhere in the Peninsula, notably in Burgos (the genealogy), even if concerned to adopt them only in summary form, and could use them in a text of primarily local and genealogical importance. One further text is not concerned with the Cid as subject, but has a reference to him which has become famous (indeed a sort of trump-card in the hands of the traditionalists). The *Poema de Almería* of 1147–9 mentions among the captains of the host one Alvar Rodríguez, son of a famous father who was, in turn, son of an even more famous father, the great Alvar Fáñez (*Alvarus Fannici*). Of him the poet says:[12]

Tempore Roldani si tertius Alvarus esset
post Oliverum, fateor sine crimine verum,
sub iuga Francorum fuerat gens Agarenorum,
nec socii chari iacuissent morte perempti.   (ll. 215–18)

'Alvar would have been the third, if he had been there [i.e., at Roncevaux] . . . and dear comrades would not have been lying dead.' The poet is in epical mood, he knows the *Chanson de Roland* (not surprisingly, if he was in fact the Frenchman Arnault, Bishop of Astorga), and the only fit comparison for Alvar Fáñez is with the heroes of it. He continues:

Ipse Rodericus, Meo Cidi saepe vocatus,
de quo cantatur quod ab hostibus haud superatur,
qui domuit Mauros, comites domuit quoque nostros,
hunc extollebat se laude minore ferebat,
sed fateor verum, quod tollet nulla dierum;

Meo Cidi primus fuit, Alvarus atque secundus.
Morte Roderici Valentia plangit amici
nec valuit Christi famulus ea plus retinere.   (ll. 220–7)

For traditionalists, this is proof that the *Poema de mio Cid* already existed, that the text which Per Abad later copied already existed (remember that sacred date of 1140) and was already famous. To them the text demonstrates that a substantial poem told how the Cid defeated the Moors and 'our Counts' (Counts of Barcelona and/or García Ordóñez and allies), and was never defeated. The poet adds that the Cid praised Alvar Fáñez although he, the Cid, was really the greater in fame, and laments that the 'servant of Christ' (the bishop, or Alfonso VI?) could not retain Valencia.

Several points (out of many possible ones) concern us here. Use of the vernacular 'Meo Cidi' by no means guarantees that the text in question was in the vernacular, as Pidal and others thought (for arguments, see Barceló, 1967–8: 19–25). Nor does 'cantatur' necessarily imply that a vernacular sung epic was being referred to, in view of figurative *Arma virumque cano*, as well-known then as now. The reference is not likely to be to the *Carmen Campidoctoris* (not only a *carmen* but, according to Wright, cast in the form of a hymn), for there is no certainty that this existed by 1147–9, and no evidence that the poem was known outside Ripoll. Yet it seems that the words most naturally bear the sense that some kind of song in the vernacular is being alluded to, and that in it Rodrigo was called 'Mio Cid'. Whether Spanish epic was later sung or chanted, we do not know;[13] some French epic certainly was, but the sole detail we have for the *Poema de mio Cid*, the presenter's explicit at the end of the MS, says plainly 'el romanz es leido', that is, 'I have now finished reading this poem to you', aloud, presumably 'from the book which I have before me'. The word 'saepe' is important too. It makes one think that a song about the Cid, well-known to all and often heard, easily remembered because short, was in the poet's mind. He expects everyone to know who is referred to by his words 'Rodericus, Meo Cidi' without further identification. In the song, perhaps two or three stanzas are to be supposed for mention of victories over Moors and Counts. But the poet does not imply that, in this song, the Cid and Alvar Fáñez were linked. His grammatical structure has lines 221–2 as a parenthesis within which details of the song are given; the main structure is based on lines 220 and 223, 'Rodericus . . . hunc extollebat', the theme of this part being 'hunc', that is Alvar Fáñez. The poet none the less tells us of a tradition whose truth we have no reason to doubt, that the Cid in life had modestly deprecated his own fame and drawn attention to the glory of Alvar. This was indeed considerable, both in the service of Alfonso VI and, after the monarch's death, as governor of Toledo, where from 1109 he withstood a fierce siege by the Almoravids. It must be recalled that in the prose *Chronica Adefonsi Imperatoris*, 'Omisso naturali ordine', sections 96–101 had told in detail of the defence of Toledo by Alvar, 'strenuus dux christ-ianorum', and he and his descendants were clearly of special concern to the writer; perhaps a memory of the Cid's praise of Alvar had come to him from a descendant, rightly proud of the fact. Further to this the *Almeria* poet was, of course, looking for a Hispanic pair-association to set beside that of Roland and Oliver, and he found one in the contemporary lives of the Cid and Alvar Fáñez, respectively first and second among the Spanish warriors of their time, without the implication that they had been associated much in history (they were not) or that they were already linked in the song he refers to. From the start of the *Poema de Almeria* the Carolingian comparison had been in the writer's mind:

> Hic Adefonsus erat, nomen tenet Imperatoris,
> facta sequens Caroli, cui competit aequiparari.
> Gente fuere pares, armorum vi coaequales.   (ll. 4–6)

It is possible that when planning his poem Per Abad, already aware of the Roland/Oliver association in the *Roland* tradition, and aware also of the dramatic utility of creating a similar association in his own work, chose Alvar Fáñez as deuteragonist because his attention was drawn to him in the *Poema de Almeria*; it is likely that Per Abad knew this.[14]

Something more can be said about this song on the Cid. Rico (1975) drew attention to 'el más antiguo cantar paralelístico de la Edad Media peninsular'. It is set down in the prose of the *Crónica de la población de Avila* of about 1255, and in later texts, with variants. The version of 1255, which people 'cantavan en los corros', can be immediately transposed into verse:

> Cantan de Roldán, cantan de Olivero,
> e non de Çorraquín Sancho, que fue buen cavallero.
> Cantan de Olivero, cantan de Roldán,
> e non de Çorraquín Sancho, que fue buen barragán.

The relevance of this to the *Poema de Almeria* is striking, with mention of Roland and Oliver showing knowledge of the *Chanson de Roland* pair, an expectation that an audience would know who they were, and a need to set up a Spanish hero beside them, indeed, instead of them. The song can confidently be dated to 1158, in view of the exploit of Zorraquín which gave rise to the song (though the deed was of local import and on a small scale, hardly of epic grandeur), that is, within a decade of the *Poema de Almeria*. The song is fascinating in all respects, not least in its parallelistic form, so well-known in the Galician–Portuguese lyric of slightly later times but much less known from Castile, and not at all, otherwise, as early as this. Parallelistic songs are capable of potentially indefinite development as the chain-effect continues; thus in our song, 'Çorraquín Sancho' might in following stanzas appear as a rhyme, and then with inversion and a new rhyme, 'Sancho Çorraquín'. Perhaps, in two or three further stanzas, the nature of his deed was briefly stated. The song about the Cid mentioned by the *Almeria* poet could have had this form. Since the song about Zorraquín was contemporary with him, and after being composed in Avila achieved a certain circulation and was long remembered, there is no problem in supposing this equally for a song, perhaps many songs, about the Cid. There is no difficulty either in recognising that a chronicler could have taken account of such songs (though without quoting or translating the vernacular words) whether he was writing in Latin in 1147–9 or in Romance at Avila in 1255.[15]

I have shown that there is no firm evidence for the existence of epic in the vernaculars of Spain before about 1200. Song, popular legendary developments, and pseudohistorical creation by interested parties concerned with persons and themes of the eleventh century and of earlier times too there naturally were. Moreover the Cid had a substantial presence in several literary works composed in the sole literary language of early medieval Christian Spain, Latin, and a further presence in Arabic writing too. That Per Abad invented the techniques of the Spanish epic genre in or shortly before 1207 is a proposition still to be argued. That he should choose the Cid as his subject was natural given the dominance of the man in legendary and literary developments during the twelfth century, and also in view of special factors linking subject and author, to be discussed later.

How can one be relatively certain of that date, 1207? The bibliography on the subject is enormous, and the arguments cannot be recapitulated here (see Magnotta, 1976: Chapter 1; and Lomax, 1977). Menéndez Pidal's view was mentioned in Chapter 1. At a later stage he made a concession: the poem was perhaps orally preserved 'hasta que a fines del siglo XII se puso el poema por escrito' (1965–6: 222), this being intended to leave the door slightly open in case it should be proved that certain late materials were included when the written version was made. Pidal may also have been aware by then of the arguments of Horrent (1964: 477), a fine independently minded though still basically traditionalist scholar, who perceived in the surviving text of the poem layers composed respectively in about 1120, between 1140 and 1150, and a 'nouveau remaniement après 1160, agrémenté de "modernisations"'. The view of the oralists seems to be that there is no such thing as a date of composition, since a poem begins more or less contemporaneously with historical events and evolves in continuous improvisations.[16] Early dates for at least the origins of the *Poema* have been imposed by traditionalists and implicitly by the oralists partly in order to explain the historical content of the work, although, as will be seen, the 'historical' contents are somewhat less factual than has been supposed, and their presence in the *Poema* can be explained in ways that do not involve a poetic tradition in the vernacular stemming from the Cid's time.

The findings of recent research combine to show that the *Poema* was composed in 1207 or a little earlier; and, I add for my part, without dependence upon techniques used earlier in a notional tradition of Spanish epic, nor upon earlier stages of the Cid-story in vernacular verse form. In order of publication, these findings are as follows:

1. In 1952 Russell's study of diplomatic in the poem – mainly of the mention of seals used by Alfonso VI and the Cid – showed that the text could hardly have been composed until late in the twelfth century. This proposition has been challenged by Fletcher (1976) and Lomax (1977), but Russell's view has not been altogether invalidated.

2. In 1957 Ubieto advanced diverse arguments based on historical and geographical references in the *Poema* to show that it could not have been composed as early as 1140, and that a date early in the thirteenth century was likely. These arguments were dismissed by Pidal (1963), but in some respects still have force. Ubieto developed his ideas further in 1972.

3. In 1962 Fradejas published a modest book, which circulated but little, in which he argued that the ideology and ambience of the *Poema* are those of the reign of Alfonso VIII and the years after 1200. This is a more subjective kind of argument, but it is not to be dismissed for that, and will concern us later.

4. In 1967 Pattison advanced a linguistic argument: certain suffixes used in the poem correspond better to a date of about 1200 than to any earlier one. This evidence has never been challenged.

5. In 1971 (a) I opined that some fictional developments in the literary personages of the poem who had prototypes in history would have needed a much longer lapse of time than that allowed by a date of 1140. Much the same was said long ago by Bello. Lomax (1977) finds this unconvincing.

6. Walker in 1977 showed that inspiration for part of the Corpes scene came from the French *Chanson de Florence de Rome*, composed, according to specialists, hardly before 1200. In 1977–8 and again in 1979 I added details of other ways in which the poet had taken ideas and materials from French epics composed in the 1180s and 1190s. Adams in two recent studies, following closely upon the work of Herslund in 1974, has similarly shown the considerable debt of the Spaniard to French epic in matters of phraseology and tense-usage; and there is more in recent work by Hook. Such borrowings from French

can hardly have occurred before the last decade of the twelfth century (see Chapters 5 and 6). These disparate but mutually supporting arguments have managed to convince some students of the question. Lomax in 1977 (in a study probably completed several years earlier) added a new argument of a political kind concerned with affairs of the reign of Alfonso VIII, concluding after review of points 1 to 5 above that:

We simply do not know when the poem was written. There is nothing to be said for 1140; 1207 has at least the authority of the only MS and fits in with the linguistic arguments of Pattison; but perhaps it would be safest to conclude merely that the poem was written in the reign, and probably the kingdom, of Alfonso VIII.

Michael in his 1976 edition of the *Poema* reviews the possibilities, concluding that 'Por tanto, las investigaciones más recientes tenderían unánimemente a fechar el *Poema* existente mucho después de 1140, probablemente hacia el final del siglo XII o el comienzo del XIII, y tal vez entre los años 1201 y 1207', implying that on his own account he finds such a dating acceptable.

The major reason for thinking the poem composed in 1207 is also the most obvious. The unique MS has an explicit in lines 3731–3, in the same hand as that which wrote out the poem. This reads:

Quien escrivio este libro ¡del Dios paraiso, amen!
Per Abbat le escrivio en el mes de mayo
en era de mill e .cc xlv. años.

Hispanic Era 1245 = A.D. 1207. The opinion of Menéndez Pidal, following Sánchez, Bello, and others, was that in what can certainly be observed as a space between the *cc* and the *xlv*, another *c* had once stood and had been erased. The view that a poem composed in about 1140 had come down to us in a MS written in 1307 by Per Abad, a scribe, passed into the standard manuals. However, it now seems certain that the MS was written in or after the middle of the fourteenth century (Horrent, 1973: 203–5), and I have argued (1973: 2–3) that the original explicit in which Per Abad gives his name and the date at which he wrote (1207) was simply copied together with the poem at that mid-fourteenth-century date, as would be entirely natural. The analogy is with tens of thousands of diplomas which, when copied anew into a revised cartulary, for example in the fourteenth century, are copied *in toto*, each with the name of him who first *scripsit* and the date of the original act, the date of the new copy being not stated. The argument about the missing *c* may be put aside, since in medieval MSS dates are often written in this way, with a space between the centuries and what follows. It may seem naive to take the explicit literally without mystifications, but I am not alone in this. The date of 1207 harmonises with what we know about internal aspects of the *Poema*, summarised as points 1 to 6 above. 'En el mes de mayo' does not imply that the poet composed his work within the one month, simply that he concluded it at that time.

Whether Per Abad was author rather than copyist is a more difficult proposition. The name *Abad* was common enough in Castile at the time. However, in 1973 I drew attention to the only Abad, and a Pedro too, who can be shown to have lived at the right time (and in a plausible area) and, from independent documentation, to have had an interest in the Cid of literature and pseudohistory. At Carrión in 1223, before Fernando III and his judges, he presented legal documents concerning a property in Santa Eugenia de Cordobilla, among which was a diploma purporting to concern Lecenio, abbot of a small monastery in Santa Eugenia and putative relative of the Cid, and purporting also to have been issued in 1075. This was a blatant forgery, as were other related documents in the series, and the royal judges very properly threw them out. The chief interest of the Lecenio diploma is that among those confirming it figure ten persons (out of eighteen lay confirmers) who are present in the *Poema de mio Cid* or in other literature about the hero. The forged diploma presented at court in 1223 may confidently be supposed the work of Per Abad, he as expert author being sent to court as the man best able to defend it; and he would have been given the task of forging it because, as author of the *Poema*, he was known to be informed about personages and background of the Cid's time. The record of the 1223 proceedings tells us that Per Abad was a layman, since he is given no ecclesiastical title, and he was accompanied by his two sons, Juan and Pedro, who would not have been there, presumably, unless already adult. One may suppose that Per Abad was a lawyer and that his sons were training in the profession; the confection of diplomas, even those that were to be rejected as spurious, was a skilled business for which professional help would be sought. If Per Abad had sons adult in 1223, he would have been amply of adult age himself to have composed the poem in 1207, and would have been born about 1170 or 1175. His legal profession, together with the dates and places of his training so far as we can guess at them, are more than marginally relevant to the nature of the *Poema*, as will be seen. To make the final link between the Per Abad who forged the diploma and the Per Abad who *escrivio* the poem requires an assessment of probabilities and cannot be a precise demonstration. My view has been reported by others without convincing them.[17]

Admittedly it requires special pleading to argue that *escrivio* means here not 'wrote out (as a copyist)' but 'wrote (as a new poetic work)'. It has long been recognised that the act of authorship in the Middle Ages was designated in Castilian by *fer*, *fazer*, *componer*, while *escrivir* was used of the act of copying. However, it may have taken time for this usage to settle down. A possible parallel for Per Abad's usage of *escrivir* for 'compose' is provided by the last stanza, 2675, of MS 'O' (written about 1300) of the *Libro de Alexandre*, which reads in part: 'Se quisierdes saber quien escreuio este ditado, / Johan Lorenço bon clerigo e ondrado / natural de Astorga . . .' Good authorities including Menéndez Pidal and – at one time – Michael have been prepared to accept that *escreuio* here means that Juan Lorenzo de Astorga composed the poem, but others have taken him to be a copyist only. It is true that the first line of stanza 2675 is metrically irregular, but so are many others in the poem. The issue is further complicated by the fact that in the other MS of the *Alexandre*, 'P' (written in the fifteenth century), the corresponding part of stanza 2675 reads: 'Sy queredes saber quien fizo esti ditado, / Gonçalo de Berçeo es por nonbre clamado, / natural de Madrid . . .' This has a first line which is metrically satisfactory, together with the verb *fizo*, but the late testimony to Berceo's authorship is as much debated as the other.[18] The *Alexandre* was composed at some time in the first half of the thirteenth century, perhaps some two decades after the *Poema de mio Cid*, and by a man who stood in some kind of relationship to Berceo and to the school of Palencia.[19] The evidence is, admittedly, unsure; we cannot guess what phrase was used at this point in the original of the *Alexandre*, and the most one can say is that in a MS written about 1300 *escrivir* was possibly used of the act of authorship.

Another line of reasoning may provide support. Since Per Abad was the first author of his kind in a Spanish vernacular, he had no tradition of usage for this concept to guide him, and opted for *escrivir* as he might have chosen one of several words. Moreover, if he was – as I argue – a practising lawyer, he would have used almost automatically the vernacular version of the Latin verb with which notaries regularly terminated their diplomas, *scripsit*. Although diplomas are formulaic, the circumstances of each differed, and to write one had an element of originality about it. The fact that the authorial explicit of the MS of the *Poema* is dated by month and year, uniquely among texts of its type, may further indicate that the author was continuing a habit of the notaries. Among those who have thought Per Abad an author of some kind (perhaps a *refundidor*) are, in recent years, Criado de Val (1970: 105–6), Riaño Rodríguez (1971), and Ubieto Arteta (1972: 189). Among objections are those of Michael (1978: note 60 to p. 48, and note to l. 3732 of the text).

In 1957 Dámaso Alonso drew attention to details recorded by two Golden-Age historians of Seville.[20] At the *repartimiento* of the city following its capture in 1248, lands were given to one 'Domingo Abad de los Romances . . . cauallero de la criacion del santo rey don Fernando' and to 'Nicolas de los Romances . . . de la criacion del Rei don Alfonso', probably son of the former; also to Martín Abad. In 1260 one of these, Nicolás 'de los Romances' was paid by the King 'por las trobas que le fizo para cantar en la su fiesta de San Clemente e de San Leandro, etc.' As argued earlier, *romance* at this time means 'long narrative poem'. The name *Abad* was common enough, but it is far from common to find it associated with literature. Was there a small poetic dynasty of Abads, Domingo being a son of Per Abad who *escrivio* the *Poema de mio Cid*, and Nicolás his grandson? Very recently Professor D. P. Seniff told me of an even more startling conjunction of names.[21] The *Libro de la montería* written for Alfonso XI (1312–50) contains in its Book III, among very numerous topographical references, two adjacent ones to 'Cabeça de Per Abat' and 'Cabeça del Cid', which Seniff locates 'in the vicinity of Cadalso/San Martín, south of Avila and northwest of Toledo'. Both would be fanciful posterior namings (that is, we know of no activities by the historical Cid in that region, so the case is not like that of the 'Poyo de mio Çid' in the *Poema*, l. 902), but could be extraordinarily significant even so. After all, it is not copyists who are remembered in this way, but poets – and heroes – sometimes are (compare, perhaps, Byron's Pool at Grantchester, and La Grotta di Byron in Liguria, La Fuente de Garcilaso, Tennyson Down, Shakespeare Cliff). All may be, of course, the merest coincidence; but there are rather numerous coincidences.

We have seen that Menéndez Pidal believed that a poem about

the Cid was composed in about 1105, received a major revision about 1140, was reworked again during the twelfth century 'hasta que a fines del siglo XII se puso el poema por escrito', and was then transmitted in a series of copies in relatively stable form until recorded for us in the surviving MS of the fourteenth century (of 1307, he thought). Horrent also believed in a series of reworkings. Such reworkings – *refundiciones, remaniements* – are fundamental to the thinking of the traditionalists, and of course, with a more extreme emphasis on improvisation, to that of the oralists. There is nothing in positivist thinking opposed to the idea of such reworkings, for we have evidence that French epic was so reworked and there are many examples of it. To take the most obvious: the *Roland* shows a variety of reworkings in its surviving texts; the Spanish *Roncesvalles* took elements from a now lost version of the *Roland*; Adenet le Roi in 1272–5 reworked a poem about *Berte aus grans piés* of the late twelfth century, not now extant; and so on. On the other hand, traditionalists inside and outside Spain have always sought to enlarge, as well as to assign very early dates to, the relatively small corpus of epic poems, for reasons examined in the previous chapter. This has led to supposition of poems where there was no more than a monastic or genealogical legend taken up by a chronicler, and it has led to assumptions about reworkings of epics where none can be shown to have existed. It now seems doubtful, for example, whether there ever was a major reworking and extension of the *Infantes de Lara* poem once supposed on the basis of the very different prose redactions in the *Primera Crónica General* and the *Crónica de 1344*.[22] The point is important for my argument because, if it can be shown that reworking was a habit of the thirteenth and fourteenth centuries in Spain, it could be held that the *Poema de mio Cid* of 1207 is likely to be a reworking of an earlier text, or an item in a whole series of reworkings, rather than the original unitary composition of 1207 which I hold it to be. In the case of the *Poema*, I have shown that no record of its existence in the twelfth century can be claimed. In the thirteenth, Menéndez Pidal thought (and most others followed him) that a major *refundición* was made. The Per Abad version, he held, was for some reason taken up by the author of the *Crónica de veinte reyes* – then dated about 1360 – and set down in chronicle prose. Meanwhile, the poem had been reworked by a *juglar* so as to produce the version which was known to the Alphonsine team as they gathered materials for their *Estoria de España* (*Primera Crónica General*) on which work concluded in 1289. This is not the place for a detailed account of chronicle composition and evolution, but recent work has greatly changed Menéndez Pidal's analysis. The *Crónica de veinte reyes* is now thought to have been redacted about 1300, and its sections on the Cid to represent the work of Alfonso's team much more accurately than does the *Primera Crónica General*. Nor is there any longer reason to suppose that there was a major poetic reworking of the *Poema*.

My view of the matter is as follows (more fully in Smith, 1980b: 418–19). Per Abad's 1207 text was copied, unchanged, and sent from Burgos to Alfonso's chroniclers in Toledo, where a prose version was incorporated in the *borrador* (preparatory draft) and was later used in the *Crónica de veinte reyes*. This is the only chronicle to represent Per Abad's text at all faithfully (though naturally it makes many adjustments, omits overtly poetic materials, etc.). Per Abad's text received, perhaps soon after 1207, an adjustment which may seem minor but was to have repercussions: someone who knew his history better than Per Abad – in this particular, at least – introduced a variant according to which, instead of 'King' Búcar being killed by the Cid as he flees from before Valencia – as in Per Abad's original – Búcar makes good his escape in a waiting boat. It has been thought that this adjustment was the work of a historically-minded chronicler, but there is reason to think that it had a poetic origin, that is, within a revised version (not amounting to a major reworking) of Per Abad's poem (Smith, 1980b: 418). The major reworking was not in verse at all, but was that produced by a monk of Cardeña when he put Per Abad's poem into prose, substantially altering its later sections and adding a large amount of pious pseudo-historical material about the Cid's last days in Valencia, his death, the taking of his body to Cardeña, his burial there, and miracles worked at his tomb. This prose *Estoria del Cid* (also known in modern times as the *Leyenda de Cardeña*) does not survive, but on being presented to Alfonso X by the Abbot of Cardeña in 1272 – as we can be reasonably sure – was incorporated more or less verbatim into the main *borrador* being built up by the Alphonsine team, displacing the version of the poem they already had (although this was to be the version preferred by, or alone available to, the *Crónica de veinte reyes*); hence it passed into the *Primera Crónica General* and on into mainstream historiography. This *Estoria del Cid* of Cardeña can be dated to the years immediately before 1272, and the sources for most of its additional materials – wholly non-Hispanic, and non-poetic too – are known (Smith, 1976*a*: 512–22). A reworking, then, of a substantial kind, there certainly was; it convinced Alfonso X of its usefulness as a historical source because of its holy provenance, and it received a large place in the chronicles, but it was a vernacular prose *pia fraus* by a monk of Cardeña, a culmination of the cult of the Cid in the monastery, and had nothing remotely poetic about it. Other variants of other stories in the chronicles, even very substantial ones, may turn out on cool inquiry to have a like origin;[23] the Fernán González story is ripe for such an investigation.

There can be no support, from what we know of the life of this text in the thirteenth and fourteenth centuries, for the notion of a series of reworkings of the *Poema* during the twelfth. When, at a late stage, further additions were made to the Cid-canon by way of new personages and incidents, they emanate again from Cardeña and similar sources, and in the first instance have nothing to do with vernacular verse. The situation of the other Cid-poem, the *Mocedades*, in the fourteenth century, is similar. A *Gesta de las mocedades de Rodrigo* was composed in the closing years of the thirteenth century in Burgos, and is summarised in the *Crónica de Castilla* of about 1300. From it there derived, possibly via a lost intermediate version, the surviving *Mocedades* poem of about 1360, composed in Palencia in the interests of the city and diocese, by a learned – if woefully incompetent – poet. There were thus two, perhaps three, successive *Mocedades* poems. The references to and accounts of this *Mocedades* tradition in chronicles and other texts of the fifteenth and sixteenth centuries, and the fine ballads that derive from it, do not lead us to suppose the extraordinary number of full poetic reworkings believed in by Armistead; they may represent very minor adjustments made by chroniclers or by others in response to local, family, and monastic concerns, and even ballad-makers were not wholly devoid of inventiveness (see Armistead, 1978, and my reply, forthcoming).

3 The poet, his ethos and ambience

I hope it can be accepted that the *Poema* is a unitary work, composed by one man at one point in time. The poem re-created materials drawn from both history and literature. The history was that of Spain, the literary sources were on the one hand in Latin and French and on the other Peninsular in nature but not, I think, in any of the Peninsular vernaculars. The *Poema* is a kind of *chanson de geste*, an attempt to emulate and acclimatise the great French genre, but it is also very much more than that, since it is an epic of a new and advanced kind, indeed, a revolutionary interpretation of an established European mode. Being new, it was experimental, and in consequence is not without shortcomings and small technical deficiencies, but these scarcely detract from its power as a work of art. To me its plot construction, its portrayal of credible human beings, its coherent ideology, its feeling for life as a continuum, its consistency of tone and style mark the poem as plainly the work of one man at one time. I do not like von Richthofen's idea about the independent authorship and precedence in time of Cantar II, especially as it requires assumptions about very early dates (1970: 136–46). The proposal of Garci-Gómez in his 1975 book and 1977 edition, that Cantar III is an independent unit, a 'razón' by a different author, seems to me ill-supported and unhelpful. Recent computer-aided studies of style confirm, as it happens, the authorial unity of the present text, but of course in themselves such studies are not conclusive since, even on oralist and traditionalist terms, in any improvisation or reworking linguistic unity would have been imposed by each performer or *refundidor* in line with his own tastes and those of his public.[1] The text as we have it is adequate for any argument about its unity, and computerised statistics will do no more than add a veneer of modernity to common sense. Nor is discussion affected by the lacunae known to exist, or by Russell's suggestion of a possibly truncated ending.[2] In any case there is strong

73

support, among critics of otherwise varying stance, for the principle of unitary composition. Those who have contributed to the study of the work as a poem, as literature, have naturally assumed that they were dealing with a unity, with the product of a single mind which could be approached as such.

What manner of man was this poet? In the absence of biographical data, anything we wish to say has to be deduced from the poem and supported, where possible, from what we know of the period. It is necessary to insist that the poet was a literate, well-informed, and cultured man, who composed in writing with a full awareness of the basis of his craft as it had been devised and developed in French. The survey of his metrics, sources, and language will prove this adequately. He had a clear sense of his public, potential rather than existing, and a clear sense too of the exemplary message which – beyond the excitement and entertainment of his drama – he wished to convey. There is no contemporary criticism or comment which would enable us to judge of his success in this, but it can be gauged from the way in which other poets followed his lead, producing a small but distinguished epic genre in Castilian in the next decades; also from the way in which the poem, with adjustments, was incorporated at length into the national chronicles, and helped to establish the Cid as the national hero. So persuasive was the poet that much of what he wrote as fiction passed – because it did not conflict with other sources – into the chronicles, and long remained part of the standard history of the realm. It is necessary to say all this, naive though it might appear, because of the notion implanted in medieval studies in recent years about the essentially illiterate nature of those who, it is held, orally improvised some of the outstanding works of medieval verse. Menéndez Pidal and his school never fell into such extremes: to them, the author of the *Poema* was a professional performing *juglar*, a minstrel, but 'entiéndase juglar docto y altísimo poeta', and, moreover, 'al hablar de juglares en el siglo XII, no quiero decir sino "poetas" que escriben para legos' (Menéndez Pidal, 1945: 92, 80).

That word 'escriben' seems literal enough, and is not a vague synonym for 'compose'. (In describing the notional *Cantar de Gormaz*, supposed ancestor or first stage of the *Poema*, to be dated about 1105, Menéndez Pidal referred to its 'redacción' at that time.) There were in about 1200 only two classes of men who were both literate (as were many nobles, merchants, etc.) and accustomed to composing in writing, as well as to verbatim copying, naturally: the clergy and the lawyers, whose medium up to that time was nearly always Latin. Sometimes a man was both priest and lawyer, as was Berceo. Although it is tempting, from the presence of Cardeña in the poem, to think it the work of a monk of that monastery, there are good reasons why this cannot have been the case.[3] Nor is it likely that the poet was a priest whose duties brought him into contact with the monastery, as Berceo's did with San Millán. The argument here is subjective, in that the *Poema* does not strike one as the work of a priest. The religious attitudes and observances attributed to the Cid and others seem to be those which would occur to a layman and are accurately represented, but no more. What is said about the archangelic visitation, Bishop Jerónimo, the death of the Cid, and other matters, is surely said with a layman's voice. Good controls are available in the poems of Berceo (including passages of epic tone) and the *Poema de Fernán González*, by a monk of Arlanza.

To identify the author as a lawyer by elimination of other possibilities is naturally not good enough. Nor can the argument be based on that Pedro Abad of the 1223 diploma. From within the *Poema* emerges all the evidence needed for the thesis that we have here a legally-trained mind and a legally-professing person at work, in the whole cast of the drama, in some episodes, and in many details. In contrast, the other Spanish epics do not have this character or wealth of detail of a legalistic kind,[4] and the same seems to be true of French epics on the whole, possibly with the notable exception of the prime version of the *Roland*,[5] a poem which in some form was certainly known to Per Abad. My thesis is by no means original but has been anticipated to some extent by others.[6] Apart from this belief that the poet was a lawyer, one may cite admirable studies by Hinojosa (1899) and others since in which the extraordinary richness of the text for historians of the law has been recognised, even though Hinojosa and others did not venture to question the reigning traditionalist view of the authorship and nature of the work. I shall refer later to the most recent inquiry, that of Lacarra; her findings are strongly in support.

My case for Per Abad as a lawyer was argued some years ago (1972: xxxiv–vi, and 1977*a*). I summarise it here, modifying a few details and adding others owed to the recent work of contemporaries. There are three general propositions:

1. The poet sees a legal aspect to many human acts. Life is conditioned by the *ira* or *graçia del rey*. The great court-room scene forms the climax of the poem, and the poet attains the summit of his art in writing it.

2. The poet wishes us to see the Cid's legal expertise and court-room rhetoric as a facet of his epic character; the Cid is a warrior and a general, but in this new kind of epic, civic and familial virtues are as important as the military, and the Cid's exemplary character is intended to be enriched in this way.

3. Ultimately, justice is not so much a matter of God's will being revealed in judicial duels, still less sought by private vengeance, as a more modern process of hearing pleas and taking evidence before impartial judges. That the Cid does proceed to exact justice in the final duels, in public and in blood, is perhaps a concession to epic tradition (that of French). Alternatively, as Lacarra proposes, the poet as part of a reforming programme is putting the case for the judicial duel, in his day still quite new, according to a set of rules and under the presidency of the monarch, as preferable to the anarchic taking of private vengeance (Lacarra, 1980a: 77–96).

These propositions seem to me self-evident. More could be made of the poet's concern with feudal relationships, banishment, the loss and recovery of honour, treason, challenges, and so on. While much medieval and other literature is about these things, without being the product of legally-trained authors, it seems to me that the prominence given to them in the *Poema*, and more tellingly, the amount of precise legalistic detail and phraseology with which they are presented, strengthens the probability that Per Abad was a lawyer. The further proofs concern these details and this phraseology, as presented in my 1977 paper (*a*) under the following heads: mention of written documents, feudal relationships, fiefs and epithets, naming of places, the first marriages, the Cortes, and finally, of general application, some of the binary phrasing. Some of these aspects are discussed below. It will suffice here to draw attention to the kinds of legal texts to which the poet refers and to areas of the law in which expert knowledge may be assumed in him.[7]

From diplomas of one kind or another, but especially of the commonly surviving kind which record gifts or transfer of land, or grant exemptions from taxes and visitations, the poet took his way of referring to certain places. Thus 'o dizen Castejon' (l. 435; also ll. 649, 2653, 2657, 2876, 2879) compares with 'ubi vocitant

Villanova', 'ubi dicent Felgario'. From the way in which confirmers of diplomas were sometimes listed, the poet adopted
such phraseology as 'Minaya Albar Fañez que Çorita mando' (l.
735), for which compare 'comes Petrus Asuriz mandante Salda-
nia'. The epithet 'el Castelano' applied to the Cid (ll. 748, 1067) –
somewhat oddly, it might be thought – may have been suggested
to the poet because the Cid of history occasionally figured among
confirmers as 'Ruderico Didaz Kastellanus' to distinguish him
from his brother-in-law (Jimena's brother) of the same name,
'Rudericus Didaz Ovetensis comes'. In this event, the poet may
have sought out in the archives diplomas in which the Cid had
figured. The listing of the royal domains (ll. 2923–6, 2977–9)
derives from their listing in similar fashion regularly in the
diplomas of Alfonso VI, and was perhaps necessary for an
audience at a time – about 1200 – when León and Castile were
again separate. The archive of Cardeña or the municipal and
cathedral archives of Burgos would have provided ample
material of this sort for the poet, but if he were a practising
notary, such documents would have been often in his hands and
their formulae second nature to him. I do not doubt that further
correspondences can be established on the lines of Hook's
admirable work (1980a, 1981b).[8]

The poet was acquainted too with local charters, the *fueros*. His
phrase 'los que comien so pan' (l. 1682) as a variant on 'los
vasallos del Çid' could have come from one of a number of texts,
such as the *Fuero de Cuenca* ('pro hominibus qui panem suum
comedunt'). The reference in line 902 to the 'Poyo de mio Çid'
shows knowledge of the *Fuero de Molina*, whose further significance will be mentioned later. *Fueros* of this type were constantly
consulted by lawyers.

For another category of references, I had in earlier work
supposed that the poet knew documents of legal and quasi-legal
standing issued by or concerning the historical Cid and constitut-
ing his personal archive, this having been deposited after the
abandonment of Valencia in Burgos or Cardeña. I now think, as
argued in Chapter 2, that the archive went with Bishop Jerónimo
to Salamanca, where it is unlikely that the Burgos poet would
have known it; the materials which I earlier thought the poet had
drawn from this archive can now, I think, be better explained as
drawn from the *Historia Roderici* composed in Salamanca, as I
shall argue in Chapter 5. But the poet knew kinds of quasi-legal

documents related to historical campaigns, perhaps more of his own time, and they gave him materials which, in his fine *verista* spirit, he could apply to his literary account of the Cid. He seems to refer to such documents in lines 1259 (the Cid orders a written roll to be made of the army in Valencia) and 1773 (spoils are divided and a written record made). On the analogy of this, a similar written record is made of spoils (l. 511) and of the agreement for the sale of Alcocer (l. 844), both of these relating to wholly fictional episodes (see also the illuminating commentary on this by Hook, 1980a: 42). A document about the historical *repartimiento* of a captured town gave the poet his guidance when describing the literary *repartimiento* of Valencia among the Cid's vassals, the different categories being differently rewarded (ll. 1245–8), and when mentioning measures then proclaimed to prevent desertion by those newly enriched (ll. 1249–62).

For the poet's other sources in the law one can refer only to his general professionalism, without precise indications. He had a clear notion of feudal hierarchy and etiquette, as anyone in a responsible position would have had; but he shows special concern with titles, ranks, precedence, and ceremonial. Some of this is necessary for the purposes of the plot, since the Cid is portrayed as of relatively low *infanzón* status but becomes sufficiently wealthy for his daughters to attract the covetous notice of the Infantes; eventually the Infantes decide that the wealth – rapidly spent – was no compensation to them for marrying so far beneath themselves, or for the loss of face suffered in Valencia. On these matters argument rages in court, for status and face are at the core of the drama and of the legal question. Sometimes the poet's insistence on proper ceremony gets him into metrically awkward situations (e.g. ll. 298, 1252). The poet–lawyer was an expert on the law relating to marriage, as shown by skilled analysts.[9] There are, of course, marriages in other epics – *Los Infantes de Lara*, *Las mocedades de Rodrigo*, *Fernán González* – but little attention is paid to them. In our *Poema*, all stages are represented with a seriousness and regard for detail which reveal the special competence of a legally-trained author. He takes pleasure in procedural subtleties which have the further useful literary effect of enhancing *verismo*, and he commands the full technical vocabulary, ritual movements and gestures, etc. The same may be said of the poet's handling of the *ira regia*, the details of the Cid's banishment, the King's treatment of the hero's followers, the progressive removal of legal disabilities, and so on. In this aspect, as in his whole handling of the Cortes episode, the poet may have had a programme of juridical reform to outline, as will be seen.

What kind of a lawyer was Per Abad? If he was the same as the one in the 1223 court case, that he forged a series of diplomas hardly stamps him as a criminal, for such forgery on behalf of a religious house or cause might fall within the range of Christian good works, while his failure to convince the judges does not mark him as incompetent, for the confection of diplomas was a very hit-and-miss business.[10] We can see within the text of the poem that the author was expert in several branches of civil and constitutional law. He was no mere outsider with an amateur interest, but a practising professional, to judge by the detail that he deals in, the precision and unapologetic air of his terminology, and his occasional mildly pedantic addition of matter not wholly relevant to plot or characterisation. He was at the least a notary, but beyond that, was acquainted with legal aspects of marriage at high social levels and with affairs within the competence of the monarch. On the other side, he made nothing of questions of canon law. Had he been a canon lawyer, one might have expected argument in the poem about the age at which the Cid's daughters might marry (they are simply said to be very young; elsewhere, the poet was specific about the 'niña de nuef años'). More would probably have been made of Bishop Jerónimo and the manner of his appointment in Valencia; our lay poet shows the Cid choosing him (l. 1300) and the Cid's captains, probably, confirming the election (l. 1310), which is contrary both to what happened in history in this case, and to normal practice (though the poet may have meant to convey that the Cid as lord of Valencia was acting with quasi-regal powers, for Spanish monarchs had long influenced, and even effected, the appointment of bishops). On the key matter of the undoing of the marriages of the daughters, about which one expects that argument should rage in court with much reference to canon law, nothing whatsoever is said. It is simply assumed that by their violence the Infantes have repudiated their wives and that the girls are free to remarry, even though it is plain that the first marriages have been consummated (l. 2703).[11] The poet also gives the impression that the monastery of Cardeña was exempt from the royal prohibition of aid for the Cid, and was able to accord him not only a welcome but also food and lodging; this makes a fine literary scene, but must fly in the face of the real situation of a monastery at the time (whether in 1081 or 1207: Russell, 1978: 94–8; and Lacarra, 1980a: 173 ff.). The poet was, then, at most a civil lawyer. But he knew Cardeña well, not merely as any Burgos man might, but more intimately, and his sentiments were with it too. The monastery has a prominent and honourable place in the poem, and material support for it is enjoined by implication (in the abbot's words to the Cid's emissary, ll. 1443–6) upon the poem's audience. The poet possibly had the Benedictine rule in mind when depicting the abbot's welcome to the Cid (Serrano Castilla, 1954). Recently Hook has shown that the poet knew the type of legal instrument in which a man came to an agreement with a monastery in respect of care for his family, and other matters, on leaving for the wars (1980b); this important addition to our knowledge makes it likely that Per Abad had acted for Cardeña or another house in just such cases.

To the above, an addition must be made. The poet drew much of his material and language from the law, but may have found inspiration of similar kinds already present in literary texts. It is likely that the trial of Ganelon in the *Roland* gave Per Abad the idea of including a similar scene in his own work. However, the Cortes scene in the *Poema* is a much more important episode than the trial of Ganelon in the *Roland*. The latter comprises only 111 lines (3747–857) in the 'O' version, but the Cortes scene occupies 447 (3061–507). Also, Per Abad narrates his trial with a much greater feeling for setting, detail, and technicality, than does 'Turoldus'. Moreover, whereas the climax of the French poem comes with the death and ascent to heaven of Roland, the trial and punishment of Ganelon appearing as a necessary but unimpressive appendix, the climax of the *Poema* comes in the court, with vindication of the Cid, together with (as the proceedings are ending) the arrival of the emissaries to propose new and nobler marriages for the hero's daughters. It is in this court scene that critics have recognised the peak of the poet's dramatic powers, in the clash of personalities and the battle of words and attitudes there fought out. It could further be argued that whereas 'Turoldus' narrates the court proceedings in terms of a somewhat archaic past, Per Abad tells his about a more recent time, and is able to convey, without anachronism, a strong message about the rule of law. It was, then, no more than a hint

that Per Abad took from this aspect of the *Roland*; the development, a triumph, was wholly his own. Some of the poet's
legalistic phraseology is documented both in the legal texts of
Spain and in French epic and law, and we cannot be sure from
which the poet took it: perhaps from both, literary precedent
confirming what he knew in legal practice (see also Hook, 1980:
note 14 to p. 35).

If it be accepted that Per Abad was a lawyer, several matters fall
into place. As argued in Chapter 1, Spanish lawyers were
accustomed to bilingual work. Not only were *fueros* drawn up in
both Latin and the vernacular, but *ad hoc* versions were made of
many kinds of Latin document so that they could be recited to
interested parties at the moment of their redaction and also read
out later in the public square.[12] Lawyers were in the forefront of a
linguistic revolution in the years after 1200, and it is entirely
logical to hold that two of them, Per Abad in 1207 and Berceo
about 1220, were responsible for the accompanying revolution
which produced two genres of narrative verse in the vernaculars
of northern Spain.

Lawyers wrote, by habit, a special formulaic language in
documents of every kind, in Latin which was often rhythmical,
alliterative, and rich in binary and balanced phrases. It has been
humorously suggested to the oralists, who use high percentages
of formulaic hemistichs as proof of the orally-improvised nature
of poetic texts, that legal diplomas which are heavily formulaic
were therefore orally-improvised too, by illiterates. What was
suggested as a joke may have a serious point, in that lawyers such
as Per Abad may quite naturally have written a strongly formulaic
style in their original verse, in addition to adopting many Latin
legal clichés directly. To a lesser degree, the same applies to
Berceo.

Some of the rightly lauded *verismo* of the *Poema* may also be
owed not merely to the author's temperament but to his legal
training. Lawyers have to be hard-headed, concerned with
detail, with property and its value, with the social status of
clients. I select one aspect of *verismo*, the geographical. That
lawyers travelled widely and often on business is obvious. When
a lawyer writes an epic, part of the setting will consist of credible
geography, even, or especially, when fictional episodes and
personages are to be set upon it. The *Poema* has always been
recognised as having a notably acute sense of geographical

realism with regard to locations and journeys. Not all the poet's geography is as accurate as Menéndez Pidal proposed (with textual adjustments) in his classic study, for recent scholars have reservations, and even when new readings or identifications are proposed, not all is clear (Criado de Val, 1970; Ubieto Arteta, 1972: 73–110; Michael, 1976, 1977). The precise location of Corpes, for example, is debated, as are points in the routes leading to and from it. Other routes are deliberately not described at all, for the poet was not producing a complete tourist guide. As for Corpes, the poet may not have intended any precise location, but one within a region suited to his artistic purposes, remote from habitation, wild, menacingly primitive. Where the poet does give details of itineraries, he probably does so because he knew the areas from his travels, and I have shown elsewhere that the poet, based in Burgos, could well have travelled as did the royal notaries along routes prominent in the poem, linking Burgos, Atienza, San Esteban, Berlanga, Medinaceli, Ayllón, etc., in the years 1201, 1203, and others.[13] One cannot demonstrate, but it is legitimate to suppose, a similar familiarity of the poet–lawyer with the valley of the Jalón, further east, and down to Molina. The legal mind provided the instinct for such geographical exactness, and the notary's experience on business gave the knowledge. That, as a poet, the lawyer was less than exact about the order of places or the duration of stages merely shows that he was either forgetful, or not concerned within his creation to be pedantically precise. There is the further point that Per Abad would have found his lawyer's instinct for geographical detail enhanced by the presence of itineraries, in some number, in French epics, whose phraseology in this regard he imitated. That San Esteban de Gormaz is 'una buena çipdad' (l. 397) and its inhabitants 'siempre mesurados son' (l. 2820) does not mean that the poet was born there or dwelled there, or in Medinaceli, as Pidal thought; possibly the poet was honouring hosts or friends made when he was on business there, but the first line was conventional enough in view of precedents in French.[14] Recently Russell has made another suggestion about the nature and sources of the itineraries in the *Poema*.[15] The poet naturally knew Burgos and used topographical detail in the opening sections of his work, and he could well have known Toledo, but it seems impossible that he could have seen Valencia, for it was in Moorish hands, despite the marvellous panoramic evocation he gives of it after hints from a French source (see Chapter 5). For his geography of the Levante and details of the Cid's campaigns, the poet was able to draw much from the *Historia Roderici*. An excellent guide to all aspects of the geography is provided by Michael's notes in his edition of the poem.

If Per Abad had been simply a cultured man with literary pretensions, a patriot keen to give Castile an epic poem, he might have produced a mere transposition of a *chanson de geste*, on the theme of the Cid but with the hero a haughty rebellious vassal of the type frequent in French; and his poem would have been replete with senseless slaughter on the Gallic model. A lawyer who was a practitioner of the traditional law of Castile would have had no reason to compose a legalistically minded poem about 1200, for he would have had no more motivation than had been present for a long time (during which, so far as we know, no poem was composed). New stimuli were involved: not only that of French epic, but on the ethical and constitutional side, in the exemplary aspect, that provided by new studies of Roman law. The standing and popularity of these in the last decades of the twelfth century impressed Walter of Châtillon (d. *c.* 1200): 'Soli regnant nunc legistae, / quibus mundus servit iste, / totus citra saecula . . .' Such studies would have attracted Per Abad as they did many others at the time. A Per Abad born in about 1170 or 1175 would have trained in the last years of the century. There seems, alas, to be no full study of the processes or instruments by which new Roman law was introduced into Spain at the time, and it may be that documentation is lacking. The thirteenth century was well advanced before Castilians going to study at the fountainhead, Bologna, are recorded for us in any numbers. Nor is there any reason to suppose any residence of Per Abad in Italy. But on all grounds it is reasonable to suggest that he went to study in France. While there as a student of law he would have acquired a sound knowledge of French, and of the *chansons de geste*, of the whole art of the epic poet in a genre then (1195–1200?) at the height of its popularity. That his knowledge of the epics was wide will become apparent in the study of his sources, and since he makes almost no mistake in handling them, we may say that his command of French was sound too. Moreover, his confident adaptation of much of the rhetoric of the French poems shows an intimate acquaintance with the genre on a broad scale. Burgos annually received thousands of French pilgrims on their way to Compostela, and had a substantial *barrio de francos*; the city was at a high point of power and prosperity in the period which concerns us, being much favoured by Alfonso VIII because of its loyalty to him during his minority, it had strong international connections especially with France (Serrano, 1935–6: II, 58, and 210 ff.; Lacarra, 1980a: 186–7), and it was the scene of several important international gatherings whose cultural consequences may readily be supposed.[16] There is thus no problem in surmising that a Burgos man could have learned French in Burgos and there heard occasional renderings of French epic or received texts of it. Yet it remains easier to suppose that Per Abad received his higher education in France and not in the Old Castilian capital, for at the time the latter may not even have had a cathedral school, and it certainly had no law studies. For these he might have gone to Montpellier or Orléans or Paris, or less probably to Toulouse.[17] The only other deduction that one can make about the poet's formation is that he received a grounding in Latin, necessary for all higher study and for the practice of law; and that he knew, at least in excerpts, certain Classical Latin texts and some medieval ones. He could have acquired basic Latin in Burgos, but better in France, and the Classical Latin literary texts would have been more accessible there. It has to be remembered that Castilian educational resources were, at the time, far inferior to those of France and Provence; also, any MSS of the *chansons de geste* and of the Latin texts in question were rare in Spain so far as we know from evidence of the times and from surviving texts.

Much of the above is supposition and conjecture. Yet it is hard to see how important aspects of the *Poema*, and hence of its author, can be explained in any other way. The poet, as will be seen, had not merely a smattering of this and that, but was a notably learned man. Also, he had a deeply serious and responsible intention in writing, and was no simple entertainer. What I have conjectured is not wildly improbable. It contrasts in several ways with what can be guessed about Berceo, who probably trained at the *studium* of Palencia under *magistri* brought from France, and wrote in the different atmosphere of heightened educational endeavour induced by the Fourth Lateran Council of 1215.

As Castro remarked (1935: 27), 'Se ve distintamente que lo jurídico y lo didáctico no es ganga que arrastre el *Poema*, sino elemento esencial de cierta concepción de la vida, base de la civilización coetánea.' We do no injustice to this observation in applying it to 1207 rather than to 1140, which Castro probably had in mind, and to a situation in which new Roman-law studies were providing novelty and excitement. The 'concepción de la vida' is idealistic rather than prosaic, as befits a lawyer with poetic inclinations. The conception is forward-looking in terms of a juridical programme, but takes its theme, naturally enough for what is cast as an epic, from a famous life and heroic moments of an earlier but not remote time. There was a danger of paradox here, which could have led the poet into agonies of anachronism, but he resolved it triumphantly just as 'Turoldus' had done when breathing the spirit of the Crusade into his *Roland*.

This programme of juridical reform is studied by Lacarra in her highly original book.[18] In defining the poet's intention she goes well beyond previous scholars who had simply illustrated the poet's knowledge of the law. She writes as an historian of institutions and social movements, relying on the specialist studies of some who have not been much read by literary critics. Her method is to study institutions as we know them from juridical sources of the period and to see how the *Poema* conforms to or diverges from them, and if the latter, why. In the operation of the *ira regia* and law on exile, of the laws on the division of booty, and those on marriage, the poet more or less conforms but with certain minor, though interesting discrepancies. The Cortes as described by the poet show several original features, and the resulting *rieptos* – challenges – do so even more. The Cortes are attended by *sabidores* who advise the King and the Cid (ll. 3005, 3070) as experts in Roman law, 'cuya presencia se hace necesaria por las muchas modificaciones legales derivadas de la adopción del derecho romano' (Lacarra, 1980*a*: 65–6).[19] The *riepto*, though occasionally in use in earlier times,[20] was first legislated for by Alfonso VII in the *Ordenamiento de Nájera*: 'Quienes han creído en la veracidad histórica del poema no se dan cuenta que el riepto no existía en tiempos del Cid como institución establecida' (Lacarra, 1980*a*: 94). The poet is advocating its more extensive use because – however much it may strike us as a barbaric ritual (and it so struck, with all other forms of ordeal, the Lateran Council of 1215) – it could serve to end the taking of vengeance privately and ensure that disputes between nobles and on questions of honour were in future resolved by public-law procedures under proper rules and under the presidency of the monarch. One may add to Lacarra's observations that considerable detail of a rather unpoetic kind is given by the poet about the correct way of staging such duels.[21] Even the poet's treatment of the *ira regia* has something programmatic about it. In operation the *ira* was arbitrary and unappealable, even though in the course of time within the poem its inequity was rectified, the royal pardon of the Cid implying acknowledgement of earlier error. In general:

En las Cortes de Toledo, según el *Poema*, triunfa el derecho público sobre el privado al ser desestimados los argumentos propuestos por el bando de los infantes de Carrión. Se propugna el concepto romano del derecho como vehículo de justicia ... El nuevo concepto del derecho público insiste en la autoridad del poder real frente al poder creciente de la alta nobleza. Los reyes, junto con los letrados, fueron quienes protagonizaron la difusión del derecho romano para defender sus prerrogativas de los ataques de la nobleza. El autor del *Poema*, al plantear el conflicto en estos términos, toma partido en defensa del derecho público, que el rey quiere implantar, y ataca el derecho vigente de la venganza privada ... El profundo conocimiento del derecho que demuestra el autor y su planteamiento del conflicto entre el derecho público y privado en los términos en que lo hace, lo definen como un hombre de fines del siglo XII. Posiblemente era un letrado defensor del nuevo concepto del derecho, que tanto la profesión a la que puede haber pertenecido, como la misma corona, trataron de implantar con especial fuerza en ese momento histórico.[22]   (Lacarra, 1980a: 100–2)

To the above I may add that it is about to be proposed, in work of which I have kindly been given notice, that the Cortes scene of the *Poema* can be analysed in terms of Roman-law procedures, in general and in detail (Pavlović and Walker, forthcoming). If this succeeds in convincing, it will add an important dimension to the thesis of Lacarra which I have adopted here.

This definition of the author by profession, and the analysis of his intention in Lacarra's terms are, I hope, accurate and credible. But this aspect is still, as we try to work our way towards the poet's motivation, no more than secondary or tertiary. There are much broader, more human aspects of the poetic ethos of the work, and hence of the author's instincts and cast of mind, which should now occupy us. If it can be claimed that the poem has a measure of universality in time and space, it must have qualities which transcend the interest of a programme restricted in application to one country and to a special moment; and it must have a message which transcends the confines of medieval epic, together with specially impressive vehicles – personages, words – by which that message is conveyed.

Epic was by tradition a virile, warlike, even bloodthirsty genre. Its protagonists travel and seek, often guided by the gods or by God, often motivated by a sacred quest for vengeance to which they are bound by the ethos of their military caste. That this sort of epic could be composed in Spain, probably after the *Poema*, is shown by the story of the *Infantes de Lara*, more in line in some ways with the typical *chanson de geste* and very popular as a theme from the thirteenth to the sixteenth century. However, the *Poema*'s civilised attitude was not without support in another epic, perhaps composed shortly after it and hardly inferior to it in quality – that of *Sancho II*, as viewed recently by Fraker in a sensitive study.[23] The *Poema* departs greatly from epic stereotypes. Certainly the Cid of history was famed as a soldier, and soldiering with the acquisition of land, booty, and power by military means were the business of his class. In the poem the Cid is properly depicted as a fine soldier, whether leading his men into battle (l. 2396), or striking great blows (l. 2424), or as a tactician (at Alcocer, etc.) and even strategist (l. 2502). He is also, of course, an inspiration to his men in the harangue and in his war-cry, and in a more practical way, is the leader who can virtually guarantee rich profits from the spoils. Within this spirited but conventional portrayal, there are unexpected notes. The Cid is not unrelievedly hostile to the Moors, and has a valued friend among them, Avengalvón, whose alliance is of great help; and he is tolerant towards the Moors he has defeated. No slaughter accompanies the taking of Valencia, for the Cid wanted to take the city over in running order; he reserves his severity for any of his men who may desert. The Cid cheerfully allows the Infantes to absent themselves from battle. The military portrayal is a well-rounded one with pleasing features, and the poem would not have been an epic at all unless it had given us a good deal of military action of diverse kinds (including, perhaps, the Cid's unarmed confrontation with the lion, and of course the duels). As far as the expectations of the groundlings in the contemporary audience were concerned, the impressive military side may have been the most important. However, I doubt if this aspect was of prime concern to the poet. His battles are mainly conventional on the French model, and his view of tactics is

simple-minded (Alvar Fáñez proposes, and executes, attacks on
the enemy from flank or rear, which always succeed: ll. 1132,
1696, 1720). The actions at Castejón and Alcocer are not at all
run-of-the-mill but are owed to classical sources adapted by the
poet (see pp. 149–53). He made little of the siege of Valencia, for
reasons suggested below (pp. 147, 193, 208). The numeration of
Moslem armies is wildly exaggerated, as in French epic. The
poet's *verismo* was, in these respects, relative. In short, his heart
was in it only to a certain extent, and in military matters the poet
hardly went beyond the lively and competent.

The true worth of the *Poema* lies elsewhere, in a civic message
equally centred upon the Cid but owing, so far as we can tell,
nothing to the Cid of history. It is here that the poet's revolutionary concept can best be appreciated. The Cid triumphs over long
adversity by reason of virtues of a civic kind. Military prowess
helped him, certainly, but his soldierly genius would have been
useless without the devotion of his men, which went beyond
what the formal feudal relationship ordained. He secured this
devotion by his fairness (l. 314) and generosity (to Minaya, ll. 492,
1806–7), by keeping his word to Christians if not to Jews (l. 1081),
by a just distribution of spoils (l. 800, and passim), by prudence in
not risking lives on foolhardy enterprises (l. 2502), by giving his
men the feeling that all was according to the divine will and even
that the deity was on his side (l. 1047), and so on. He takes a
proper pride in his own efforts (l. 1935) but only after recognising
that all is divinely ordained (l. 1933), a theme which has been
movingly enunciated by Jimena when, at the moment of her
husband's exile, she prayed for heavenly protection for him, and
when God's archangel appeared to him. The Cid rises above the
miseries – material and psychological – of exile, by ironical
expression of good cheer (l. 14), and is immediately answered by
the united affection of the people of Burgos (ll. 16b–20), the
blessing of the little girl (l. 43), the adhesion and help of Martín
Antolínez (l. 66, etc.), and the hospitality – in defiance of the royal
command? – of the monks of Cardeña (ll. 243 ff.). Men flock to the
Cid's banner; they are not greedy adventurers, but include men
of substance who have a lot to lose because the King will
confiscate their property (l. 77). These men encourage the Cid in
his moment of deepest sadness at parting from his family (l. 381).
The Cid's qualities and demeanour have won him the right sorts
of aid when most needed. Later, the hero's confidence in his

captains is rewarded by their devotion. Even the results of Pedro Bermúdez's impulsive disobedience of orders are entirely positive (ll. 704–14). The Cid maintains his confidence in the treacherous Infantes up to the last possible moment, at least in public for the protection of his honour and for the good discipline of army and household. It is the Infantes, rotten to the core, who alone have not allowed themselves to benefit morally from the Cid's example. Those who have so benefited gain material rewards too.

The Cid's conduct in exile is clearly intended by the poet to be exemplary in a special way. As noted earlier, the poet chose not to take the facile course of making him a merely rebellious vassal. The prototypes of this in French epic must have seemed to the poet to illustrate nothing much beyond the cult of the ego and self-justification in rivers of blood. At all times in exile the Cid is philosophical and dignified. At the moment of banishment he does not rant; the banishment is accepted as God's will, and the trouble-making faction at court is blamed (l. 9, echoed by Jimena, l. 267) as the human instrument, rather than the King in any personal way. What follows has been misinterpreted by sentimental critics. Pidal thought that the exiled Cid was showing special restraint in refusing to fight the King; he based this view on *Partidas*, IV, xxv, 10, which indeed allow an exile to make war on his monarch. But as Lacarra points out (1980a: note to p. 21), the *Fuero Viejo* – known to us only in Pedro I's redaction, but of much earlier origin than the *Partidas* – forbade the exile under all circumstances to fight against the monarch, so the Cid was simply obeying the law. It was surely then common prudence for the Cid to hasten away from a possible clash with the royal forces (ll. 527–8, and 532) after he had, for several sound reasons, taken Castejón from the Moors even though these were on terms of written truce with Alfonso. The Cid was legally in the wrong, and he knew it. For the rest, the poet's emphasis is on the Cid's obedience to the law as well as on his prudence. An early suggestion by Alvar Fáñez, that the Cid's fifth share of the booty from the raid to Alcalá and the capture of Castejón should be sent to the King, is apparently not proceeded with. Later, in sending a share of the spoils to the King, the Cid was, on the first two occasions (after the victory over the army from Valencia, thirty horses; after the capture of Valencia, one hundred) merely obeying the law, as Guglielmi reminds us.[24] According to the

Fuero Viejo, the monarch was still the 'señor natural' even of the man in exile, and was entitled to his share of the booty won by that man. Often in the poem, the Cid renews his protestations of loyalty to Alfonso, properly continuing to regard himself as a vassal of the King even in exile, his 'señor natural' (ll. 895, 1272, 1339, etc.), and the Cid lives in the constant hope of being received back into favour. His first plea for reconciliation is deemed premature (l. 883), but the Cid's emissaries have made the plea precisely in terms of the *Fuero Viejo* as quoted by Guglielmi. The passage of time, the Cid's ever-respectful conduct, and – perhaps most telling of all – the hero's growing power in land and wealth, eventually secure the reconciliation in carefully graded stages (Alfonso's public utterance of goodwill, ll. 1875–6; private assurances to the Cid's messengers, l. 1898b; ceremonial public restoration of favour, l. 2034). The Cid's third gift of booty after the defeat of Yúçef, 200 horses, was perhaps still in accord with the requirements of the law, but the Cid generously added to this the great tent of the Almoravid emperor (ll. 1789–91). This part of the story, then, is an illustration more of the proper workings of the law than of any special sentiment on the Cid's part, but it does show that an extra demonstration of generosity and respect may tip the scales of justice at the right moment.

The whole progress of the Cid from the material and psychological abyss of exile up to the restoration of full civil status, with the acquisition of wealth and power beyond anything he had possessed earlier, is a masterly demonstration of the principle that dignity in adversity and obedience to the law bring due rewards. The law is not in itself unjust, the poet implies. Its application in the Cid's case by the King may have been arbitrary and excessive, but it must still be obeyed, and the injustice will be rectified in due course. All those with the Cid see their legal disabilities removed (ll. 886–7, 890–3), and are enhanced in both status (l. 1213) and wealth (ll. 848, 1086, 1245–7), a fact on which the poet becomes sententious (l. 850). In this part of the poem the Cid's progress forms a natural structural backbone to the narration, and represents, of course, the age-old theme of the testing of the hero, as defined by Dunn (1970: 117–18).

The poet's exposition of the nature of kingship, and of the relations of lords, vassals, and subjects to the monarch and among themselves, is plainly exemplary in intention also. He does not indulge in this because anything radically new was occurring to change these things in the years about 1200, but because Roman-law studies were making intellectuals more conscious of the issues involved, adding theoretical reasoning to what was current practice resulting from long evolution. Possibly the poet was influenced also by the French epics of his day in which these same questions were argued (Cotrait, 1977: 188 and 221 ff., with reference to the Fernán González story). From a structural point of view, and now from a legalistic or ethical one, the relations between the Cid and the King can be seen as a basic theme of the poem (Walker, 1976; with references to work on this aspect by Correa, de Chasca, Dunn, Gilman, Hart, and others). Walker proposes that the first half of the poem – in which the restoration of royal favour marks an almost exact mid-point – concerns the testing of the Cid as vassal, the second half then concerning the testing of the King as lord. There is even a remarkable series of parallels in the way in which the Cid and King prepare for the 'vistas' at which reconciliation will occur, detailed by Walker; the terms are partly formulaic, but still significant, and the application of epic epithets to the two may have further sense in establishing the equation. Now the King is to be tested by having his political judgement shown as faulty, in making the marriages between the Infantes and the Cid's daughters, and by being called upon to vindicate the Cid and repair his honour. The King passes his test by acknowledging his responsibility for the marriages (l. 2950), calling exceptional Cortes (only the third of his reign, l. 3129), and there adjusting procedure in a way helpful to the Cid. Finally, he presides over the judicial duels, having taken care to ensure that in the period leading up to them, the Cid's champions are protected in hostile territory (ll. 3475–9). Alfonso has learned, after an initial error, to be a just king, and to recognise and support human worth in his vassal the Cid. In Dunn's analysis, this corresponds as myth to the theme of 'the king released from evil counsellors'.

That the poet made a considerable adjustment in this regard to what had happened in history shows his instinct for the power of a simple story-line and plain exemplarity. In history the King banished the Cid in 1081, took him back in 1087, banished him again in 1089, and never removed the ban. Walker observes that 'An intelligent and patriotic man like the poet must have felt that this was one of the great tragedies of his country. I am suggesting that one of his aims in writing his poem was to replace the unhappy historical truth with a more inspirational poetic truth' (1976: 266).

Within the *mesnada*, viewed as a microcosm of the State, further exemplary traits are present. The bonds are of both legal and ordinarily human kinds. All are members one of another, and the outrage upon the Cid's daughters is a dishonour not only for the Cid but for all (ll. 2941–2); it is three of the captains who utter the challenges in the Cortes and hence fight the duels. As Guglielmi reminds us, the Cid is depicted as carrying out to the letter his feudal duty towards his vassals, paying them (l. 314), feeding them (l. 304), securing husbands for Jimena's ladies and providing a dowry for each (ll. 1765–6). The Cid consults his captains on both military and civil matters (ll. 670, 1941), and Alvar Fáñez discharges a feudal duty by giving unsolicited advice (l. 1251). These are minor, undramatic matters, but they serve to complete a remarkably full picture of exemplary relationships.

The Cid's family is a yet smaller microcosm, rich in love and harmony. The Cid's paternal – almost patriarchal – role is dominant as it must have been in the reality of the medieval family; one might describe it as despotism tempered by good sense and tenderness. Jimena is given no truly active role, but her gentle, feeling personality comes over well in her prayer and in her parting from the Cid. We know that on the model of numerous French epics, Per Abad felt that he should include a 'prière épique' (of a kind discussed below, pp. 159–60), but to put it into Jimena's mouth in the setting of the abbey church of Cardeña was a master-stroke. Similarly, the daughters are affectionately portrayed (ll. 269b, 275–6, etc.). Too small at this point even to be named by the Cid, Jimena, or the narrator, they are none the less prominent in the hero's thoughts because their eventual marriages – at this low point, on what possible basis? – are of vital concern (ll. 282–2b). This is as much a hint about paternal duty as an indication by the poet of the progress of his plot. Eventually the girls will have their marriages simply announced to them (ll. 2188–9) by their father, after he has consulted his captains but not Jimena. The Cid had grave doubts about the matches (ll. 2082–5), and he frankly voices these to Jimena and the girls (ll. 2196–204), but the marriages must take place because the King wishes it, as a move in the power game. In a difficult situation the Cid puts a good face on the matter, talking of the honour which the marriages will bring (l. 2198) and firmly laying the legal responsibility where it belongs, with the King. Earlier, the presence of the womenfolk in Valencia has been related, chivalrously and charmingly, by the Cid to the military theme (ll. 1633–56, especially 1648 and 1655; again, 1748–9). The women in the poem are not mere ciphers, and their presence and the themes related to them serve to illuminate exemplary facets of the hero.

We do not know (but can conjecture: see Chapter 7) how the poet came to make the fruitful decision that the marriages should be the mainspring of his plot. He had no historical or literary antecedent for so doing. Once he had decided, he went far beyond the perfunctory in giving the women scenes and words, and he used them to show a domestic and intimate side of the hero which is not common in epic. Perhaps he was impressed by what the *Historia Roderici* records about the maltreatment of the women by the King, a possibility discussed in Chapter 5. It is not likely that the presence of 'Dame Guiborc' in the French William cycle, the only possible parallel for Jimena, gave Per Abad any hint for his work. It has been held that the attention given by the poet to family and domestic matters diminishes the epic status of the work; in a strict definition, this may be true, but the gain in ordinary human appeal is enormous.

Within the character of the hero himself, the poet is concerned to exemplify the greatest civic virtue of all: *mesura*. Many have commented on this. It is akin to Roman *gravitas*, compounded of dignity, calm, a certain stoicism; also of prudence and good sense in facing decisions, and tact and consideration in dealing with others, especially the weak. The quality may manifest itself in the way a man speaks (l. 7). It is linked to major themes of the poem at all points, for example in all the Cid's dealings with the King (indeed, the poem could be read as a manual of diplomacy), and in his conduct at court. It includes practical precautionary measures such as the wearing of arms to court, duly concealed (l. 3076). The hero's reaction to news of the Corpes outrage is all *mesura*: he 'sat and thought' for a long time (l. 2828), then raised his hand and clutched his beard, speaking just five lines, weighty and precise, ironically thanking God for the 'honour' which the Infantes have done him, swearing by his beard that they will not get away with it, and that he will still make good marriages for his daughters. But this is not only *mesura* as a pious, stoical pose, made advisable by the need to reassure his captains and servants who are listening. The Cid's period of reflection has been used in part to master his grief, but also to calculate the legal and political odds. He can already see that his case for vindication will be strong, for the King had made the marriages and must help to secure amends for their breaking. The case is so put to the King by the Cid's emissary (ll. 2936–52). Politically, the Cid can see that although his daughters have suffered, they will not lack suitors of equal or higher rank, for he has been further enriched since marriage first entered the heads of the Infantes. Furthermore, by careful action, the party of the Beni-Gómez family at court will be finally discredited if the Cid, with the King as a more than benevolent arbiter, triumphs in the assembly. The Infantes by their violent act have played into the hero's hands. The important thing for the Cid, on hearing of the outrage, was precisely not to be as violent as they. The expectations of an audience still, in 1207, might well have been that the Cid should at once seek out the Infantes and exact in blood a vengeance for the wrong done to his daughters and the dishonour to himself and the *mesnada*. Under a centuries-old code, the Cid would be a less than normal man – and very much less than a hero – if he failed in this duty. Well on into the fourteenth century, such exaction of vengeance could still be celebrated in literature (the *Infantes de Lara*, and much in French). The poet must have judged that part of his public was ready to consider an alternative, particularly in view of the way the Cid's character had been built up earlier in the narration. If there was to be blood as well as a civic vindication, and the Cid does eventually demand it, this was to be executed in a legally-sanctioned way under the eye of the monarch.

Mesura, on the other hand, is lacking in the Cid's adversaries: not only in the Infantes, constantly and by nature, and less seriously in the Count of Barcelona ('muy folon', l. 960), but also in García Ordóñez ('mal irado', l. 1859) and, most memorably, in Asur González who disgraces himself by appearing in court half-dressed, drunk, and offensive (ll. 3373–81). The Moorish leaders Tamín, Avengalvón, and Yúçef are notably dignified, only Búcar appearing mildly ridiculous. The poet was making a point about mankind in general, not a racial one.

The quality of *mesura* is most necessary in a civic hero, a likely creation of an author whose profession was the law. In this regard the Cid far outshines any protagonist of French epic,

Roland and Charlemagne not excluded, as a model for later generations. Amador de los Ríos argued in 1861 that the Cid in this way represented 'el carácter nacional personificado ... y reconcentrado'. Menéndez Pidal much developed this in various of his works, sometimes in narrow Castilian terms as a result of 1898 Generation attitudes. At this point the foreigner holds his peace, or murmurs not too audibly '¡Ojalá!' He notes that a fellow-Hispanic, Rodríguez-Puértolas, has reacted violently against much of what has been said of the specifically Spanish virtues of the Cid (1977). It is probably pointless to defend the poet's idealised portrayal of his hero as having anything necessarily Spanish, still less Castilian, about him. He is better viewed as a human exemplar portrayed by a poet of Castilian birth who had been educated in a broad way beyond the mental horizons of the Peninsula and of his time, for Latin and Roman law were for all men.

The poet can have had no special model in mind for the Cid's character. The hero is an amalgam of qualities which the poet admired, as a lawyer, in diverse men of his time: governors, administrators, churchmen, lords and also vassals, other lawyers, perhaps in perfectly ordinary individuals seen in roles of husbands and fathers, even peasants of patriarchal mien. It was not merely a personal question, but the thought that the progress of the State would depend upon the cultivation of many Cids. After all, there was nothing extravagant or superhuman about the hero he portrayed. The Cid stood, a natural leader, a head taller than those around him, but his feet were visibly planted on ordinary ground. The poet gave the Cid a few moments of proper pride, but usually he is plain-spoken, unsententious, even humorous in a variety of tones: a man among men. Where the French poet showed Roland ascending to heaven, a soldier–martyr in the great war between the forces of light and darkness, the Spanish poet depicted the Cid dying in what we may assume is domestic peace, adding as narrator the briefest prayer for his salvation (l. 3727). The poet's sureness of touch, his own *mesura*, was with him to the end.

It is plain that Per Abad did not intend to portray either an archaic or contemporary reality, despite his noted *verismo*. He looks ahead, to a better juridical and therefore human future. As I put it some years ago: 'This is a poet who looks back into the past in order to point a way forward; he unfurls the Cid's "seña cabdal" in the hope that a people will follow it.' This, after all, is what exemplarity, moral messages, and a programme of juridical reform (if Lacarra is right) are all about. Yet the poem is by no means devoid of contemporary notes. It may well be that political and military preoccupations of the years about 1200 in Castile figure, by implication, in the *Poema*. This aspect of the work could hardly be assessed while a belief in its early date, and close association with the period of the historical Cid, persisted. In 1962 Fradejas argued that the spirit and some details of the poem could best be explained in relation to events of Alfonso VIII's reign. Critics made little of this at the time, but Lacarra's work now shows that this idea is sound and helpful.

In June 1195 a large Almohad army crossed the Strait, began campaigning, and at Alarcos on 19 July 1195 inflicted a terrible defeat on the Castilian army. It seemed to some well beyond the Pyrenees that a new Moslem peril threatened, and there was general alarm. Castile's situation became more desperate when the Leonese seized their advantage and, renewing hostilities of a few years earlier, began to raid into Castile, with the aid of Moslem units. Peace was patched up and to some extent guaranteed by a dynastic marriage, in 1197, in which Alfonso IX of León married Berenguela, eldest daughter of Alfonso VIII of Castile. Although this marriage was dissolved in 1204 at the Pope's behest (the spouses were within the prohibited degrees of consanguinity), peace was firmly established by the Treaty of Cabreros in March 1206. After this Castilian thoughts could turn to vengeance for Alarcos. It is almost to be expected that a poem of 1207 should reflect thse stirring events. The *Poema* is generally inspirational in that it shows how free men could flock to the banner of a notable leader, serve with confidence and devotion, and win generous reward, perhaps sharing in the glory of some spectacular conquest comparable to that of Valencia. The example of Castile's great commander in battle against the Moors was modernised and held up, very much in the way that the example of Charlemagne and Roland, campaigners against the Moslems of Spain, was held up by 'Turoldus' for the French of about 1100, as the barons and armies sought recruits to hold Syria and Palestine against the Moslems. In the *Poema* there is a further dimension, in that the Cid serves to exemplify 'social mobility': the Cid as *infanzón* rises by his efforts to great achievements, to near-royal status in Valencia, and ultimately sees his daughters

married into the royal family of Navarre and that of 'Aragón'. The
light of these achievements shone on all who had been with him:
'a todos alcança ondra . . .' More practically, men could hope to
enrich themselves by the spoils expected from campaigns envisaged in 1207. Booty from Moslem sources in the later years of the
twelfth century was again of importance, and the *fueros* of that
time enact regulations about it: 'Hay que llamar la atención de
cómo en la mayoría de los fueros se consideraba a la hueste como
una sociedad formada para la ganancia' (Palomeque Torres,
quoted by Lacarra, 1980a: 48). In a society in which a money
economy was beginning to flourish, the *caballeros* received their
share of the spoils in coin (ll. 515, 2467, 2509), and even the Cid's
swords when won by him were valued in cash terms (ll. 1010,
2426), though later in the poem they were to be charged with
symbolic and heroic values. A *caballero* received double the sum
to which a *peón* was entitled, but a key line is 1213, 'los que fueron
de pie cavalleros se fazen': after the capture of Valencia, so great
were the spoils that everyone was enriched, with the direct
consequence in terms of social mobility that any foot-soldier now
owner of a horse and sword was, indeed, a *caballero*. Perhaps a
memory of such enrichment and ascent survived in Burgos
among men whose ancestors had fought with the Cid and
returned as *caballeros villanos*, retaining and transmitting that
status. In any case, one cannot gainsay the value of the poem as a
sort of recruiting-poster for 1207. Even losses suffered by the
Cid's men, in action against huge Moslem armies, are hearten-
ingly small (e.g. only fifteen killed in the battle against the
Valencian army, l. 798). Literature spilled over into life a few
years later when reports of the battle of Las Navas said much the
same.[25]

Yet literary example may have been just as powerful a guide to
the poet as anything in the life of contemporary Spain, so that one
cannot positively aver that Fradejas and Lacarra are correct.
Mention of the advantages of serving a good lord, the material
rewards of loyalty, and the duties of the lord towards his
vassals, are commonplace in French epic with its wholly feudal
ethos. A recent study of *Girart de Roussillon*, a poem of about 1180
which Per Abad probably knew, makes this clear (Hackett, 1980).
In *Girart* the landless young men take service with great lords as
soudader and are paid and protected by them. More down-to-
earth than some *chansons de geste*, *Girart* provides numerous

instances of the monetary considerations involved in campaigning, mentioning not only gifts but booty in monetary terms, and the promises made by commanders to their men before battle as an incitement, also payments to the *soudader*, and so on. The Gascons are detached from their feudal duty to Girart by a bribe, and the royal palace is burgled. The practical motivations of service and warfare are prominent, then, in this remarkable poem, but it is by no means unique.

Lacarra rightly insists that the social mobility exemplified in the poem is a strictly limited one. There is no justification for the view sometimes expressed that the poem is a 'democratic' one in spirit, a meaningless concept for its time. Nor is the poem generally anti-noble in feeling: the Cid's hostility is directed solely at García Ordóñez and his allies, the 'malos mestureros', and later at the Infantes and their family. The particular reason which the poet may have had for this hostility will be discussed in the next chapter. All one can say is that the enemies and villains represent the old nobility of blood, entrenched in positions of power, while the Cid represents both nobility of blood (of lesser status) *and* personal worth, energy, and sound moral sense. Those entrenched at court view the Cid's rise with alarm: 'En la ondra que el ha nos seremos abiltados' (l. 1862).

The poet is manifestly anti-Catalán in feeling, or is at least disposed to show the Catalán Count up as effete, blustering, unwarlike, and his army as ineffective. Yet there was no motive in the years around 1200 for such a portrayal, and the main reason for the poet's splendid episode is simply that he found rich materials for it in the *Historia Roderici*, as will be seen. Whether the poet shows hostility to León is arguable. Sound motives for such hostility existed a short time before 1207: the Leonese had not helped Castile at Alarcos, and after it had raided Castilian border areas with Moslem units among their forces – this, after Alfonso IX of León had sworn fealty to Alfonso VIII at the Cortes of 1188. Clearly implications of treachery against Alfonso IX, perhaps against the Leonese generally, would not be unexpected in a Castilian work of 1207.[26] However, it is by no means sure that such sentiments can be discerned in the poem. Many have thought that the King, Alfonso VI, is viewed unfavourably because he had been King of León alone (1065–72) before assuming also the crown of Castile. However, in the poem he is indifferently 'el castellano' and 'el de Leon', the alternation depending on the demands of rhythm and assonance; towards the end of the poem he is the just ruler of a united realm (ll. 2923–6), and only his habitual oath '¡par Sant Esidro . . . !' might have reminded a Castilian public of his Leonese years. Nor was the Beni-Gómez family so wholly Leonese as has often been thought. They were so originally, and their broad lands around Carrión (together with Sahagún, Valladolid, etc.) had at various times in the eleventh and twelfth centuries been within Castile and León, being incorporated definitively into Castile in 1182. Lacarra thinks this last fact sufficient to remove any sense of the part-Leonese nature of the family from the poet's mind when writing in 1207 (Lacarra, 1980a: 262), but the issue may not be so simple, as the poet was obviously well acquainted with parts of the family history and has one of his personages utter a eulogy of its earlier worth (ll. 3443–4). The possibility that in selecting the Infantes as villains the poet was conveying an anti-Leonese prejudice, one still general in Castile at the time, cannot be dismissed.

Menéndez Pidal thought, from the variety of backgrounds from which the Cid's captains came, that the poem had a certain national value and that the Cid himself (the historical and literary Cids being, in his view, an undifferentiated compound) was a Hispanic hero who fomented 'la idea unitaria hispánica'.[27] Lacarra thinks this can hardly be justified, concluding rather that the presence of 'Martin Muñoz el que mando a Mont Mayor' (l. 738, etc.; in Portugal), and of 'Galin Garçia el bueno de Aragon' (l. 740, etc.) may reflect the growing unity of Christian states in the years leading up to the campaign of Las Navas. A significant date is 1206, when (Santo) Domingo de Guzmán was encouraged by Innocent III to preach a bull urging all Christians to unite against the Moslems of Spain. Needing men for his final attack on Valencia, the Cid sends his heralds not only to Castile but to Aragón and Navarre (ll. 1187–8) in the same spirit; as a result, 'grandes yentes se le acojen de la buena christiandad' (l. 1199).

The chief interest of the years up to the campaign of Las Navas as it may be present in the poem lies in the nature of the war itself and religious attitudes to it. The Spaniards always showed a practical approach to warfare with the Moslems, and on the whole were not given to undue ferocity or mindless slaughter. They by no means shared in the conventions repeatedly depicted in French epic, according to which Moslems were pagans or the devil's agents, meet for extermination or forced conversion. The presence of French Cluniacs in twelfth-century Spain, while it may have stiffened Christian resolve and spirituality, did not cause the Spaniards to adopt French extremities of view. In the *Poema* the Cid revels in battle and kills many Moors single-handed; but when victory is secured, relatively civilised procedures prevail. Alfonso's written truce with the Moors of the Castejón region is mentioned (l. 527): a normal enough fact of history, and one which the poet inserts without emphasis. The surviving Moors of Castejón are restored to liberty and their town is not razed (ll. 553–4), 'que de mi non digan mal' (l. 535); at the Cid's departure, 'los moros e las moras   bendiziendol estan' (l. 541). The Moors of Alcocer are expelled from the town, as a security precaution, but return to it after the Cid's victory, and are not left destitute either (ll. 801–2). Again, at the Cid's departure, the Moors express sorrow, weep, and even pray for the hero (ll. 851–6). The spoils of Castejón, hard to transport, are sold back to their owners for easily carried coin, the Cid accepting the Moors' estimate of value (ll. 518–21). At no time are captured Moors retained or sent elsewhere for what they might fetch as slaves (l. 517), though this is for practical reasons rather than on any principle (l. 619); none the less, they are not to be pointlessly killed (l. 620). In his Valencian campaign, the Cid pitilessly devastates the countryside year by year (ll. 1172–3) in order to deprive the city of food, and the poet feelingly portrays the suffering of the population (ll. 1174–9). After its fall, Valencia is despoiled and property is distributed among the victors (ll. 1245–6), but the people are not otherwise harmed.

This account of the Cid's methods is more or less in line with historical reality, though shorn of the grosser brutalities which, away from the battlefield, did sometimes occur. The account has a certain programmatic value for relatively decent conduct by Christian campaigners of the early thirteenth century. It must be stressed that in this important aspect the Spanish poet deliberately refused to follow the examples of French epic, so well known to him. His portrayal is careful and detailed, to the extent that some of his lines cited above do not help the action forward or enhance the epic theme, but are more in the nature of asides or considered afterthoughts.

The poet goes further than this. Although he does not show

Moors actually fighting as part of the Cid's host (as they certainly did in history), they may be taken to be present in it, following the Cid's call to his tributaries for help in the Valencian campaign (ll. 1107–10). Earlier, the army of the Count of Barcelona has contained men of both religions (l. 968). More striking is the depiction of Avengalvón, ruler of Molina, as an ally of the Cid, especially as it has been doubted whether in history he could have acted as the poem says (Lacarra, 1980a: 196–201, with mention of studies by Huici Miranda and Sancho Izquierdo). He is not merely an ally, but is on genuinely warm terms with the Cid (ll. 1464, 1480, etc.). He provides hospitality for the Cid's messengers and womenfolk as they journey through his lands, and he is conspicuously generous beyond the minimal obligations (ll. 1488, 1490, 1535, etc.). Avengalvón is a 'necessary' ally; each needs to keep on good terms with the other in the prevailing circumstances. But there is more to it than this. Avengalvón is, though a Moor, a much more honourable man than the Christian Infantes. Following the discovery of the Infantes' plot to murder him, he gives them an indignant lesson in good conduct, in part the outcome of bitter experience, in part a publicly uttered warning to the Infantes' wives to be on their guard. The Moor overcomes with difficulty his inclination to punish the Infantes then and there (l. 2688) and restore the girls to their father (l. 2679); his implicit warning turns out, in Corpes, to be amply justified. This is on all scores a most remarkable sequence of incidents, fitted perfectly into the plot structure and helpful for the development of characters. Although Avengalvón was a historical person, the scene owes nothing to any historical memory. Per Abad created what was to become – though not fully until the sixteenth century – an important literary type: the noble Moor. It is as though the poet, beyond a need to feel that among enemies there are occasional figures who command respect, natural to any people on a war footing, is suggesting to the authorities of his day the need to discriminate in the coming campaign, to seek useful allies among the established local rulers of Al-Andalus while not neglecting the main task of defeating the alien Almohads. In human terms, says the poet, better an Avengalvón, though Moslem, than self-seeking and treacherous nobles, though Christian, such as the Infantes. As a Moslem, Avengalvón kissed Alvar Fáñez on the shoulder, 'ca tal es su

husaje' (l. 1519), but the God of Christian and Moslem is almost
One in the Moor's appeal to him (l. 2684), as earlier in the prayers
of the Moors of Castejón and Alcocer.

The poet did not wholly neglect the idea of crusade, though it
was not native to Spain, but one feels that he hardly welcomed or
comprehended it. There was slight precedent for the crusading
ideal within the Peninsula, but only when French or other foreign
influence became involved. In 1172 when Alfonso VIII marched
towards Huete to defeat a Moslem incursion, the papal legate
Jacinto who was with the army declared the campaign a crusade,
announcing spiritual benefits for those taking part. In the years
leading up to Las Navas papal interest was direct from 1206, and
Innocent III proclaimed the Crusade in January 1212. In the
poem, the author presents Jerónimo as full of crusading zeal on
his arrival (ll. 1293–5), but further reflection of this is limited to the
bishop's announcement of absolution and indulgences for those
dying in the coming battle (ll. 1703–5). Even this, more than a
contemporaneous note – entirely appropriate, one may add –
depends rather on literary precedent: that of Archbishop Turpin
in the *Roland*, who absolves the soldiers in the same manner, and,
just like Jerónimo (ll. 1708–9), has the honour of the 'primeras
feridas' (*Roland* 'O', ll. 1487–509). This poetic portrayal of the
bishop owes much to Turpin, not inappropriately, since he was
of French origin in history and was so recalled in the poem (l.
1288). It is only in the battle with Yúçef that warfare reaches the
level of a struggle between divine and devilish powers on the
French model, in Yúçef's exclamation about Christ (ll. 1632–4)
and the Cid's equally dramatic response (l. 1655). For the rest,
religious observances do not go beyond the conventional, but on
the Cid's part they are frequent and fervent. It may be intended
that the fighting leaders of 1207 should be reminded of their duty:
the Cid promises to pay for a thousand masses at the altar of the
Virgin in the Cathedral (Santa María) of Burgos, in return for her
aid (ll. 221–5), and later he does so pay (l. 822). The Cid sends 500
marks to Cardeña (l. 1285), and on receiving them the abbot
reminds the emissary that the Cid's renown will continue to grow
if he remembers the monastery again in this way (ll. 1443–6). In
conquered Valencia, the Cid richly endows the new bishopric
(l. 1304).

One can see that the poet's choice of subject was entirely right.
As shown in Chapter 2, the Cid's legends and literary *persona* had

grown in the twelfth century more than those of any other potential candidate for epic honours. As will be seen, the poet probably knew much of the twelfth-century literary record. As a man of Burgos or its region, he would have been aware of the Cid as the major local hero, and disposed to give Vivar and Cardeña, as well as the city, due prominence. Per Abad as a lawyer may also have had a special interest in the Cid because of the hero's reputation as a legist, which owed nothing to any literary or legendary development (Entwistle, 1929: 11–13). The special circumstances of the years about 1200, and the poet's use of them in his work, also demonstrate the naturalness of his choice of subject and explain some of the ways in which he developed it (though it is important to bear French literary precedent in mind also). The literary urge, the impulse to create plot and characters, remains primordial, and any practical contemporary message or programme of juridical reform secondary. The power of the poet's words joins all elements together in a convincing unity.

4 Metrical structures

'Al estudiar la versificación de nuestro Cantar, notaré con Restori [1887] que la importancia del *Mio Cid*, como documento métrico, supera a su importancia como poema nacional, como monumento histórico y como obra de arte.' So Menéndez Pidal in 1908. The priority may seem misconceived, but this aspect has given rise to a vast and distinguished bibliography,[1] and this chapter should be considered to be at the core of my thesis. If as I claim Per Abad composed the first Castilian epic, he invented a metrical system for it. His work was experimental and hence not without shortcomings, and these, while scarcely affecting one's admiration for the literary artefact, have a special interest because they can show us a good deal about the poet's sources and working methods.

The general assumption has been that Spanish epic, including the *Poema*, employs age-old habits of versification, which had grown up autonomously on Spanish soil and were necessarily as ancient as the historical materials which are the themes of the poems. Such is, I think, the traditionalist view. At one time the effort of scholars went into trying to crack the secret of the *Poema*'s versification, their idea being that copyists had disturbed what had originally been a metrically regular composition in terms of assonance and length of line; and completely regular restored texts were produced. Menéndez Pidal's work – and his analysis of the metrical structures presented in the MS remains fundamental – showed that the system involved a constant and inherent variability of line-length (i.e., that irregularities were not the work of copyists exclusively, though there are disturbances of this sort), and that this was characteristic of the Old Spanish epic genre as a whole. Even so, in his critical edition of the *Poema* (1911), Pidal did make a large number of adjustments to the MS readings designed to bring very short and very long lines towards a middling norm, and he regularised the far from perfect system of assonances. His ideas and work on these aspects, as on most others, immediately won the support of most scholars and makers of literary histories. A few post-Pidalian studies of these matters have great interest, but none takes the radical line I am adopting here (Maldonado de Guevara, 1965; Hall, 1965–6; Strausser, 1969–70; Adams, 1972; Cázares, 1973).

Menéndez Pidal concluded his survey of studies up to 1908 by saying that the metrics of the *Poema* and other epics were 'la maraña de una versificación primitiva irregular, ajustada a leyes totalmente desconocidas para nosotros', without attempting to guess at the antiquity of the system. There is indeed no evidence of any kind before the *Poema* of 1207 of what such a system might have been, had it existed. The *Chronica Najerensis*, even on the traditionalists' terms (that the chronicle gives summaries of a number of vernacular epics), gives no hint about metrical forms, having in its Latin no echo of those clichés and phrases which are typical of known vernacular epics and which hypothetically might have given clues. There are two further arguments in favour of Per Abad's primacy. One is that since he was a powerful inventor in other ways – of characters and motivation, of a well-knit and fast-moving plot, of a fine style for both narration and direct speech – there is no reason not to credit him with a capacity for metrical invention also, naturally with models in other languages if not in his own. We know that Dante first used *terza rima* and Boccaccio first used *ottava rima*, that Santillana wrote the first Spanish sonnets in experimental hendecasyllables, and that Boscán and Garcilaso later introduced the whole corpus of Italian metrics, with accompanying sensibility and much else besides, into Spanish. Per Abad was not necessarily less talented than these as a 'maker'. The other argument is that, after all, vernacular literature as a whole was being created in Spain in Per Abad's time. Someone first used Navarrese to redact the brief *Corónicas*. Someone began vernacular prose by redacting the *Anales toledanos primeros*, by translating the *Fazienda de ultramar* from Latin, and works of science and wisdom from Arabic. These things do not happen casually, as one might say they do when an incompetent notary redacted a diploma in which the language is visibly more Romance than Latin. They are the result of a decision taken with the purpose of a text and the nature of its reading or listening public in mind. In verse the adventure is greater. Nobody has ever doubted that *cuaderna vía* was invented by Berceo, or possibly by the author of the *Libro de Alexandre* (these poets may be the same person); as mentioned earlier, the metre has been shown to derive from the French alexandrine, with additional influence of Latin rhythmic verse, and was probably developed at the *studium* of Palencia under the guidance of French *magistri* (Dutton, 1973). This parallel is of special importance, for *cuaderna vía* was devised for distinctly learned use in expressing religious and classical themes drawn from the Latin tradition, although, significantly, it could embrace an epic theme also, that of Fernán González. The relationship of these two main narrative modes, *cuaderna vía* and epic properly so called, was close at all points, most notably in the general manner of narration and in rhetoric; and if Berceo invented the one, there is no reason why Per Abad should not have invented the other a few years earlier. Both were to be fruitful initiatives, and in both the examples set by Latin and French were to be paramount.

Before the argument can be taken further, we have to consider the textual basis upon which study of the metrical system must rest. This is not as clear as one would like. The unique MS of the *Poema* is a strange thing, unlike any other in Spanish or in French (in the latter, of course, hundreds of epic MSS survive), as anyone can appreciate from the facsimile published in 1961. For long it was held that this text had suffered from careless copying, more recently that its defects result from dictation to a scribe by a minstrel who was relying on his memory and unable to get laisses and line-lengths right because of the artificiality of the circumstances (the minstrel being bereft of his musical accompaniment; but he could have asked for this, presumably, or supplied it himself?). However, although there are certainly some copying errors, it is now possible to assert that the MS has far fewer of them than was once thought, given the basic irregularity or relative freedom of the metrical system, and recent editors – Michael and myself – have been inclined to leave the MS readings much (not totally) as they are. On the one hand, the text makes good sense for the most part, and we do not need to fiddle with it in order to understand it or enhance its poetic qualities. On the other, it makes even better sense structurally if we can begin to see it, as I do here, as an experimental work. For this to be valid, one has to concede that the present MS was copied in the middle years of the fourteenth century from a text very close to the original of 1207, so that it represents fairly accurately the state in which Per Abad left his composition, that is with the defects and oversights inherent in any draft. As for the proposal that the text has suffered because of defective dictation by a minstrel, although at first sight this might seem to explain why some lines are wrongly divided, it is clear from the few cases in which whole lines are transposed that this could not have been the process; medieval copyists sometimes did transpose lines, like modern compositors, because their eyes wandered, and this has nothing to do with the dictated word. We also know (as Pidal showed) that a corrector went over the work of the copyist of the surviving MS and made rectifications based on the example from which the copyist had worked.

As will be shown, it will almost always be improper to correct imperfect assonances in order to make them conform, or to take too rigid a view of laisse-structures, for freedom and variability are inherent in the poet's system at least in the experimental stage. Nor must we add lines which appear in chronicle accounts but have been thought to be missing from the poetic MS. The chroniclers were perfectly capable of adding explanations or adornments, or filling imagined lacunae, even in a form vaguely resembling verse, and recent investigations have emphasised this.[2] What we must do is adjust the line-lengths of the MS on many occasions, not by adding or suppressing words, but by redividing the lines. Examples are 16–16b, 69–69b, 269–269b, on whose rearrangement editors more or less agree. One can suggest how these mistakes arose. It might be that the fourteenth-century copyist overran the line shown in his model, as a modern might do when preparing a typescript; but since other poetic MSS from Spain hardly show this kind of error, it is a less likely explanation. Better, it may be conjectured that at some stage a copy was made in which the poem was written down in continuous lines as though it were prose; from this, the surviving MS was made and the text reconstituted as verse, though less than perfectly. This is no idle conjecture, for much medieval verse was set down as prose in order to save space on costly parchment. Examples from Spain include the texts of the *Carmen Campidoctoris*, the *Auto de los reyes magos*, the *Disputa del alma y el cuerpo*, the *Mocedades de Rodrigo*, one MS (419 of the Biblioteca Lázaro Galdiano) of the *Vida de San Ildefonso*, and 'aljamiado' MS 'A' of the *Poema de Yuçuf*.[3]

How did Per Abad create his system? There are advantages in taking rhyme before the other aspects. We know that assonance existed in Hispanic lyric before 1207 both in Mozarabic (if recent criticism has left any Romance *kharjas*) and in Galician, and we can suppose it to have existed in Castilian lyric too although we have no texts from this early period which show it.[4] Assonance was firmly established in the usage of medieval Latin and in French. But assonance cannot be considered in isolation from the laisse or verse-paragraph in which Per Abad groups his lines. Even though he might have learned the practice of assonance from Galician or Castilian lyric, or from Latin hymns and songs, these would not have given him the patterns of combination which he needed, for lyrics and hymns are firmly strophic, with syllabically regular lines which assonate alternately or in other patterns. Per Abad can only have learned his practice of assonance jointly with his practice of the laisse, that is in French epic. As we have seen and shall see constantly, there is no problem about postulating the poet's knowledge of and general debt to French texts, and hence in affirming that he imitated the metrics (in this regard) at the same time as he imitated the rhetoric, certain episodes, and many topics, of those texts. There is nothing new in such an idea, for one of the first students of the *Poema*, Bello, advanced it, and many have done so since.[5] But Per Abad was not simply trying to write French alexandrines and doing it badly, as some have thought. The matter is more complicated and more interesting than that.[6]

Per Abad's rhyming system allowed, first, for occasional assonances which we may call approximate or imperfect (I use this word in a technical, not a derogatory sense; after all, if Per Abad was an innovator, he had no standards of 'perfection' in his own language against which to measure himself). Early editors were prepared to tolerate some of these. Menéndez Pidal in his critical edition thought that imperfect assonances were the result of careless copying, and he detailed processes which could have led to this, but even so, it is not easy to see why any copyist should deliberately have upset notionally perfect rhymes. Certainly in a few cases of rhyme-words the fourteenth-century scribe (or a predecessor) modernised, perhaps unconsciously, for example in writing 'señoras' (l. 3450) in place of the archaic feminine 'señorcs' which the rhyme requires. These any modern editor will restore. But it is hard to imagine a copyist writing the 'en buen logar' (l. 2155) of the MS as 'en buen recabdo', which is Pidal's emendation, for here no modernisation was involved; 'logar' with stressed *á* can stand as an approximate assonance which concludes a laisse rhymed in *á-o*. Transpositions of hemistichs by a copyist are hard to imagine too. Some disturbance of word-order could, perhaps, be allowed to have occurred if the poem were written down as prose at some stage, the order of words in prose being then used with consequent disturbance of rhymes; thus in line 2635 the MS has a second hemistich 'una noch y iazredes' in a laisse rhymed in *ó(-e)*, and, since this is not even an approximate assonance, Pidal and others have restored the order 'y iazredes una noch'.

When, having made a few allowances of the kinds mentioned above, we return to the MS, we can begin to see that Per Abad's system gave a good deal of liberty. Perhaps finding a single rhyme strictly maintained throughout a laisse that might extend to over a hundred lines rather monotonous, even though this was what the general model of French epic authorised, he produced an occasional couplet within the laisse whose rhyme differs from that of the generality of the laisse. For example, in laisse 9, rhymed in *á-o*, he made lines 124–5 into a couplet with rhymes 'gañó' – 'sacó' (that is, maintaining *á-o* but with different stress). Or the rhymes of a couplet may bear no relation to those of the laisse, as in 'caridad' – 'Bivar' (ll. 720–1) in laisse 35, which is rhymed in *ó(-e)*. Furthermore, the argument about the possible monotony of a long laisse does not greatly apply, for although laisse 9 has seventy-four lines, laisse 35 has only eleven. Such couplets with apparently anomalous rhyme usually make good sense, and are sometimes especially emphatic (lines 720–1 are a good example), so there is no reason to correct them on any semantic ground. One such couplet, therefore, is dubious on the very score that it does not make a satisfactory sense-unit (ll. 1071–2). There are in all some seventeen such couplets (ll. 15–16, 124–5, 127–8, 720–1, 820–1, 826–6b, 827–8, 967–8, 1071–2, 1195–6, 1644–5, 1866–7, 1910–11, 2675–6, 2753–4, 2962–3, 3053–4). Early editors were content to let most of them stand; Michael and I have agreed, and there is no reason to think them alien to the poet's system at least in its experimental stage. The alternative is to regard such couplets as forming small independent laisses; several, such as ll. 826–6b and 827–8, make good sense in this way, while others, such as 820–1, are less pleasing.

The poet wrote many lines whose last word does not give a perfect rhyme, such lines being especially frequent as a laisse is concluding and another starting. These are of two types. The first continues the assonance of the laisse which is ending but belongs semantically to that which is starting, for example 'grado' (l. 570), which continues the *á-o* rhyme of laisse 28 but is associated in sense with what is coming in laisse 29. A second type partakes of the rhyme of neither laisse but is completely independent, e.g. line 404, 'fue çenado', attached neither to laisse 18 in *á(-e)* nor to 19 in *ó(e)*. In five instances there are couplets, such as lines 1195–6, occupying such transitional places. In all some thirty change-overs of laisse are affected in these ways, one-fifth of the total in a work of 152 laisses. The practice seems, then, to be willed, at least experimentally: it has something to do with the linking of laisses. It may be that the practice is an imitation of the independent lines and half-lines which feature in certain *chansons de geste* probably known to the poet (Smith, 1979: 39 and note), and that he was toying with such a system but not confident enough in it to follow it consistently. As with the couplets, such lines usually make good sense and there is no reason to think, as Pidal did when correcting them all, that scribal corruption produced them.

Other types of approximate assonance occur within the laisse. Some of these conserve the stressed vowel which is the basis of the rhyme of the laisse, but follow it with a different unstressed vowel. Such are 'heredades' (l. 460) in a laisse rhymed in *á-a*, 'consegar' (l. 1256) in a laisse rhymed in *á-o*, together with all cases of 'Alfonso' and 'Jeronimo' within laisses generally rhymed in *ó* (-e). Pidal corrected all these, but Michael and I accept many of them in our editions, Michael justifying the acceptance in part on the analogy of French practice as known to Per Abad.[7] Less satisfactory are the occasional lines whose end-words have vowels not in common with the rhyme of the laisse (e.g. ll. 1043, 1045, 2645). These are hard to justify as part of any system and have no analogues in French; however, they all make good sense, and it seems best to conclude that they are tentative lines which the poet would have improved in some later version. Again, it is not proper for an editor to emend these lines unless he is himself composing that hypothetical improved version on behalf, as it were, of a long-dead colleague (and it is in this sense that Pidal's great edition can be applauded). The rhymes of *ué* with others in *ó* (e.g. 'muert', l. 2677) are tolerable in the terms suggested here, and do not require archaising to bring them into line ('muort', etc.).

It is hard to know, on my terms, how to class the licence known as the 'paragogic -*e*' by which, for example in laisse 128, among many rhymes in -*ó* one finds occasional words in -*ó-e*, all rhyming together. This may have been taken from the practice of contemporary lyric, and it was certainly to be the practice of other epic texts (notably the *Roncesvalles*, in whose surviving fragment paragogic -*e* is actually written on all the rhymes that have, etymologically, simply *ó*) and of the ballads. Such an addition seems to derive from poetic forms composed to be sung, in which a fixed number of syllables and equality of syllables in the rhyme-words would be essential when words are to be accompanied by a repetitive tune. Within the stressed system of Per Abad's lines (as will be argued) the pronunciation of a paragogic -*e* would have been less essential, but a musical accompaniment – not amounting to a fully repetitive tune – may all the same have required it, and the example of the *Roncesvalles* fragment shows that it was to become a natural part of the system. All one can say is that Per Abad's text is the first to give a hint of the paragogic -*e*, still without writing it,[8] and that this at least has no parallel in French or Latin.

It seems natural enough to suppose that the poet took from French his notions of the coherence of the laisse, the practice (not rules) for starting and ending one, etc., together with the technique of the *laisses similaires* ('series gemelas') at which he occasionally tried his hand. The practices are well analysed, in brief, in the introduction to Michael's edition, and they are shown to derive from those of French by Herslund (1974: 80–1).

The great metrical problem of the *Poema* is its line-structure. As mentioned above, in many instances these structures have been disturbed by copyists, but editors have largely agreed about necessary redivisions. Once these have been effected, the task is to see what system Per Abad tried to create.

What models could the poet have had for heroic verse around 1200? There was much in Latin, of different kinds, which he could have known; but since we cannot identify textual borrowings which he made directly from Latin poems, the possibility that he imitated Latin verse-structures is best regarded as secondary and left for later consideration. It seems obvious, and is the recurrent thesis of this book, that an apprentice Spanish author of about

1200 would have turned to French to learn his craft. He imitated the French system of laisse and assonance, and it seems likely that his line-structures have something to do with those of French epics. Lines embody, after all, the formulae and topics which the poet drew in abundance from French, as will be shown. There is, again, nothing notably new about such a proposal, long ago formulated by Bello; but Bello and others thought that the author of the *Poema* had simply made a poor effort to transpose French lines into Spanish, whereas I think the effort is to be viewed in a much more positive way.

It seems that in any case Per Abad could not have learned much for his purposes from the lines of existing vernacular verse in the Peninsula. Lyric in Mozarabic and Galician showed a variety of line-structures, but most were shorter than Per Abad needed for his epic measure, and in particular, they had no caesura. The same was presumably true of Castilian lyric at the time, and it seems that the double octosyllable, later to become so dominant in Castilian verse, was not then so powerful as to persuade the poet to adopt it. It is true that a proportion of the lines of the *Poema* do conform to this double octosyllable, but I think this a coincidence or at least an unintended result, and the proportion is not sufficiently high to warrant the attempts that have been made to adjust all lines of the text to conform to this pattern.

Among the *chansons de geste* which, as we know from recent studies,[9] Per Abad was probably acquainted with, various metrical forms are represented. In decasyllables constructed 4 + 6 are the *Chanson de Roland* (in a version related to 'O' or 'V⁴'), *Raoul de Cambrai*, *La Prise de Cordres*, *Amis et Amiles*, and *La Chevalerie d'Ogier*. In decasyllables of the type 6 + 4 is *Girart de Roussillon*. In alexandrines measured 6 + 6 are *Fierabras*, probably the lost version of *Berte aus grans piés* (known in Adenet's reworking of 1272–5), *Florence de Rome*, and *Parise la duchesse*. The possibility that Per Abad imitated some of these French lines, especially the alexandrine, and mingled with the results the native octosyllable, was discussed by early scholars, but the inquiry began on a false footing because – as was natural to those whose ears were attuned to ancient and modern French verse, and to most types of Spanish verse – it was based on counting syllables in Per Abad's text, which led inevitably to the conclusion that he was merely an incompetent imitator.

The way forward is to dismiss the syllable-count as irrelevant and to consider the poem's lines in terms of stress. It seems that the first to envisage this was Delius in 1851, but others who have thought the same since, with varying confidence, include Restori, Gamillscheg, Leonard, Aubrun, Clarke, Navarro Tomás, Maldonado de Guevara, and Hall (see Magnotta, 1976: 171–3). Pidal's view is fundamental here. While his first statement referred to the system's 'leyes totalmente desconocidas para nosotros', he later opined that 'el principio rítmico que rige la irregularidad métrica del *Cantar* es tan vario, que no es fácil de precisar'. Alonso, Horrent, and others have echoed this, accepting that 'principio rítmico'. Recently Adams, starting without any preconceived idea about the metrical structures, has reaffirmed both the stress principle and the essential variability of its application, showing that many hemistichs in which a proper name or a formula is present are varied in length syllabically by inclusion or omission of a preposition, article, etc., but are of metrically equal value:

[These lines] cannot merely be the work of a short-sighted scribe or of an oral poet who has lost his sense of rhythm. They are both constant and syllabically irregular. They are intrinsic criteria and must mean that, of the schools of thought mentioned earlier, . . . only that which sees the poem in terms of stresses is anywhere near a 'regular' solution to the problem of the poem's metre. (Adams, 1972: 118–19)

A number of arguments in favour of an accentual solution can be advanced:

1. One does not need to adopt the views of the oralists – that epic was sung and offered, newly improvised on each occasion, to a listening public – in order to affirm that epic was a *public* genre, presented either by a professional minstrel who reproduced a memorised text, or by a performer who read aloud from a manuscript in his hand. A system of stresses is natural to an art involving declamation (though this cannot have applied to French epic, for a reason mentioned below).

2. If there was a musical accompaniment to epic in Spain, Menéndez Pidal's conjecture cannot be bettered:

'Pero nada sabemos de cómo los juglares exponían al público las Gestas; y a pesar del nombre de Cantares, aun cabría otra suposición tratándose de unos versos tan extremadamente irregulares como los del *Mio Cid*: que no se cantasen propiamente, sino que se acompañaban de un simple tonadillo de recitado, el cual llevaría una modulación más saliente para el acento de la cesura y para las sílabas finales de cada verso.'
(1908–11: I, 102–3)

This implies a system of strong and weaker stresses.

3.   Some of those who have postulated an accentual system, such as Restori, have thought it a continuation of primitive Germanic habits, which in Hispania would be those of the Visigoths. This naturally fitted in with traditionalist ideas about the 'latent state' of epic and other phenomena, and with the essential 'germanism' of Romance epic. This latter part of the standard canon of belief has – on the metrical side – recent adherents (Maldonado de Guevara, Hall, and Strausser). Such an idea – that epic in Spanish has a stress-system which in some way continues that of Gothic verse – is implausible, because metrical systems surely die with languages, and there was no Gothic in Hispania after about A.D. 600, no written texts of Gothic being known to have survived for imitation by later poets. The thesis is superfluous in any case for, as will be shown, excellent models of stressed verse existed in Latin and were likely to have been known to any cultured person of Per Abad's time.

4.   The metrical system of the *romances* (ballads), which seems to have resulted from the evolution of one type of epic line, certainly has a stress pattern; even if there is syllabic regularity, as is the case from the sixteenth century onwards, this is secondary.

5.   The claim made by the author of the *Libro de Alexandre* in his second stanza, that his work is constructed 'a silabas contadas, ca es grant maestria', need not imply that the epic poets in their craft of *juglaría* were incapable of counting their syllables correctly, but may mean that the epic poets did not count syllables at all, their verse having a different, accentual basis.

There is nothing, then, which would prevent us *a priori* from considering that the system of the *Poema* is accentual; quite the reverse. The modern reader can readily appreciate the force of the stresses and the often rhythmical nature of the verse by reading a section of it aloud, and one may suppose that a minstrel or other presenter of the poem in its time could have given a certain artificial extra emphasis to the stresses, especially if accompanied by an instrument.

The way has been cleared for a detailed presentation of the case that Per Abad devised his system following French models. Yet the matter is not simple, given that the diverse French lines all have a syllabic basis, and that Per Abad's probably have an accentual one. That there must be some bond between them is undoubted in view of the close textual parallels adduced in what follows. I mark the certain and probable stresses on the Spanish lines, and their syllabic count too.[10] We may take first the French decasyllables 4 + 6 which Per Abad imitated in whole or in part:

Set cenz cameilz e mil hosturs müez (*CR* 'O', 129; see also 31, 184)
e sín falcónes e sín adtóres mudádos (*Cid*, 5)   5+8

Puis se baiserent es buches e es vis (*CR* 'O', 633)
besó le la bóca e los ójos de la cára (*Cid*, 921)   5+8

Franceis decendent, a tere se sunt mis (*CR* 'O', 1136)
firiéron se a tiérra, deçendiéron de los caválos (*Cid*, 1842) 6+9

Par tute l'ost funt lur taburs suner (*CR* 'O', 3137)
en la uéste de los móros los atamóres sonándo (*Cid*, 2345) 7+8

Tu n'ies mes hom ne jo ne sui tis sire (*CR* 'O', 297)
cuemo yó so su vassállo y él es mío señór (*Cid*, 2905)   8+6

S'irons veoir a Cordes la fort cit (*Prise de Cordres*, 2123)
Hirémos vér aquéla su almofálla (*Cid*, 1124)   4+7

Grans fut li deus a celle departie (*Prise de Cordres*, 647)
Grándes fuéroñ los duélos a la departiçión (*Cid*, 2631)   7+7

c'est Herchanbaus, si l'ai oït conter (*Raoul*, 6381)
aquéste era el rey Búcar, sil oyéstes contár (*Cid*, 2314)   7+7

In decasyllables 6+4:
Firaz les, chevaler, pos tant i pert! (*Girart de Roussillon*, 1287)
Firaz les, chevaler, pos vos comant! (*Girart de Roussillon*, 1300)
¡Firíd los, cavalléros, tódos sínes dubdánça . . .! (*Cid*, 597; see also 720, 1139)   7+7

In alexandrines:
Riche cheval en destre de Sulie ou d'Espaigne (*Florence*, 169)
e buén cavállo en diéstro que va ánte sus ármas (*Cid*, 1548) 7+6

De pennes et de drais, de riches cendaus d'Andre! (*Florence*, 451)
mántos e piélles e buénos çendáles d'Andria? (*Cid*, 1971)   5+8

La forest fu parfonde, li bois haus et foilluz (*Florence*, 3776; also 4019)
los móntes son áltos, las rámas pújan con las núes (*Cid*, 2698)   6+8

Et Miles l'an desfant, li traïtres provez! (*Parise*, 432)
S'il ne fait recreant, le traïtor prové (*Parise*, 442)
a aquél rey Búcar, traidór provádo (*Cid*, 2523)   5+5

Vienent à Valancines, une bone cité (*Parise*, 787)
de siniéstro Sant Estévan – una buéna çipdád (*Cid*, 397)   8+7

The most diverse line-lengths, then, on a syllable-count, came from Per Abad's pen when he was following models in French decasyllables, and the same when he was following alexandrines. Moreover, some of his lines based on alexandrines emerged shorter, syllabically, than some of those based on decasyllables. Clearly, the poet was not following a model slavishly. He was not translating, but as a creative artist took what he wanted and adapted it. Sometimes the difference in grammatical structure between the two languages makes for a metrical difference ('li traïtres provez' = 'traidor provado'), or the contextual grammar demands an adjustment ('De pennes et de drais' = 'mantos e pielles'). Even when the imitation is closest, as in 'Grans fut li deus   a celle departie' = 'Grandes fueron los duelos   a la departiçion', we see that it was not the poet's intention to follow the French syllabic structure, for here 4+6 and 7+7 are equivalent. In any case, there was no point in trying to make individual lines conform to the structures of their French originals (notionally, the poet could have written as a first hemistich *'grand fue el duelo', four syllables echoing the four of French), for the lines directly based on French are only a small percentage in the poem as a whole and do not specially dominate. Whatever we discern must be part of a system of general application.

The reason for marking stresses on the Spanish lines above then becomes apparent. But stress, unlike the identity of the syllable, is to some degree a variable or personal matter. We cannot be precisely sure how Per Abad stressed his lines – beyond asserting, naturally, that there was a stress on the last etymologically accented vowel at the end of the first hemistich, and another, also etymological, on the main rhyming vowel; and we cannot know how presenters handled the matter. For example, in line 597 above, the second hemistich, on which I have placed three stresses, may really have only two: 'tódos sines dubdánça'; while the first hemistich of line 5 may well have only one stress, 'e sin falcónes'. Nouns and verbs obviously carry more stress than prepositions and particles, while adjectives and adverbs vary in emphasis. The consideration may not be wholly one of grammatical priority, however, since the poet was (as will be seen) strongly conscious of alliterations and vowel-harmonies, and may thus have placed stresses in ways which, while not anti-etymological, would not occur to a modern speaker. What does seem certain is that in this 'public' verse, the stress can never be anti-etymological, for that would strike a listening public as unnatural; hence I do not think that the ingenious stress-system proposed by Aubrun (1947) is valid.

Bearing this uncertainty about some stresses in mind, one can still say that the number of stresses in the line is as variable as any count of syllables. Lines that are typical and also pleasing to the ear – that is, to the modern ear – are those having stresses in the pattern 2+2 or 2+3, but first hemistichs having three stresses are by no means displeasing (e.g. ll. 1648, 2278, 2631). Hemistichs having one stress only are not poetically defective and need no addition in order to complete their sense or structure: perhaps 'e sin falcónes' (l. 5) with one stress only, while in line 2631 one might scan 'a la dèpartiçión', with a minor or secondary stress on *dè-*. Sometimes, the French source assures us that a hemistich is textually sound even though it may seem short, since 'a la departiçion' = 'a celle departie'.

Sometimes one can recognise that a line has a French source, but we find a number of lines (all in poems which we can hold were probably known to Per Abad) which could hypothetically have been that source, and these have differing structures. Thus the line:

¡en sos àguisamiéntos   bién seméja varón!   (3125)

marks a high point in the poem, when the Cid presents himself after due preparation, with total visual and corporeal conviction, at the Toledan court. The poet has made a good adaptation of a French cliché, learned in one or more poems. In decasyllables 4 + 6 there was:

S'il fust leials, ben resemblast barun   (*CR 'O'*, 3764)

Cil au cor neis   resanble bien baron   (*Prise de Cordres*, 598)

and also, in alexandrines:

Quant li rois fu montez, bien resambla baron   (*Florence*, 1125)

From one of these or from all, Per Abad made a line of 7 + 7 syllables, or of 1 + 3 stresses. It might be thought that he was simply producing a Spanish alexandrine, which regularly was to have 7 + 7 syllables as an equivalent to the 6 + 6 of French, and the case would not be an isolated one. But the fact that the poet in other instances produced very varied results from French alexandrines prevents us from relating line 3125 specifically to *Florence* rather than to the lines of *Roland* and the *Prise de Cordres*. Similar is:

fáta Valénçia   duró el segudár   (l. 1148; compare 2407) which has analogies both with a French decasyllable:

Li enchalz durét   d'ici qu'en Sarraguce   (*CR* 'O', 3635)

and with an alexandrine:

Deci à Vauvenice   ne finent de chacier   (*Parise*, 1992)[11]

At times we catch the poet almost with his pen in his hand, working with results which show their experimental nature. I said in an earlier paper that the poet found, or recalled, a detail in *Florence* which interested him for his description of battles:

Que donc veïst abatre   et paveillons et trez   (l. 2529)

and I then suggested erroneously how and why the poet expanded this. Deyermond and Hook (1981–2: 27–8) have now identified this motif in other French epics and have shown that the cutting of cords and pulling up of pegs are present in them, so it is more proper to say now that Per Abad combined details perhaps drawn from several texts:[12]

Tánta cuérda de tiénda   i veríedes quebrár,
arancár se las estácas   e acostár se a todas pártes los tendáles
                                                          (ll. 1141–2)

The first line of this comes out well, and the first hemistich of the second; but the rest is a disaster, for even if we count only three stresses (and 'todas' could well carry another), and even if we note that the alliteration of stressed *a* has its attractions, the second hemistich of line 1142 remains heavy and clumsy. Evidently this was an experimental line, of the sort that the poet might have improved in a final version. Editors have contributed towards that improvement. Restori and Lidforss omit 'a todas partes'. The poet used the idea again:

veríedes quebrár tántas cuérdas   e arrancár se las estácas
e acostár se los tendáles,   con huébras eran tántas   (ll. 2400–1)

with better results, though the first hemistich of line 2400 is heavy, and one remains unsure whether a half-line of four stresses was intended within the system. However, one can see that at this second attempt the poet improved on his earlier one. He perceived (giving support to the emendation of Restori and Lidforss) that 'a todas partes' would not really fit, especially if he wished to vary a little by introducing the 'huebras', not present in any French model so far identified. He seems also to have elaborated the word-music: not only does 'huebras' echo 'cuerdas', but the vowel-sequence of 'cuerdas e arrancar' is echoed in 'huebras eran tantas' among the still dominant notes of *á*.

A good example of the tentative nature of the poet's work, and one which illustrates the perils of textual emendation on metrical grounds, is provided by Jimena's prayer. The tradition and sources of this have been the subject of distinguished studies, mentioned in Chapter 5 (what follows was published by me in 1977–8: 14–16). The prayer is a moving one and serves to introduce Jimena effectively on to the literary stage. None the less, it has features which are less than fully satisfactory but can be explained by the poet's attentiveness to his French sources. He found the following about the life of Christ in the alexandrines of *Fierabras*:

Puis alastes par tere .xxxii. ans passés   (l. 1178)

and adapted it as:

por tiérra andidíste .xxxii. áños, Señór spirítál   (l. 343)

That is, he had the unhappy notion of putting the equivalent of the whole French line into his first hemistich (and it is no help to think that possibly the '.xxxii. años' might go into the second). Perhaps some devout prompting led the poet to add 'Señor spirital', or more likely, since this phrase too has precedents in French, he had to seek a rhyme-word in *á(-e)*, and nothing in the French suggested one. Perhaps the poet could have concluded by following *Fierabras* exactly and writing as a second hemistich '.xxxii. años passados', giving an approximate assonance in which *á* continued the stressed vowel of the laisse, and producing a satisfactory caesura after 'andidiste'; but he did not. Later comes a passage of great importance:

Longinos era çiego   que nunquas vio alguandre,
diot con la lança en el costado   dont ixio la sangre,
corrio la sangre por el astil ayuso,   las manos se ovo de untar,
alçolas arriba,   legolas a la faz,
abrio sos ojos,   cato a todas partes,
en ti crovo al ora   por end es salvo de mal   (ll. 352–7)

For this Per Abad had before him as he composed, or had an extremely accurate memory of, no fewer than three French passages:

Quant Longis vous feri   de la lance trenchant,
Il n'avoit ainc véu   en trestout son vivant;
Li sans li vinst par l'anste   juques as ex coulant,
Il en terst a ses ex,   tantost en fu véant   (*Fierabras*, 946–9)

Et Longis vous feri   de la lance es costés;
Il n'avoit ainc véu   de l'eure qu'il fu nés;
Li sans fu par la lance   duques as puins coulés;
Il en terst a ses ex,   tantost fu alumés   (*Fierabras*, 1207–10)

Et Longins de la lance, biau Sire, vos ferit;
Aval parmi la lance li sang clers en salit,
Il an tardi ses euz, alumer li féis;
Ses pechiez pardonas, qu'il te cria merci   (*Parise*, 813–16)

Line 352 of the *Poema* echoes 947 or 1208 of *Fierabras*; line 353 of the *Poema* nearly translates 1207 of *Fierabras*; and so on. But the Spaniard combined both passages of *Fierabras*, for if 'astil' = 'anste' of the first, 'costado' represents 'costés' and 'manos' represents 'puins' of the second. One then notes that 'dont ixio la sangre' (353) imitates 'li sang clers en salit' of *Parise*, 815, which is not found in *Fierabras*; however, Per Abad combines this with a line of *Fierabras*, 948 or 1209, for Spanish 'la sangre' = French 'li sans'. Yet all is not well. The passage is fully coherent, but the poet has 'la sangre' twice, inelegantly, in successive lines, and line 354 is too heavy with its four probable stresses in the first hemistich ('corrió la sángre por el astíl ayúso'). These defects the poet would surely have remedied in a later version. Modern editors have taken to themselves the right to do it for him. Pidal omits 'la sangre' from line 354; Bello omits 'la sangre' and also 'ayuso'; Restori and Cornu omit 'por el astil'. But nobody has a right to suppress anything, since the study of the sources – an aspect overlooked by the traditionalists, who do not believe in them – proves that 'la sangre' has to figure twice, in view of the two sources followed by the poet, that 'ayuso' must stand, since it echoes 'aval' of *Parise*, and that 'por el astil' is essential too in view of 'par l'anste' of *Fierabras*. Examples of this kind, perhaps less telling, occur throughout the poem. It is no more up to modern editors to polish Per Abad's generally admirable work than it is up to scholars to rewrite *Don Quijote* in order to harmonise the affairs of Sancho's donkey or the names of his wife.

In numerous other instances Per Abad echoed the thought or adapted the materials of a French line or couplet, without sufficiently precise verbal parallels for us to be able to compare metrical structures. It seems, for example, that the lines:

a las sus fijas en braço' las prendia,
legolas al coraçon ca mucho las queria.
Lora de los ojos, tan fuerte mientre sospira   (ll. 275–7)

echo those of *Raoul* in which Gueris takes his small nephew in his arms at a farewell:

Gueris le prent en ses bras maintenant,
Parfondement del cuer va soupirant   (ll. 348–9)

Two French lines have been expanded into three in Spanish, and no hemistichs precisely correspond. An unusual word in Spanish as well as similarity of phrasing may lead us towards a possible source, as when:

vistios el sobregonel; luenga trahe la barba   (l. 1587)

appears to be based on:

Il s'agenoille; vestue ot sa gonnele   (*Raoul*, 1757)

but Per Abad has switched the hemistichs; perhaps for reasons of rhythm or from need for an assonance in *á-a*. One may suggest that while the poet began by writing hemistichs and lines which nearly translate hemistichs and lines in French (not necessarily those which figure in the surviving text and are noted above, but lines which were no more than tentative jottings), he was not often so slavish in his imitation, but quickly asserted his independence. In any case, his contexts and grammatical structures were often to differ from those of French. He had a good story to tell and strong personages to move about his stage, and energy to carry him along without overmuch dependence on particular sources for long at a time.

The same can be demonstrated in the multitude of formulaic hemistichs (to be discussed as a system in Chapter 6) which the poet adopted from French. Second-hemistich 'a guisa de varon' (ll. 1350, 3154, 3563) echoes 'en guise de barun' (e.g. *Roland* 'O', 1226, 1889, 1902, 3054), six syllables of French making a simple two-beat half-line in Spanish, with ready rhyme in *ó*. There is a variant 'a guisa de muy pros' (l. 2847) based on the variant 'en guise de produme' of *Roland* 'O', 3264, while for a different assonance Per Abad has 'a guisa de menbrado' in lines 102, 131, 3700, representing '. . . membré' of French. In studying the extensive catalogues of such formulaic borrowings which Herslund and Adams have compiled, one can see that on the whole Per Abad respected the placement in the line which he found in French, so that a formula devised, with variants, for second-hemistich use in French remained a second-hemistich formula in Spanish. This is natural enough, given the facts that such formulae often have a useful line-filling function, and have vowels which are easy to fit into series of rhymes. But 'a guisa de varon' can be used to end a longer second hemistich in lines 2576 and 3525, and 'a guisa de menbrado' is used as a first hemistich in line 579. The formulaic half-lines which most closely conform to French must, one feels, have been an early part of Per Abad's system, for they are mostly simple, and almost all have two stresses; and they were elements in the wholesale adaptation of a formulaic system which the poet recognised as a fundamental part of French epic rhetoric.

The formula might consist of as little as one word, 'sabet' or 'sepades', in part emphatic but in part also a mere line-filler. Per Abad used it commonly, imitating, I think, the usage of *Raoul*:

Miex li venist,   ce saichiés par verté   (l. 389)

Rien ne li donnent,   se saichiés, si ami   (l. 644)

Ocis l'eüst,   sachiés a esciant   (l. 3100)

This formulaic 'saichiés' in *Raoul* occurs at the start of the second hemistich. In the *Poema*, of twenty-four instances of 'sabet' or 'sepades', twenty occur in that position and only four at the start of the line, so that even here, with an apparently easily-movable single word, French usage was on the whole respected.[13] That neither close imitation of French nor mere line-filling was, however, much in the poet's mind may be judged from some of the lines he produced with the formula, for example:

Otro dia mañana   pienssan de cavalgar;
es dia a de plazo,   sepades que non mas   (ll. 413–14)

in which, after providing an elegantly leonine anticipation of 'cavalgar' in the vowels of 'mañana', the poet emphasises the key word 'plázo' and severely marks it with the admonitory echo of 'sepádes' and 'más'. To count syllables or stresses does not make one's ear insensitive to the real qualities of Per Abad's verse, and it is noteworthy that in this instance, as in many, he found only a skeleton in his French model; the clothing in poetic flesh is entirely his.

When we put Per Abad's numerous French-based formulaic lines together with the non-formulaic lines and groups of lines which the poet modelled on French sources, we have a substantial corpus. It is likely that it was in composing this corpus, upon immediately available models, that Per Abad served his apprenticeship as Spain's first epic poet. As I have argued, he had no predecessors in the Spanish vernaculars to follow, and it was natural for one fired by enthusiasm for the epic ideal to realise that ideal on the technical side by following the precedent of the dominant French genre. But he did not try to imitate the syllabic structures of French epic, even though one of them – the alexandrine – was successfully acclimatised in Spanish by Berceo or the *Alexandre*-poet a few years later. I suggested earlier that with sure instinct Per Abad sought to create a 'public' poetry, trusting his voice and ear – which was in imagination already the ear of his potential public – and that he was not concerned to produce something that would look well on parchment; for this, a set of structures built on stresses was entirely suitable. One could add that since he felt a special urge to make his personages live in direct speech – a feature of his work which has long been regarded as a triumph – he tried also to harmonise the rhythms and emphases of ordinary speech with those of verse; some poetic inversions would be allowable, even necessary (given the dignity that epic language must have), but in moderation.[14]

Numerous students of the *Poema* have held, in differing ways, that its line-structures resulted from an imitation of French metres. But their proposals now seem unsatisfactory because most of them insisted that the imitation was a defective one, or because they remained wedded to a syllable-count in Spanish. Restori in 1887 came close to what I regard as the right approach, though of course he wrote in traditionalist terms and did not regard the author of the *Poema* as any sort of innovator:

Io credo ed è forse l'ipotesi più accettabile, che gli endecasillabi francesi (4+6) e meglio ancora la cadenza che li governava, fossero ben noti e comuni. Da ciò una irriflessa tendenza ad ammettere quel verso e quel canto; l'orecchio assuefatto a quella misura vi si conformava più o meno liberamente sicchè poeti e ascoltatori neppur sospettavano quanto a formare in essi una tale assuefazione avessero contributo i cantori d'oltralpe. Imitazione incosciente: è la sola formola che parmi possa spiegare, da una parte, le grande conformità di verso e di serie tra Francia e Spagna, dall'altra tutte le libertà e le irregolarità che i giullari spagnuoli si permettevano.   (Quoted by Magnotta, 1976: 155)

Perception of the 'cadenza' and the 'grande conformità' is entirely correct, but the notion of the 'irriflessa tendenza' and 'imitazione incosciente' is not. Certainly I think Per Abad's work experimental, but there was nothing 'incosciente' about it. He was too good an artist in other respects for us to believe that he wrote anything that was not consciously willed, even if some of it was to be left in a tentative and slightly untidy state. One must then argue in one of two ways about his creation of stressed line-structures. That he was a cultured man acquainted with French and some Latin texts now seems incontrovertible. He could have known his French texts in Burgos, on the basis of a reading knowledge of French together with some auditions of poems; or he had lived in France and acquired a true possession of the language both spoken and written. In the first case, his imitation of French metres was conditioned by the fact that he read lines of *chansons de geste* giving them a false Spanish intonation; that is, in reading aloud – as medievals did – from the MS before him, he placed a Spanish-type stress on individual syllables which no longer had one in French. Hence, the alexandrine:

Ríche chevál en déstre de Súlie ou d'Espáigne   (*Florence*, 169)

seemed to him to have an accentual basis of 3 + 2 stresses, in no wise different (to his Spanish ear) from the decasyllable:

Gráns fút li déus a célle departíe   (*Prise de Cordres*, 647)

whose rhythm he then reproduced in the impressive line:

Grándes fuéron los duélos a la dèpartiçión   (l. 2631)

And so on in other instances. On this view, Per Abad was not imperfectly imitating lines (by failing to represent their syllabic structure correctly in Spanish), but was misinterpreting their nature (by assuming that they worked on a stress principle). However, I do not think this first possibility a likely one. As argued earlier, it is easier on all scores to suppose that the poet had lived and trained in France rather than been self-educated in Burgos. In that event he could not have misinterpreted the nature of the French metrical system, for he would have been acquainted with it not only in private reading and by listening to more frequent renditions of the *chansons*, but in relation to the speech-rhythms of spoken French also. His transposition of French lines into Spanish, and of a syllable-count into a stress-system, was thus a more artificial and deliberate act. Since the poet was often combining features of French sources (as in Jimena's prayer) and adapting a formulaic system common to many texts, it is easier to suppose that he worked from a well-stocked memory rather than by poring over manuscripts on his desk in search of materials, though he may have continued to read or re-read these also, in Burgos.

In addition to the five *a priori* reasons which may dispose us to seek a stress basis in Per Abad's line, it is important to note (as was hinted when the third reason was stated) that, while stress-systems may seem alien to the Romance languages in their middle and modern phases, the parent of them all, Latin, had them in abundance at several periods. It can be argued that the more popular forms of Latin verse were always so built, the introduction of the hexameter and other modes of 'classical' prosody being undertaken as a wholly learned imitation of Greek. In the rhythmical sequences or the hymns of the Church,

Per Abad like any moderately cultivated man of about 1200 had
an ample store of stressed Latin verse, for example:
> Stábat máter dolorósa
> iúxta crúcem, lacrimósa . . .

Goliardic song of the twelfth century may well have been familiar
to the poet also, in Spain, but more likely in the student taverns of
a French university, as the mugs were banged on the tables:
> Pòtatóres èxquisíti
> lícet sítis síne síti,
> et bibátis èxpedíti
> et scyphórum ìnoblíti . . .

That this is octosyllabic too is beside the point. Very much to it, in
addition to the strong end-stresses, is the frequent enrichment of
end-rhymes (in the same song, 'potestis/modestis', 'te prestare/
pede stare') and the love of alliteration both of consonants ('Qui
potare non potestis') and of vowels ('exeat ab hac cohorte . . . si
recedat a consorte'), techniques which Spanish in the hands of
Per Abad was well able to adopt, as will be seen. This kind of
Latin verse could have been more familiar to Per Abad as student
and reader than the classical hexameters of Virgil and Statius, or
the medieval imitations of them by such as Walter of Châtillon.
We are in territory adjacent to that of the poem *XV signa ante
Judicium* in the tradition which lies immediately behind Spanish
cuaderna vía, as cited by Dutton (1973: 84):
> Antequam Judicii dies metuenda
> veniat, sunt omnia mundi commovenda,
> nam per dies quindecim mundo sunt videnda
> signa nimis aspera, signa perhorrenda.

It was at one time suggested that the metrical system of the
Poema was based on imitation of the classical Latin hexameter and
pentameter, imperfectly realised. The editor who first published
the poem in 1779, T. A. Sánchez, thought so, and the possibility
was taken up again by Amador de los Ríos, who very specifically
associated the poet's lines with 'la tradición latino-eclesiástica'.[15]
Since then discussion of the idea has hardly taken place, a result,
perhaps, of the general neglect of Latin traditions in the Peninsula in their relevance to vernacular culture. While sequences
and hymns of the Church, and rhythmic Goliardic verse, could
have conditioned Per Abad's ear, he had good models of stressed
Latin verse closer at hand in texts which – as we can now see –
were altogether relevant to both the materials and techniques
of his poem. The recent book of Martínez has a section of the

greatest importance for my argument here (1975: 223). Discussing the *Poema de Almeria*, he begins by acknowledging, as others had before, that 'el poeta ha usado en una buena parte de sus versos el ritmo acentual ... en lugar de seguir el cuantitativo, como requerían sus hexámetros latinos'. The words omitted are: 'muy parecido al de la épica vulgar', with the hint that the *Almeria* poet might have adopted his accentual system from that source. However, this is unacceptable on my terms, because at the time that the *Poema de Almeria* was composed (1147–9) there is no evidence that a vernacular Spanish epic existed. Martínez himself dismisses this possibility shortly after, for the general richness of biblical phraseology adapted for the *Chronica Adefonsi Imperatoris* and the *Poema de Almeria* 'hace pensar que nuestro autor tuvo como modelo la poesía de los *Salmos* más bien que la de los juglares'. In this Martínez could well be right, but I am not concerned here with what lay behind the *Poema de Almeria*. It is the further parallel between the line-structures of *Almeria* and the *Poema de mio Cid* which is important, and which is briefly treated by Martínez. Noting that many of *Almeria*'s lines are leonine, e.g. 'Parvorum dux est, adolescentum pia lux est', Martínez observes that this structure encourages such parallelistic sequences of lines as are found both in the Psalms and in Jimena's prayer in Per Abad's poem ('fezist ... ', ll. 331–2; 'salvest ... ', ll. 339–42). The rhythmic principle is important too:

A pesar de las divergencias rítmicas, causadas por las exigencias semánticas de una y otra lengua, es bien evidente que en ambos textos la disposición de los acentos finales de cada hemistiquio tiende hacia un mismo principio regulador; esto es particularmente válido para el acento final del segundo hemistiquio que es el verdadero portador del ritmo en la épica vulgar.

Martínez perhaps does not go far enough, and it was not his purpose to say more about this aspect. However, I think he was right to perceive a clear relationship between the metre of *Almeria* and that devised – half a century later, in my view, though this was not Martínez's – by Per Abad. A typical stanza of *Almeria* is

> fácta séquens Cároli, cui compétit áequiparári.
> Génte fuére páres, armórum ví coaequáles.
> Glória bellórum gestórum pár fuit hórum.
> Extítit et téstis Maurórum péssima péstis,
> quos máris aut áestus non protégit, aut sua téllus.   (ll. 5–9)

The structure in hemistichs is plain. The leonine rhyme occurs in all five lines, and may be fully consonantal ('bellorum/horum') or assonantal ('pares/-quales', 'aestus/tellus'), also assonantal with an unstressed vowel not reckoned ('Cároli/-ári'). The stresses are in a varied pattern but often strong, 3+2, 3+3, 2+4, etc.; and are often emphasised by repetition of the vowel, for example of ó in line 7. Further alliteration of consonants is frequent, as in 'pessima pestis'. The similarity of these features to those of Per Abad's system is startling. All aspects of the latter are present in *Almeria*, one could say, except of course that *Almeria* has lines grouped in stanzas of five, without end-rhyme, whereas Per Abad's are grouped in laisses and assonate throughout after the French fashion. The nobly heroic air of the *Chronica Adefonsi Imperatoris* with its integral *Poema de Almeria* might have attracted Per Abad enough for him to adopt some features of its versification.

Whether the poet knew, or needed to know for his purposes, other Latin verse of twelfth-century Spain, is less easy to say. The *Carmen Campidoctoris*, immured in Ripoll, was probably not known to him.[16] The hexameters of the *Carmen de morte Sanctii regis* reconstructed by Entwistle are often built on rhythmic rather than classical patterns, and are frequently leonine too both in full rhyme and in assonance (Entwistle reconstructed in accordance with patterns and licences authorised by the near-contemporary *Poema de Almeria*). The epitaph of Sancho II at Oña is in hexameters of classical form, but three of its four lines are leonine, two in assonance and one in full rhyme; other epitaphs of the period share these features. Much of the Latin verse composed in France and elsewhere in the twelfth century, which Per Abad might have known during a stay in France, is rich in the features discussed here, even over-elaborate in its rhythmic and rhyming effects.[17] But the poet had ample materials in the Latin tradition of his homeland on which to work, including relatively ancient ones which have recently been considered in a new and very interesting way by Wright.[18]

In considering how to organise his work for public presentation, the poet seems to have recognised the advantage of dividing it into three sections, with appropriate phrasing for the information of his audience (ll. 1085, 2276). Sections one and two conclude with tranquil moments in which the hero can contemplate the summits of power which he has attained (victory over the Count of Barcelona, and massive booty; the marriages of his daughters to the Infantes), while the third ends also in tran-

quillity with the Cid's death after his final triumph. This
structural aspect is well handled by the poet, and as has often
been noted, each section probably corresponds to what could
conveniently be presented to an audience in one session. The
poet may have taken the idea of such a division from French epic
(Smith, 1977b: 151–4; and for the French background, Rychner,
1955: 48–54). *Fouques de Candie* is divided into six sections, but
there is no other evidence that Per Abad knew this poem. A text
which Per Abad probably knew is *La Chevalerie d'Ogier* (about
1185), which is divided like the *Poema* into three sections with
appropriate phrasing at the divisions. There is, of course, an
important difference: the French poems are very long, *Fouques*
having 14,916 lines and *Ogier* 12,346, so that within them, one
could say that breaks in the narration were necessary for the
relaxation of presenter and public in a way that they were not in
Per Abad's much shorter work. None the less, the Spaniard
rightly saw advantages in so dividing his poem, and may have
imitated the practice of *Ogier*. It is noteworthy also that Per Abad
imitated French nomenclature here: both *Fouques* and *Ogier* refer
within their texts to each section as a 'chanson' (e.g. *Ogier*, ll.
3103, 9552) even though the whole poem is a *chanson de geste*, and
Per Abad calls his section a 'cantar' as he ends it (l. 2276; also a
'gesta', l. 1085).

I argue, then, that when Per Abad conceived the idea of
composing the first Spanish epic, and knew that he should create
for it an adequately public form, he had a considerable range of
models in contemporary French and Latin. Both were dominant
in their times, widely known to cultured people, and of an
authority which not only invited imitation but positively imposed
it. From French epic the poet took his system of assonances and
laisses, varying the former slightly, and he probably took from it
too his tripartite division. He also took from French a formulaic
rhetorical system, some grammatical practices, suggestions for
several episodes, and a number of individual lines; but, for a
variety of reasons outlined above, he resolved not to adopt any of
the French line-structures known to him, with their syllable-
counts and virtual regularity, but to create patterns of stresses in a
relatively free system. His decision rested upon a deliberate
reinterpretation of French structures, perceived accentually not
syllabically; and this was reinforced or perhaps preconditioned
by much that he observed in the various forms of twelfth-century
Latin verse.

Although I think the French example was primary and the Latin secondary – because vernacular French epic was so much more immediate and necessary to the poet, and because his borrowings from French much outweigh those from Latin – the latter has its special importance when we consider the extraordinary phonetic elaborations with which Per Abad adorned his work. These had gone unperceived until de Chasca began the study of them (1972: Chapter 11) and I carried the inquiry further (1976b); very recently Adams (1980b) has refined the analysis.[19] I summarise here, for some indication is needed for a due appreciation of the poet's achievement. These phonetic elaborations seem to be unknown in French poems – naturally enough, given the lack of strong word-stress and different vocalic system of that language – but were common in twelfth-century Latin and proved readily adaptable to Spanish. Features mentioned earlier in this chapter as asides now come to be central. De Chasca more or less limited his observation to the fact that internal or 'vertical' assonance often links the endings of first hemistichs, as in:

Luego fablaron ifantes de Carrion:
'Dandos, rey, plazo ca cras ser non puede.
Armas e cavallos tienen los del Canpeador'   (ll. 3467–9)

Two or three lines may be linked in this way, sometimes four and even five . The assonance may not be continuous, but in a pattern ABAB (e.g. ll. 411–14), AABBA (ll. 3074–8), etc. De Chasca claimed that 987 first hemistichs, that is 26.5%, are linked in this way; even though this figure must be reduced somewhat, the practice is too frequent for the fact to be the product of accident. Of it de Chasca remarked that 'En nuestro *Poema* la rima interna me parece siempre estéticamente satisfactoria, sea por el instinto mencionado, sea por un propósito artístico evidente.' But his findings are only a beginning. Similar internal assonances of varying kinds are richly present in the poet's lines. To de Chasca's 'vertical' assonances must be added many 'horizontal' ones, sometimes within the hemistich, as in:

el castiéllo de Alcoçér en pária va entrándo   (l. 569)

¡en el nómbre del Criadór que non páse por ál!   (l. 675)

or embracing the whole line, as in:

Bién puébla el otéro, firme prénde las posadas   (l. 557)

metióla en sómo en tódo lo mas alto   (l. 612)

or, with greater elaboration of the same principle:

Mio Çíd e sus conpáñas caválgan tan aína   (l. 214)

passáron las águas, entráron al cámpo de Toránçio   (l. 545)

las carbónclas del yelmo echó gelas aparte,
cortól el yelmo que legó a la carne   (ll. 766–7)

These lines exploit a sequence of stressed vowels. The repetition
may be of a sequence of stressed and unstressed vowels:

Passaremos la sierra que fierá es e grand;
la tierra del Rey Alfonso esta noch la podemos quitar
(ll. 422–3; *ié-a, ié-a, ié-a; ó, ó*)

en San Pero a matines tandra el buen abbat   (l. 318; *a-á, a-á*)

To such cases must be added the numerous lines in which a
grammatical construction is repeated or in which some antithesis
is stated, such as:

Esto feches agora, al feredes adelant   (l. 896; *é-e-a, é-e-a*)

Leonines of the type identified earlier as common in Latin verse
of the twelfth century are frequent too, both in assonance:

Estas palabras dichas, la tienda es cogida   (l.213)

a las sus fijas en braço' las prendia   (l. 275)

and with full rhyme:

Mucho era pagado del sueño que a soñado   .   (l. 412)

quinze moros matava de los que alcançava   (l. 472)[20]

Rich rhymes are common too. There may be one extra vowel
before the normal two of the end-rhymes:

Yas tornan los del que en buen or*a* nasco.
Andava mio Çid sobre so buen c*a*vallo,
la cofia fronzida: ¡Dios, commo es bien b*a*rbado!   (ll. 787–9)

or two, or even three:

Levaron les los mantos e las piel*es* armiñas
mas dexan las maridas en brial*es* y *en* c*amis*as   (ll. 2749–50)

Dixieron los alcaldes quando man*festados* son:
'Si esso plogiere al Çid non gelo v*edamos* nos;
mas en nuestro juvizio assi lo mand*amos* nos'   (ll. 3224–6)

Consonantal alliteration is perhaps more obvious, but it requires
more attention than it has received from students of the *Poema*. It
is the secret of some of the poet's best lines:

Con lumbres e con candelas al corral dieron salto   (l. 244; *k, l*)

linpia salie la sangre sobre los çiclatones   (l. 2739; *l, s+ç*)

e que non parescan las armas, bien presos los cordones
(l. 3076; *k, p*)

These varied possible harmonies sometimes come together in a
display of artistry perhaps reserved for special moments. After

the sadness of abandoning his home and after the generally chilled and embarrassed reception in Burgos, the Cid's party reaches Cardeña with its human warmth and spiritual reassurances. The bells are rung for joy:

Tañen las campanas   en San Pero a clamor   (l. 286)

The heavy beat of the bells requires a ponderous rhythm of 2 + 2 stresses, but the line is not intended to be slow. One can hear in it a lively onomatopoeia both of the bell striking (*k* . . . *k*) and of its echoing vibration (nasals *m*, *n*, *ñ*, *-mp-* twice, and possibly a lingering final *-r*), and for once it does not seem excessive to say that the line is enhanced by sense-through-sound. At other times no such additional sense is conveyed, but one can confidently say that the poet has disposed the elements of his line with special care:

Grandes son los gozos   que van por es logar
quando mio Çid gaño a Valençia   y entro en la çibdad
(ll. 1211–12)

in which one notes *g-g-g* in line 1211 and *ç-ç-ç* in line 1212, the *ó* of line 1211 echoed by two others in line 1212, and in both lines a stressed *á* which anticipates the *á* of the end-rhyme.

An analysis of passages containing sequences of place-names produces the conclusion that the poet's natural affection for them (as a lawyer to whom they were of professional concern, in diplomas and listing of bounds) led him to adorn their mention with vowel-harmonies and alliterations. In my previous study I so analysed lines 396–401, which no-one had previously mentioned as containing verse of any distinction, and from which one line – firmly linked in every possible way to adjacent lines – was removed by Menéndez Pidal, in an insensitive moment, to another place. Names of kingdoms, too, used in the Cid's *pregón*, by which he calls for volunteers, come significantly into an equally splendid passage analysed in the earlier study (ll. 1187–91). I ended the detailed part of that study with mention of the ways in which Per Abad decorated the name of Valencia, the Cid's greatest conquest, in order to enhance its poetic force. This may be in a tone of doom, when the city is under threat:

Déntro en Valénçia   non es poco el miédo
(l. 1097; also 1098, 1155, 1174, 1191)

or in a neutral tone when an administrative detail is given:

diéron le en Valénçia   o bién puéde estar rico
(l. 1304; also 1299, 1306, 1308)

or in a voice of pride and triumph:

Alégres son por Valénçia   las yéntes christianas
(l. 1799, and many more)

On a rough count, in about half the cases of mention of the city –
which is perhaps to say, whenever he was able – the poet
anticipates or echoes the vowel-pattern of the name in these
ways. Often, to aid his purpose, 'Valençia' is prominent at the
end of the first hemistich. As always, other word-play may come
into this, as when the Cid greets the women in one of the grand
moments of the poem:

'¡A vos me omillo, duéñas!   Grant préz vos he gañado,
vos teniéndo Valénçia   e yo vençi el campo'   (ll. 1748–9)

'Valençia' is still the key-word, proudly echoed by 'vençi' and
perhaps anticipated by 'prez' (-ç). But the 'dueñas' and the 'prez'
are inseparable now from the city, and the hero can both bow to
the women and then lift his head in triumph in two successive,
complementary actions that are parallel in their vowel-structures
(vós me omíll-, yó vençí).

At this point one realises than many of the poetic inversions
may respond not only to an effort to dignify epic language (with
French usage as a precedent) but to metrical needs. These may
include the need to ensure an end-rhyme, as is obvious; but often
the effect is to enhance a rhythm or make a vowel-harmony, as in
the Cid's weighty pronouncement:

si desóndra i cabe   alguna cóntra nós
la póca e la grant   tóda es de mio señór   (ll. 2910–11)

Further good examples are provided by:

grándes averes priso   e mucho sobejános   (l. 110)

los avéres que tenémos   grándes son e sobejános   (l. 2541)

Perhaps, indeed, all instances of dislocation of normal word-
order would respond to such reasoning.[21]

Naturally, I have selected examples which most suit my
purposes. Those lines which most impress us by their content
and within their context often turn out, on second glance, to
participate in one or more of the techniques I have described.
Lines and sections which have them are numerous throughout
the poem. I refrain from quantifying them because percentages
do not help much and are readily overturned by the next analyst
to use the computer. This is not to deny that the poet wrote a lot of
lines which are flat, though passable, and some which are
downright bad; and that there remain some lines which seem
defective even within his fairly free system, and which he might
have corrected in a final polished version. I see no lack of logic in

holding on the one hand that Per Abad invented his metrical system and in large measure used it successfully, while confessing on the other hand that in some respects his work remained experimental or untidy here and there. After all, there are largish areas of pot-boiling mediocrity in Shakespeare; Wordsworth enthusiasts regret much of what he left; and every major poet can be faulted somewhere. The equivalent of the Person-from-Porlock who, in Per Abad's case, took him away from what should have been his more polished version, may have been an urgent messenger from abbot, judge, or king, who had a task for the lawyer–poet and, moreover, offered a definite fee.

Beyond the surviving text of the poem, beyond the original, must have lain scraps of parchment on which the poet began his apprenticeship, hammering out lines as he considered his French models (perhaps in memory only) and tuned his ear to the rhythms and phonetic elaborations of Latin verse. It is not necessary to think that he began his work at any other than the obvious point – the start, since, as will be seen, he had French guides for certain early sections, including the first surviving lines, a direct knowledge of Cardeña and sources for Jimena's prayer there, and then two battles available in Latin prose on which to base his first military actions (with battle-scenes available in common formulaic fashion in numerous French epics). After that, a few essential facts of history and a substantial source in the *Historia Roderici* gave him the outline and much detail with which to finish his first *cantar* and carry the narrative up to the conquest of Valencia. The confidence gained, then, in techniques (including metrical ones), grew steadily and took the poet towards the mature triumph of the third *cantar*. Precisely how he composed cannot be conjectured. One has the impression that a medieval poet, conscious of his duty to his *mester*, and particularly of a duty to a noble subject, composed more laboriously than a modern. However, as I said in my earlier study:

I do not think that we need to envisage Per Abad working out in detail, precisely and mindfully, all his patterns of sound and rhythm. No-one can create good verse in that way. I think that a poet in command of his craft often employs what we in our pedantic way analyse as 'techniques' in a fashion which is not deliberate or willed on each occasion. If the instinct is there, and the fire of enthusiasm for a particular subject, the poet simply gets on with his composition with a minimum of planning.

De Chasca's view is pertinent also:

La naturaleza misma de la composición en verso exige al poeta atender tanto a la armonía de los sonidos como a la adecuación de los significados. A veces los sonidos se repiten con resultado feliz, pero sin intervención consciente. Pero si el poeta es bueno, obra inconscientemente en su ánimo creador un instinto por el que las palabras, rimadas a veces, se atraen por la fuerza de una misteriosa afinidad.

Et après? Just as Berceo after devising *cuaderna vía* in about 1220 had imitators who continued the school until the days of López de Ayala about 1400, so Per Abad had imitators who continued the epic genre and its metre into the late fourteenth century. We know little about the diffusion of the *Poema*, but enough to say that its rhetoric and some of its details were well-known to Berceo and other *cuaderna vía* poets, that it passed to Cardeña and thence in modified prose form on to the royal chroniclers, that it was still sufficiently known about 1300 to provide models for certain features of the lost *Gesta de las mocedades* (continued in the surviving *Mocedades* poem of about 1360), and that in some debased form it was still available perhaps late in the fourteenth century for ballad-makers to use it as a quarry. Burgos was a good centre for diffusion, whether aided or not by nearby Cardeña. Whatever the details of the process, the *Poema* was both available and attractive enough to inspire others to imitate it within Spanish, and, in the decades following 1207, in some cases with new hints from Latin texts and from French sources, the other epics of Castile were composed. There would be substantial agreement, I think, that the next epic in order of composition was the *Cantar de Sancho II y cerco de Zamora*, to which later a section on the *Jura de Santa Gadea* was added, partly for the inherent drama of the episode, partly for local pride in Burgos (where associated relics, such as the 'cerrojo' or bolt, were easily produced in the church of Santa Agueda associated with the *Jura*), partly in order to give a reason for the mistrust between Alfonso VI and the Cid with which the *Poema* opens. All this may have amounted, as Horrent thought, to a substantial cycle of poems on the Cid. The *Jura* was certainly the work of a Burgos poet, and the *Cantar de Sancho II* may well have been also, since the Cid figures prominently in it. Moreover, certain features, such as the relative abundance of named minor personages, the precision of the geography, and the strong juridical interest recently emphasised by Fraker, link this work rather strongly with the *Poema de mio*

Cid. Eventually the *Cantar del rey don Fernando* (so mentioned by one of the chronicles) was reworked as an independent poem. Soon other poets took up, from monasteries and families, other Castilian stories which already had, upon a historical base, accretions of legend and pseudohistory with heroic potentiality (*Los Infantes de Lara, El infante García*, perhaps others). In Navarre, at a date unknown, someone translated or adapted a now lost version of the *Chanson de Roland*, producing the Hispanic *Roncesvalles*. As an answer to the excessive claims made by French chronicles and epics about Carolingian conquests in Spain, a poet, possibly Leonese, composed the totally fictitious epic of *Bernardo del Carpio*. After 1264 a monk of Arlanza composed a *cuaderna vía* epic on Fernán González, taking much from other epics in more popular style. In 1236 Lucas de Tuy and in 1243 Rodrigo Jiménez de Rada began to take account of epic stories in their Latin chronicles, just as had begun to happen in France; but Jiménez de Rada complained that the poets had begun to interfere with serious historiography. In the 1270s Alfonso X's chroniclers succeeded to some extent in harmonising epic verse and Latin historiography, though perfectly aware that the latter was the more trustworthy.

We have some 500 lines of the *Infantes de Lara*, 100 of *Roncesvalles*, and some 1160 of the *Mocedades*. Good sections of *Sancho II* can be constructed with some confidence from chronicle redactions and ballads. From these one can see – notably in successive analyses by Menéndez Pidal – that epic poets after 1207 adopted Per Abad's metrical system just as *cuaderna vía* poets used Berceo's. In both cases there was modification and evolution of a minor kind. The relative freedom of line-lengths which Per Abad allowed himself seems to have been progressively restricted, but the system never became a rigid one, and it retained its accentual basis. Possibly there was some influence from the *cuaderna vía* genre of narrative verse, in the direction of greater regularity of line. In the fourteenth century one can see, in the Palencian *Mocedades*, that one type of line created by Per Abad was coming to be construed syllabically as well as accentually (though still quite free), and it is this which eventually evolved into the ballad line of 8 + 8 or 16 syllables, naturally enough, as a substantial group of early ballads consisted of epic episodes and fragments slightly recast. Greater regularity was needed when the ballads were set to fully repetitive tunes, but some licences continued, and accentual patterns in addition to syllabic ones can still be strongly perceived in the *romancero*.

It is noteworthy that when the *Roncesvalles* was composed in Navarre it was done in Spanish epic metre, not in some newly-devised version of a French metre in which its model was written. The materials might be French, but the verse-structure was native, having by then been established for perhaps a century. Only the Arlanza monk felt obliged to follow the monastic precedent of Berceo's *cuaderna vía*, even though much of his *Fernán González* is epic in spirit.

The fragments of *Roncesvalles* and of the *Infantes de Lara* are rather dull as verse, and the surviving *Mocedades* can only be called execrable. None shows the slightest awareness of, or wish or ability to imitate, the phonetic elaborations and structural effects which Per Abad so richly added to his poem. Yet there is much of this in the ballads: alliteration, vowel-harmonies, prominent use and phonetic echoing of place-names, even the creation of musical jingles for their own sake (*Fontefrida*, *Moraima*, etc.). Epic prosifications usually give no clue to the poetic virtues of the originals; one could not guess Per Abad's power of words from the redaction of his poem in the *Crónica de veinte reyes*. But there is an important exception. What can be reconstituted of the *Sancho II* poem is distinctly impressive as verse, and some of Per Abad's techniques can be discerned in it. I do not think he was the author, but if *Sancho II* were composed in Burgos not long after the *Poema de mio Cid*, as seems likely, it is natural that its author should have paid Per Abad, now Master of another Apprentice, the tribute of close and admiring imitation.

5 Historical, literary, and other sources and motives

Per Abad composed an epic poem, not a historical work in verse of the kind represented by the *Carmen de Hastingae proelio,* Ambroise's *L'Estoire de la Guerre Sainte,* or the *Poema de Alfonso onceno.* He created a drama with a plot, a series of climaxes artistically disposed, and personages who live a literary life speaking words invented for them by the poet. His drama has, beyond the immediate entertainment and excitement, a moral and exemplary aim, and is by no means devoid of actively ideological and contemporary references. The poet felt no special duty to record or respect or even to use the facts of history. If he knew them, he used them only when it suited his entirely literary purpose to do so, and he invented freely, though conscious of limitations imposed by existing traditions and memories about his comparatively recent subject (Lacarra, 1980a: 219–20; Dunn, 1970: 110). In any case it is sure that the poet's perception of history was not the same as ours; not as a result of any idiosyncrasy, but simply because he was a man of his time.[1]

It seemed to Menéndez Pidal and his school that the wealth of apparently historical detail in the poem – whose quantity they much enlarge – could be explained only by postulating a continuous verse tradition which extended from a composition soon after the death of the Cid in 1099, by someone who had known him and a great deal about his life from at least 1081, down to the poem in the form now surviving. The same idea was applied to other epics in Spain and, of course, in France and elsewhere; it was inherent in Romantic thought. Certainly it can be agreed that within the small Spanish epic genre there was a wide range of variation in this respect, from *Sancho II,* whose poet found good literary materials almost ready-made in the facts of history, to *Bernardo del Carpio* and the *Mocedades,* which are almost wholly fictional. Our *Poema* comes somewhere in the middle of this range. Those who have acclaimed its fidelity to history – and who have, for some reason, counted this a literary virtue – have perhaps been misled not only by Pidal's sustained and brilliant argumentation (applied not only to Spanish poems but, in 1959, to the *Roland*), but by other factors.

In the first place, it is true that the poet used some basic facts about the historical Cid's life from 1081 to 1099 as his framework. But one must not develop from this the belief that other poetic events, recounted by the poet on precisely the same level as the historical events, were therefore historical also even though not recorded independently for us. This fallacy has plagued discussion of these matters.[2] Furthermore, the facts of history were radically adjusted by the poet for sound literary reasons: for example, the Cid's two captures of the Count of Barcelona are reduced to one, and a fine literary episode is built on this; and the Cid's two banishments by Alfonso are reduced to one, with a single reconciliation which endures to the end, since by this means the poet made a useful framework for his plot. Second, the poet used as personages many who can be shown to have lived in the time of the historical Cid, with correct names and places of origin; but it is uncertain whether in history any of these persons was associated with the Cid, or acted as the poet makes them, and in one important case – that of Alvar Fáñez – it is sure that the action is wholly poetical. Third, the poet tells all with an air of fact. As narrator, he does not differentiate. He states no sources and does not intrude any comment on the action, except for rare semi-proverbial observations. He simply sets the wheels in motion and leaves them to spin, as any good literary creator does. He does not insist, as French epic poets often do, on the truth of his tale ('vere chanson', etc.), nor claim to be outdoing others in veracity and quality. By his silence on these things he effectively asserts that he is offering factual material, not because he could (or wished to) guarantee its historical truth, but because this is the natural way of the story-teller. In this he in no way differs from, for example, Juan Ruiz with his marvellously convincing presentation of the Doña Endrina episode as something which had happened to him, while we know it to be re-created from the *Pamphilus*. Fourth, the poet's specially strong sense of *verismo* is not to be confused with fidelity to historical truth. That the 'niña' is nine years old (l. 40), that Jimena is accompanied by five ladies (l. 239), and that Avengalvón has the hooves of his guests' horses shod (l. 1553), are admirable *verista* details, which help to convince us of the general human authenticity of what is being recounted. No traditionalist has ever gone so far as to defend the historical existence of the 'niña', still less her precise nine years. But Menéndez Pidal regarded the same kind of *verista* detail in line 2814 as a sort of trump-card for traditionalism. The Cid's daughters are succoured by Diego Téllez, about whom details are given: he lived at San Esteban, and was Alvar Fáñez's man. Certainly he had a historical existence, at the right time. But there is no proof that he was ever at the place mentioned or involved in any way with the Cid, and his presence in the *Poema* – in an action which we know to be totally fictional – must have a different explanation from that hitherto advanced. From an artistic viewpoint, it is obviously better to have a credibly named individual in this incident, rather than the nameless 'labrador' who replaces him in most of the chronicle accounts. But Pidal went much further, arguing that since Diego Téllez's existence in history can be proved, there must be an element of historical truth in what the poet narrates about his part in the rescue of the Cid's daughters, and thus, by extension, in the Corpes episode itself. Here, artistic *verismo* has deceived a too historically-minded critic. The same may be said about geographical *verismo*. That the places and routes in the poem had a real existence on the soil of Spain is a strong artistic feature, but does not persuade us that poetic events associated with them occurred there in history. After all, no-one has ever claimed that, because *Vindilisora* is Windsor, anything recounted in *Amadís* actually happened there.

Within traditionalist belief – that the poem preserves a good deal of history and does so because a poetic tradition stemmed from nearly the Cid's own day – there was naturally little to explain. The few new features recognised as fiction had crept in as the poem evolved, as free invention by the *juglares* (the moneylenders, the lion, etc.); and such elements were, it was sometimes implied, naughty intrusions which soured the pure milk of *historicidad*. There was almost no question of any study of sources, since history itself, within a wholly autochthonous flow of epic, was itself the original source.

In placing the *Poema* at 1207 and regarding it as an original creation of that moment, I must naturally show from what sources the poet gathered his materials and motives. I classify these in six groups.

1. The Burgos tradition

We may surely assume that a cultivated Burgos man of 1207 would have had a general notion of Rodrigo Díaz, the most famous son of the city. He would have known that the hero's ancestral home was at Vivar nearby, and that he was born there or in a house in the city; that he had a brilliant early career and rose to prominence under Sancho 'el Bravo'; that he married Jimena; that Alfonso later to be known as 'el de Toledo' banished him; that he campaigned long in the Levante, defeating the Count of Barcelona, taking Valencia, and greatly enriching his men; that his daughters married into the ruling families of Navarre and – was it? – Aragón, the former marriage being specially important because several monarchs, including the Alfonso now reigning in Castile, descended directly from it. Precise dates and the numeration of kings would not come into such a tradition, but the rest was sound enough. To such information, local legend of an undramatic kind might have added (although the poet could well have invented such things for himself): that on that spot down by the river, the Cid and a few followers had camped at the moment of exile, the lowest in the hero's fortunes; that Burgos had felt itself unable to defy the royal command and help the hero, except that perhaps one defiant *burgalés* – was his name Martín? – had alone given cheer and material aid. These, it seems to me, are the sort of modest additions to a core of historical data which legend fosters about a place and a person, some not devoid of folkloric or symbolic connotation,[3] some plainly inspirational. To this the poet, a Burgos man, further added topographical details.

2. The genealogical tradition

That the poet knew some genealogical traditions seems certain, either in oral or written form. In the Middle Ages a strong clan sense in powerful families ensured a knowledge of who begat whom, and in some parts written king-lists and pedigrees survive better than other kinds of record, as in Anglo-Saxon England and medieval Wales. In the eleventh and twelfth centuries the keeping of such genealogies on scraps of parchment may have been common enough in noble families and by their lawyers, if only to ensure correct inheritance and avoidance of marriages within the prohibited degrees. That a Burgos man could have had knowledge of the Cid's genealogy and ancestors presented to him orally – but not necessarily accurately – seems possible. That he could have had access to a written genealogy is likely, especially if the inquirer were a lawyer whose habit it was to seek and prefer written sources. That lawyer was not interested in the Cid's ancestors, as known after a fashion, much embellished, in the *Historia Roderici* and as currently of concern in Burgos because of the then recent invention of the 'jueces de Castilla'. It was the Cid's marriage and issue that were vital. The information may have been available to the lawyer–poet in a form akin to that used by the Navarrese *Linaje* before 1194, which says:

Este meo Çid ovo muyllier a dona Xemena, nieta del rey don Alfonso, filla del conte don Diago de Asturias; et ovo en eylla un fijo e dos fijas. El fillo ovo nompne Diago Roiz, et mataronlo moros en Consuegra. Estas dos fillas la una ovo nompne dona Cristiana, la otra dona Maria. Casó dona Cristiana con l'ifant don Romiro; casó dona Maria con el conte de Barcalona. L'ifant don Romiro ovo en su muiller la fija de meo Çid al rey Garçia de Navarra, que dixieron Garçia Remiriz.

That Jimena was of the blood-royal (as also stated by the *Historia Roderici*, 921.10) was, then, probably known to the poet, but he resolved to include only a vague allusion to her rank ('menbrada fija dalgo', l. 210) and for the rest to give the impression that she was of equivalent class to the Cid as portrayed in the poem, an *infanzón*; that is, the poet was not concerned to dignify the hero by stating Jimena's origins (in history, the match had been a highly honourable one for him), but rather to show the Cid making his way by his own efforts to a position of power in which he overcame higher nobles. The poet remains silent about Jimena's origins even when the lowly status of her daughters is scornfully emphasised by the Infantes in the Cortes and Alvar Fáñez is replying. Here the poet's dramatic sense predominates over a fact of history which was known to him, as often, and it is not for others to criticise him. As for the son Diego, first known to us in the *Linaje*, the poet simply decided not to use him. He was not mentioned in the *Historia Roderici* (except that this text says vaguely that the Cid and Jimena had 'filios et filias', 921.11), probably because he went as a boy into the royal service. No place suggested itself for him in the poet's scheme, even though it might seem to us that the 'hero's son' motif is an obvious one.

The *Linaje* then states, correctly, that Cristi(a)na married Prince Ramiro of Navarre, from whom descended García Ramírez. He took the crown of Navarre in 1134 as 'el Restaurador', and his daughter Blanca married Prince Sancho of Castile – Sancho III who ruled briefly in 1157–8 – their son being Alfonso VIII of Castile (1158–1214) who was thus the Cid's great-great-grandson, as the poet probably knew from other sources. The *Linaje* adds that the King of Navarre ruling at the time the text was written, García, similarly descended from the Cid. It is this, together with other ramifications, which leads the poet to state in the triumphant line 3724 (much-debated, but not to be read as embracing *all* the rulers of the Peninsula) that 'Oy los reyes d'España sos parientes son'. To this splendid conclusion, a historical as well as a literary truth, the Cid's struggles in adversity and rise from lowly status have led. The other marriage, of María to the Count of Barcelona, had less importance in genealogical consequences. The poet almost certainly knew the proper names of the hero's daughters, but resolved not to use them. While *Sol* is documented as a by-name for *María* (and thus might have had historical tradition behind it in this instance), this does not apply to *Cristina/Elvira*. However, *Elvira* was much the better known of the two, as a royal and noble name, and the poet may have made the change for this reason. It may be that metrical considerations were involved: the possible hemistich *'doña Cristina e doña Maria' would have contained two more syllables than 'don Elvira e doña Sol' which the poet chose and regularly used, and his laisses rhymed in *ó* were to be far more numerous than those rhymed in *í-a*.

When the ambassadors come into court to ask for the hands of the hero's daughters for their masters, it is for princes of Navarre and Aragón (ll. 3395–6, etc.). If the poet had access to information akin to that of the *Linaje*, he would have known that the Cid's younger daughter married not a prince of Aragón but a Count of Barcelona. Since I think that on the whole the poet's historical information was quite good, and that in his legal professionalism he liked to be careful about such things, it will not do to say that he made a mistake by writing Aragón instead of Barcelona. Nor can it be argued that, since Catalonia and Aragón were united from 1137 under the Crown of Aragón, an audience of 1207 would be expected to take the general term 'Aragón' as including Catalonia at an earlier stage. It may be that, as has been argued, María was indeed briefly married to Prince Pedro of Aragón before marrying the Count of Barcelona, so that the poet has his facts right for the time envisaged; but then his source could not have been the *Linaje* or another text related to it, and we know of no other at that date. It is better to reason that, just as the poet neglected Jimena's royal blood and said nothing about the son Diego, and made other radical adjustments to history, he had an artistic reason here too. The poet had shown up the Catalans as unwarlike and their Count, in an extensive portrayal, as effete and effeminate, and it may have seemed to him that to say at the end of his work that the hero's daughter had married a similar man was not a fitting conclusion, however true in history.

As for the date of the Cid's death, the *Historia Roderici* gives it as 'mense iulio', the *Linaje* as 'el mes de mayo'. We have no means of knowing the true date beyond saying that it was in the summer of 1099. The poet says 'el dia de çinquaesma', that is, Whit Sunday – surely a poetic choice made for religious reasons (though confirmed, for what it is worth, by the *Linaje*, since Whit Sunday in that year fell on 29 May).

3. Written historiography

The *Historia Roderici* provided a rich source of material for the poet. That it could have been available to a Burgos author about 1200 is likely enough, to judge by the number of copies postulated in Pidal's stemma and by the fact that the work was later used by the Alphonsine chroniclers. The special interest of Cardeña in the Cid (and the fact that in the work it is clearly stated that the Cid was buried there) could have ensured that the monastery would acquire a copy; the *Cronicón de Cardeña*, known to us only in its 1327 redaction, has a passage about the Cid's vengeance against the Riojan lands of García Ordóñez which is based on the *Historia*. Some dependence of the *Poema* upon the *Historia* has occasionally been suggested, but the question has not been studied in detail or resolved.[4] It seems to me certain that Per Abad knew it. He made no precise textual borrowings from it, understandably enough if he found its Latin inexpressive and unsuited to adaptation into the verse of a different language, but there are quite strong echoes, as will be seen.

The poet selected his materials from the *Historia* with care, having the lines of his plot already firmly in mind. Parts of the Latin text were of no concern to him: the opening genealogy and the life of the Cid up to his exile in 1081; the Cid's activities in Saragossa in the service of its Moslem ruler, hardly apt for a poem about a Christian hero; Alfonso's first pardon of the Cid and the latter's return to Castile, 1087; Alfonso's second decree of banishment, 1089; the Cid's oaths about his conduct at Aledo; his vengeful raid into García Ordóñez's lands. The complicated account given by the *Historia* of the Cid's campaigns and diplomacy in the Valencian region did not deflect the poet from his intention to handle this aspect in a much simplified and even unduly abbreviated form (well justified by Hook in artistic terms, 1973), though here he still took some hints from the *Historia*. Per Abad disregarded the *Historia*'s note that the Cid died in July, and was not concerned with what it says about the years during which the Christians held Valencia after the Cid's death.

The poet followed the *Historia* when creating three major episodes of his work: the banishment of the Cid, the clash with the Count of Barcelona, and the Valencian campaign, together with other isolated hints. The *Historia* tells a detailed story (921.12 ff.) about how Alfonso sent the Cid to Seville and Córdoba to collect tribute ('paria'), and how the Cid there became involved in defending the King of Seville against the King of Granada, the latter aided by Christian knights. At Cabra the Cid defeated the Granadine force, capturing García Ordóñez and other Christians, taking tents and spoils from them, and holding them prisoner for three days. On his return to Castile the Cid was accused 'causa inuidie' (922.27) of misdemeanour. The next year the Cid, to avenge a Moorish raid, made an incursion into the Moorish kingdom of Toledo, returning with booty and many captives; certain 'curiales inuidentes' (923.17) misrepresented the Cid's action to the King, who exiled him. This account was adopted by the vernacular chroniclers in detail. It is likely that a summary of it, taken from the *Historia* but with details added from a French poetic source to be mentioned later, was made by Per Abad at the start of his work, since he needed to state a reason for the Cid's exile and also to involve García Ordóñez in the affair (for the latter was to occupy the role of enemy of the Cid and villain in the poem). The French source would have persuaded Per Abad of the need to include such a passage, and it provided a precedent. This introductory passage could well have been in prose (as the historical introduction to the *Mocedades* poem of the fourteenth century was to be), the verse beginning only as the Cid prepares to leave for exile, that is, a few lines before the twelve-line passage reconstructed by Menéndez Pidal, which precedes the extant verse text. This prose passage would have mentioned Seville, the victory over Granada, the taking of spoils, the brief captivity of García Ordóñez, and the return to Castile. It would not have complicated matters by referring to the Toledan incident at this point. Further reflections of the Cid's Sevillian expedition, taken from the *Historia*, occur later in the poem. The 'parias' are mentioned in line 109, after which the Cid's agent, Martín Antolínez, tells the moneylenders – as an indication of the Cid's financial soundness – that the hero kept back some of the royal tribute, producing the accusation which led to his banishment. This idea may have come to the poet from the *Historia*'s statement (922.21) that the King of Seville 'addidit super tributa munera et multa dona que suo regi detulit', the poet perhaps reinterpreting the last word. The Cabra incident is recalled, with offensive details, by the Cid in the Cortes, after Ordóñez has insulted the hero (ll. 3280 ff.). The banishment 'causa inuidie' and at the hands of the 'curiales inuidentes' is echoed in words of the Cid, 'mios enemigos malos' (l. 9), and of Jimena, 'malos mestureros' (l. 267).

The two battles in which the Cid defeated the Count of Barcelona, 1082 and 1090, are recounted by the *Historia* at 926.16 ff. and 942.1 ff. On the first occasion the history says that the Cid held the Count captive for five days, taking spoils and then releasing him. This occupies only fourteen lines. The account of the second capture at Tévar[5] is merged with the first by the poet, who needed no duplication in the progress of his plot; but it is recounted by the poet as occurring early in the Cid's exile, that is, more in relation to the real event of 1082. This episode in the *Historia* is quite exceptionally lively, detailed, and dramatic, and these qualities must have impressed the poet and led him not merely to conclude his first *cantar* impressively with the Cid's victory over the Count, a semi-royal personage, but to expand his story at this point into a fine dramatic cameo in which he could indulge his talent for characterisation and for a variety of tones in direct speech, as has been noted by critics in excellent studies. The *Historia*'s account of Tévar occupies some 170 lines of print. Its tone is set by the Cid's preliminary message to his ally the Moorish King of Saragossa, that 'Comitem uero et suorum bellatorum multitudinem omnino uilipendio et sperno' (942.8), which is the tone adopted in the poet's episode. Much of the *Historia*'s space is occupied by the full texts of a letter, indignant and insulting, which the Count sent to the Cid, and by the latter's reply (Menéndez Pidal being surely right to insist, against others who had thought these rhetorical exercises, that the letters are authentic). This exchange of messages is briefly echoed in the poem: in the Count's protest (ll. 961 ff.), with the message in line 975 and the Cid's reply (ll. 976–8), and a final message from the Count (ll. 979–82). The Count's reference in the poem to previous hurts suffered from the Cid (ll. 961 ff.) is possibly developed from the Count's words in the *Historia*, 942.25. In the battle, according to the *Historia*, the Catalans began by charging downhill (946.3), which the poet took up in 'Ellos vienen cuesta yuso' (l. 992). After the battle the history says, with unwonted detail, that the seated Cid refused to allow the Count to sit down in his tent when he came to beg mercy; indeed, 'sed foris extra tentoria eum custodiri a militibus suis iussit' (947.5), from which the poet took hints for his lines 1012–13. A victory banquet is prepared for the Cid and his men (947.7), which gave the poet the idea for his banquet ('grant cozina', l. 1017), and also, by extension, for the Count's refusal to participate in it, and for his fatuous hunger-strike and battle of wills against his captor. Eventually the Count and others are released without ransom in both texts; the spoils suffice (*Historia*, 946.21; poem, l. 1084). Within the general tone, the effeminacy of the Count – who even though desperately hungry demands a finger-bowl before eating – may have been suggested also by the *Historia*. The Cid's letter to the King of Saragossa, intercepted by the Count, evidently made similar accusations ('nostris uxoribus nos assimilasti', 942.31; references to 'nostre mulieres', 943.3; and in the Cid's reply, 944.15). The *Historia*, then, gave the poet an outline and some hints; most of all, its detail, rich texture, and distinctive tone suggested to Per Abad that here was an episode with fine potential for poetic and dramatic development.[6]

The early stages of the Valencian campaign are narrated by the poet in some detail, for logic required him to show how the Cid subdued parts of the Levante, secured tributaries, and increased his power before launching his attack on the city itself. He does this in ten laisses, indicating a period of three years for these operations (l. 1169). Most of the place-names mentioned by the poet in this section could have been taken from the *Historia*.[7] It has been noted that the poet mentions the Cid's occupation of Murviedro (Sagunto) out of historical order; in the poem, the Cid takes it before Valencia and uses it as a base for the assault on the city (ll. 1095, 1196), whereas the *Historia* says he captured it several years after Valencia. However, the poet may have been misled by the *Historia*'s note, corresponding to the year 1089, that 'hoc enim fecit et dux de Muro Uetulo' (933.18), 'he – Alcadir – made him (the Cid) also *dux* of Murviedro'.

Elements of the *Historia*'s account of the action at Valencia itself were used in a free manner by the poet, partly out of order, as he composed his episode. The conquest of the city was the high point of the hero's military career, but the poet seems to have been concerned to abbreviate the military narration. It has been suggested that this was because in 1207, Valencia (again Moorish from 1102, and to remain so until 1238) lay outside the Castilian sphere of interest, having been allotted as reconquest territory to Aragón by a treaty of 1151. The reasons may rather be that, on the one hand, the *Historia* told a somewhat diffuse story about the politics and stages by which Valencia was taken (in addition to being besieged), and the poet would not have found it easy to make good verse out of this; on the other hand, the poet probably had little idea of a large Moslem city, and had never himself seen a siege, while other literary factors can be conjectured too.[8]

One adjustment the poet made was to displace the coming of Yúçef with his army from Morocco until well after the Cid's capture of Valencia, whereas the *Historia* shows Yúçef already in Spain, though inactive, in 1093. Hence the *Historia*'s mention of how Yúçef gathered his army and crossed the Strait with it (957.13) is displaced by the poet to his lines 1625–9. But reference to the Emperor Yúçef ('el rey de Marruecos') is still made earlier in the poem: in line 1181 the starving Valencians send to him for help, as in *Historia*, 957.25. The moving account of the hunger inside Valencia (ll. 1174 ff.) corresponds to *Historia*, 958.19, but the poet has also drawn here on the lengthy account of the sufferings of the people of Murviedro in 964.13 ff. ('Jam enim nos et uxores nostre et filij atque filie fame proculdubio moriemur', 964.19, = 'fijos e mugieres   ver lo murir de fanbre', l. 1179). The Cid's concession of a 'plazo' to Valencia so that the city may seek aid (l. 1208) corresponds to the concession made in the *Historia* (957.18) and to another granted to Murviedro ('placitum', 964.31). The spoils of Valencia are immense (poem, ll. 1214–18; *Historia*, 958.30 to 959.5; perhaps 'Todos eran ricos   quantos que alli ha', l. 1215, = 'uniuersi sui facti sunt diuites et locupletes',

959.4). The Moorish reaction to the loss of Valencia is in both texts (l. 1622; 959.5 ff.). The size of the army sent to recover the city is given by the *Historia* as 'C.L. milia militum' (959.20), probably – according to Pidal – a copyist's misreading of an abbreviated *c* for *circa*; that is, in a better text, 'L. milia militum' suggested the poet's 'con l. vezes mill de armas' (l. 1626), transferred to Yúçef's expedition. The victory of the Cid over Yúçef produces the *Historia*'s longest description of spoils (960.11 – 960.18), echoed in lines 1772–92 of the poem. Here even details correspond, in that the poet's 'tiendas' = 'tentoria', 'armas' = 'diuersis armorum generibus', 'vestidos preçiados' = 'uestium pretiosarum', and 'cavallos' = 'equis et palafredis ac mulis', naturally with further details of the poet's invention. Finally, the poet knew of the Cid's conversion of the chief mosque of Valencia to a cathedral, and its dedication to 'Santa Maria' (ll. 1668–9), as in *Historia*, 968.2.

The poet's debt to the *Historia* was, then, considerable in respect of these episodes. He may have picked up further details from it. At 931.11, the *Historia* summarises a diploma of 1089 (possibly falsified, as noted above), by which Alfonso gave the Cid possession of all lands he might conquer from the Moors, 'iure hereditario'; this is reflected in the poetic Cid's insistence that Valencia was the 'heredad' of himself and his family (ll. 1607, 1635). At 935.25, on the occasion of the second *ira regia*, according to the *Historia* the King 'quod deterius est, suam uxorem et liberos in custodia illaqueatos crudeliter retrudi . . . mandauit', perhaps recalled by the poet when Jimena, on being reunited with her husband, exclaims 'Sacada me avedes de muchas verguenças malas' (l. 1596); the line is otherwise mysterious, since all that the poem has conveyed hitherto was that Jimena and her children were living comfortably in Cardeña. Of the situation of the Moorish forces at Bairén, the *Historia* says that 'ex altera parte erat mare' (962.18), possibly echoed in the panoramic view of Valencia, 'e del otra parte a ojo han el mar' (l. 1614). Of more general application was the accusation, in the letter of the Count of Barcelona to the Cid, that 'montes et corui et cornelle et nisi et aquile et fere omne genus auium sunt dij tui, quia plus confidis in augurijs quam in Deo' (943.12). Several times in the poem, the Cid takes the auguries in this way (ll. 11–12, 859, 2615), the poet turning the Count's scornful accusation into a special skill of the hero (since the omens turn out to be correct), and making a dramatic feature of it (since suspense is created). The poet also found in the *Historia* (962.26) a useful model for the harangues which the Cid addresses to his men before battle. The soldierly piety of the Cid when he prays for victory, and afterwards sees God's hand in it and gives thanks for it, regular observances in the poem, have models in the *Historia* (964.1, 962.33, 963.7, etc.).

It was suggested in Chapter 2 that the *Chronica Adefonsi Imperatoris* may have given the poet the idea of making Alvar Fáñez the Cid's principal lieutenant. He did not know from local tradition or historical sources – nor do we know today – of any specially constant companion or feudal associate that the historical Cid may have had. But he saw, from the most famous epic of his day, the *Roland*, that a Roland needed an Oliver, and that the possibilities of his plot would be enhanced in drama and characterisation by the presence of such a deuteragonist at the hero's side, without the contrast of qualities and clash of temperaments presented in the French poem. Thus Alvar Fáñez is constantly present in a variety of roles. He is also important as one who initiates dialogues and reacts to the Cid's words. In history we know of no special link that Alvar had with the Cid, and it seems from the evidence that he cannot have been much, if at all, in the Cid's company during the exile and Valencian years. Nor had he any reason to act with or for the Cid, for he had a distinguished career in his own right and in the royal service. That the poet chose him to be the Cid's deuteragonist was a tribute to the reputation which Alvar left in several historical sources, and particularly to his presence in the *Poema de Almeria*.[9]

4. Literary texts: Latin

In an earlier paper I proposed that the poet drew his Castejón episode (ll. 415–73) from Sallust's *Bellum Jugurthinum*, sections xc and xcI, and his Alcocer episode (ll. 553–610) from Frontinus's *Strategemata*, II.v.34, with further hints from III.x.2 (Smith, 1975). The Sallust text tells how Marius took the town of Capsa in Numidia from Jugurtha's supporters, by waiting in ambush overnight until the townspeople opened the gates at dawn and went out to their fields, the remaining townsfolk and those dispersed outside the walls falling easy prey to a sudden Roman attack. Eleven detailed points of similarity, all in order though without precise verbal borrowings, were listed. A further possible parallel occurs when Marius, before the attack on Capsa, sends an officer off with the cattle won as booty to a safe place where his treasury and stores already are, partly with the idea of concealing his main objective – Capsa – from the enemy; this could have given Per Abad hints about the diversionary raid to Alcalá on which the Cid sends Alvar Fáñez. The Frontinus episode concerns an action during the Slave War in which Crassus destroyed an enemy force by coaxing it out of its unassailable encampment: Crassus left his command tent pitched, with a few men concealed in ambush, and led his army away; when the rebels, imagining him to be retreating in disorder, emerged from their camp and charged after him, Crassus and his army appeared in battle order to defeat the rebels and occupy their camp. Although one or two details in the poem's account are unclear, and can be interpreted in different ways, Frontinus's text serves to elucidate these points to some extent, though not fully. In their main lines the Frontinus text and that about Alcocer are in quite close agreement, having some ten points of detail in common, all in proper sequence, and to these may be added the further hints to be found in iii.x.2, a similar ruse, more briefly told, practised by L. Scipio in Sardinia in 259 B.C.

There remain, naturally, substantial differences between the Latin texts and the poem. The Capsa episode seems roughly to correspond to that of Castejón in terms of geography and the size of the forces involved, but Crassus's action against the slaves was on a large scale, for in it 35,000 men were killed, and the objective was a camp, not a small walled town, so that the Alcocer adaptation of it is different in nature and magnitude. Further, the Latin texts are brief and compact, though full of incident, whereas the poet's adaptation is relatively extensive. However, expansion of any source, particularly when material is adapted from concise Latin into a vernacular verse medium, is inevitable, and it was natural for the Spanish poet to add dramatic and imaginative material as well as to fill up his lines metrically. Thus, while Marius's leading of the charge towards the gates of Capsa, 'ipse intentus propere', is represented by the line 'Mio Çid don Rodrigo a la puerta adeliñava' (l. 467), the poet adds lines in which the hero is depicted at the gates with drawn sword, personally killing fifteen Moors inside them (ll. 470–1). Even an apparent negative may be taken up by the poet. Sallust says that Marius's men were ordered not to stop to collect spoils while the Romans were charging towards Capsa, 'neque milites praedari sinere'. But medieval discipline and instincts were not those of Romans, and the poet – reminded of the loot by Sallust's word 'praedari' – shows the Cid's men rounding up Moors and wandering cattle apparently while the charge towards Castejón was in progress (ll. 465–6). There remain, in any case, similarities substantial enough for one to assert with confidence that Per Abad received his inspiration, in considerable detail, from Sallust and Frontinus.

This proposal of classical sources, though startling, has seemed acceptable enough to some. Michael adds a further point of similarity between the reference which Sallust makes to Marius's concern for his water-supply, which I had prematurely dismissed, and line 526 of the poem (note to l. 525 of his edition of the *Poema*). Russell guardedly approves of the idea, adding that the poet may have misunderstood Frontinus with regard to the abandoned tent (1978: 53). Hook supports, by implication, the case I made by suggesting a similar source for lines 704–11 of the poem (1979*a*). As the Cid's forces drawn up outside Alcocer await the Moorish onslaught, the Cid's standard-bearer Pedro Bermúdez, who 'non lo pudo endurar', shouts his intention of charging into the enemy with the standard, expecting the army to follow and thus battle to be joined. The source for this is Caesar in *De Bello Gallico*, IV.25: on the first expedition to Britain, the standard-bearer of the Tenth Legion leaps into the water from his ship, bearing the eagle and wading ashore, whereupon the legion follows and attacks the waiting Britons. Five points of detailed similarity to the passage in the poem, all in sequence, are noted. Hook dismisses the possibility of a coincidence, concluding that the poet knew this part of Caesar's text. I think this entirely right. As Hook observes, the incident inspired by Caesar follows upon the episodes of Castejón and Alcocer inspired by other classical writers. Moreover, all three are of the same kind in that they deal with military matters. Hook's discovery of the source in Caesar greatly assists the case for the poet's knowledge of the other two Latin passages, since they form a small series.

Objection to my case for the poet's use of Sallust has been taken by Chalon (1978*b*). He takes my eleven points one by one, claiming that the Spanish verse-lines are not sufficiently precise echoes of Sallust for inspiration to have come from there. He also draws attention to differences of context. Chalon's idea of the

Castejón episode is that the poet is retailing, with adjustments and displacement to a different period, the story of the Cid's retaliatory raid into the kingdom of Toledo in the summer of 1081. I had already borne this possibility in mind at the start of my 1975 study, and after discussion, dismissed it. Nothing that Chalon now writes has caused me to change my mind. Of course the poet, writing in verse in a different language in 1207, does not precisely echo the Latin, and of course the contexts are different. The poet was not rewriting Sallust *in toto*, nor writing of Roman wars. He borrowed an attractive episode and used it in the context of a poem already under way, which imposed its own conditions. Chalon's major weakness is that he detaches the Castejón episode from that of Alcocer, with which it is in sequence, and which is also from a classical source, and he nowhere mentions the second one.

Chalon implies some surprise than an early Spanish poet could be thought to have known and imitated a classical writer. This surprise is natural, and to be respected when it comes from one of Chalon's open-mindedness (for he does not simply decry my proposal on grounds of traditionalist or any other theory). In my 1975 paper I devoted some space to the question of how the poet could have known Sallust and Frontinus, and Hook does the same with regard to Caesar. Sallust was quite well-known in twelfth-century Spain, and there is no difficulty about Caesar. Of Frontinus there is no trace before 1207, and this writer was not well-known in the Middle Ages elsewhere in Europe. But it is not necessary to think of complete texts of these authors. It may rather be a question of some *florilegium*, some series of short excerpts compiled for use either as a military manual (including, then, most desirably Vegetius; but the inclusion of Caesar on the standard-bearer would be hard to justify for such a purpose) or, more likely, as a means of instruction in Latin and rhetoric. There is no great difficulty in supposing such a compilation to have been in use in some instructional setting in Burgos or in the Cardeña library, though admittedly there is no trace of such a compilation there.[10] The proposal made earlier, that Per Abad received his higher education in France, where access to such classical materials and to rhetorical training was easier than in Spain, is therefore worth retaining.

If, beyond this, the poet's use of such sources still seems startling, that is only because of received ideas about the popular, jongleuresque authorship and nature of Spanish epic. The sources – modest enough, in all conscience – fall well within the range of the cultivated man whose picture is building up. From his point of view as literary craftsman, he needed these episodes to form his logical story of the Cid's progress. The *Historia Roderici* says that the Cid on being banished went to Barcelona and thence to Saragossa, without military action on the way. In the poet's invention, on being exiled the Cid crossed the frontier and immediately began to 'earn his bread' by fighting. The two episodes from classical sources show the Cid with a few hundred men able to take small defended towns, not by assault but by ruse. The episodes illustrate facets of the hero not found elsewhere, notably the talent for ruse and bluff, essential to all great commanders. From his victories in these fictional episodes, the Cid is able to make a first present to Alfonso, to win more recruits, in short, to begin his rise towards great power and towards the return into royal favour. The poet's literary logic is impeccable. His geographical logic was too. Castejón was and is where the poet places it, now Castejón de Henares. Alcocer exists only in the poet's verse, but he located it in a perfectly rational setting in the valley of the Jalón. The search for it by critics imbued with *historicista* attitudes has been arduous and amusingly fruitless.[11]

The episode of the lion with which the poet begins his Cantar III may at first glance seem slightly childish, but it is of great importance in the progress of the plot and for the characterisation, and is by no means devoid of subtleties. Strongly symbolic connotations have been perceived in it by some, notably by Bandera Gómez. Here the Cid is a Christ-figure, and line 2294, '¿Ques esto, mesnadas o que queredes vos?' resembles Christ's words to the disciples: 'Quid timidi estis, modicae fidei?' (Matthew 8.26); further, the 'viga lagar' (l. 2290) represents the Cross (Bandera Gómez, 1969: 82–114; the tradition of lion-symbolism in literature is surveyed by Garci-Gómez, 1975: 172–206). Hook in response to this and to other studies inclines to dismiss the idea of any elaborate symbolism or religious connotation, as is surely right in view of the nature of the poet's work in general (1976). Yet one cannot reject the possibility that in this passage the poet had the biblical text strongly in mind, in view of some six similarities between the poem and Matthew 8.23–7, in which Christ is awakened by the disciples during the storm at sea, and rises from his bed. As Hook remarks, 'Given the influence of the biblical text and biblical modes of expression in the Middle Ages, these similarities might quite well be unconscious', and he adds that they might well be fortuitous too. My impression is that there is something in the parallel, and that in view of the indication of Latin sources in Sallust, Frontinus, and Caesar, the possibility that the poet formed his episode partly with the biblical text in mind or before him must be retained. It is in these terms that Hook concludes. These may not be the only biblical resonances in the poem,[12] and as will be shown in Chapter 6, the poet probably took isolated phrases and *topoi* too from the Bible, as is natural enough. I entirely concur with Hook in rejecting the notion of the Cid in this passage – which Hook describes as 'resolutely secular' – or anywhere else, as a Christ-figure. The Cid eventually acquires a sort of patriarchal dignity, but this is owed more to literary descriptions of Charlemagne than to anything biblical.

A source in medieval Latin is to be stated for the episode of the moneylenders. There is a substantial and lively bibliography on this for, as I remarked elsewhere, 'the episode . . . is something of a touchstone for discussion of the Cid's morality and character, the poet's intention and sense of humour' (bibliography is listed in the editions of Michael and myself; a new survey is that of Salvador Miguel). If viewed in unreal terms in relation to the strict progress of the plot, the episode is irrelevant, for the poet could have dealt with the Cid's need for cash in a couple of lines. But he makes a fully dramatic scene out of it, at length (ll. 78–200), and reverts to the matter (ll. 1431–9). He demonstrates in it a fine range of powers both narrative and dramatic, as in the Count of Barcelona section, with many subtleties and notes of humour and farce, and he fits it all neatly into the topography and social reality of Burgos. While free imagination using this social reality might explain the episode, it has long been related to standard folk-motifs and to a variety of sources, but Menéndez Pidal in 1913 indicated that much the most likely of these was Tale xv of the *Disciplina clericalis* of Petrus Alfonsi, a converted Jew born in about 1062, who compiled this collection of *exempla* from oriental sources. This work was well-known in Spain during the Middle Ages, and had effects in many parts of Europe. Tale xv concerns a pilgrim to Mecca, and in outline and in a number of details – notably those concerned with the chests in the deception of the moneylenders – one can readily agree with Pidal in seeing in it the immediate source for Per Abad. On such authority traditionalists have accepted this source, perhaps surmising that the poet knew it in oral form; this is possible, but in view of the demonstration of his Latin written sources in this chapter, it is simpler to say that he knew it in a MS of the *Disciplina*. This episode and its context are related by Burt (1979) to the 'Exodus pattern', and I would by no means deny that the poet may, in a general way, have had biblical precedent in mind; but this, and the 'ironic reversal' which Burt identifies, should surely have led him to describe the poet as something other than a 'juglar', as he repeatedly does.

5. *Literary texts: French*

That the *Poema* owes a good deal in many respects to the example of French epic was plain to one of the first serious students of the text, Bello, in an early publication of 1823 and others later. The question has been vigorously debated ever since, sometimes on patriotic rather than scholarly lines.[13] The course of the debate to 1970 may be followed in Magnotta's survey.[14]

A good deal of the debate has centred on the debt which the *Poema* may have owed specifically to the *Chanson de Roland*, almost always cited in its 'Oxford' version. Bello did not begin it in that way, for the simple reason that during his period of work in London (1810–29) the *Roland* was not known to him, since it remained unpublished until 1837; Bello worked on the MSS of other epics in the British Museum. In recent times the seemingly incontrovertible dating of the *Poema* to about 1140 had the effect of restricting comparisons to the *Roland*, since there were very few other French epics which could be dated with it to the years before 1140 (and the relatively early *Couronnement de Louis* and *Chanson de Guillaume* are unrewarding in this respect). The whole investigation was distorted by this dating. When Curtius – rightly, as many would now think – perceived in the *Poema* certain *topoi* drawn from French texts, he was obliged to think that the Spanish work could not have been composed before 1170–80, and his findings were indignantly rejected by Menéndez Pidal. Pidal himself did not, in early days, by any means reject the idea that the Spanish poet had drawn upon French examples for a limited number of features, notably the enumeration with *tanto* (e.g. l. 726), demonstrations of grief and the phrase *llorar de los ojos*, and the description of battles. He summed

up in 1913 by saying that 'Un juglar de gesta castellano, en el siglo
XII, no podía ignorar el *Roland* y otras gestas anteriores referentes
a las guerras de Carlomagno en España' (though it was by no
means plain what those 'gestas anteriores' might have been).
Moreover, 'el argumento y el espíritu general del *Poema* son
completamente otros que los de las *chansons*' (as all will readily
agree) . . . 'De modo que la cuestión puede quedar en terreno
firme, reconociéndose en el *Cantar* un fondo de tradición indíge-
na, y una forma algo renovada por la influencia francesa.' In a
long note, he then listed other similarities of phrasing, pointed
out by others: 'Pudieran señalarse otras frases del *Poema del Cid*
análogas a las de las *chansons*, pero que no relevan imitación
inmediata, siendo resultado general de la fraternidad de las dos
lenguas y literaturas.' The introduction to the 1913 edition of the
poem in Clásicos Castellanos which included the foregoing
remarks was reproduced unchanged in Pidal's 1963 book,
presumably showing that he saw no need to modify anything in
it. Meanwhile Horrent in 1956 judiciously reassessed the evidence for the influence of the *Roland* on the *Poema* (taking into
account all versions of the former); he insisted on the profound
differences of ideology between the two works, but concluded:
'En efecto, creo que hay motivos que asientan que el juglar
español no ignoró del todo el poema francés, o más bien su
versión española.'

Yet there is much in the *Poema*, as Bello and Curtius and others
had shown, which relates to French epics of much later date than
the *Roland*. Pidal himself seems to have been nonplussed by
similarities which stared him in the face but which were
inexplicable on his dating of the *Poema*. In his 1913 introduction
he mentioned Rajna's indication that there was some link
between the episode of Pippin and the lion in *Berte aus grans piés*
(known only in Adenet's reworking of 1272–5) and the lion
episode of the *Poema*, but he dismissed it on various grounds.
Pidal himself noted similarities between a prayer in *Fierabras* and
that of Jimena, but he could not resolve the problem because the
known redaction of *Fierabras* is 'de hacia el año 1200' and,
although this 'debió de tener otra forma anterior', he could not
well put this before 1140. On the general question of the Spanish
debt to French epic he was, then, open-minded in his early days,
and he recognised that in later periods a variety of French epic
themes known in Spain were used as sources for ballad materials;

but in later life, the effect of his work on the *Poema* was to insist on its original autonomy, since the *juglar* who (he held) composed the notional *Cantar de Gormaz* at its core, to be dated about 1105 or 1110, could not well have known even the *Roland*. In the 1970s the view of the relation of the *Poema* to French epic has been revolutionised by the finding of new sources and parallels, made possible only by the recognition that the *Poema* was composed not before about 1200 and that its author was hence able to draw upon a considerable range of French texts. What follows is to be taken in conjunction with what has been said about metrical aspects in Chapter 4 and remains to be said about stylistic matters in Chapter 6.

On the means by which Per Abad knew his French texts I have speculated in earlier chapters. Menéndez Pidal thought that Spanish *juglares* listened to French *jongleurs* perform their works along the pilgrim road or in the suite of travelling lords, etc., thus acquiring the few largely superficial borrowings whose presence in the *Poema* he recognised, and as mentioned earlier, such auditions of French poems in Burgos are entirely possible. Horrent, cited above, thought that with regard to the *Roland* the Spanish *juglar* who composed the *Poema* knew 'más bien su versión española'; but there is no reason to postulate a Spanish version of the *Roland* or of other poems at this date, and there is no evidence for their existence. A more radical view of the transmission process was taken by Riquer: 'El poeta que escribió el *Cantar del Cid* conocía bien la epopeya francesa. En su biblioteca particular, o en la del monasterio o de la corte a que estaba adscrito, figuraban, sin duda alguna, varios manuscritos de *chansons de geste* que podía leer en su lengua original.'[15] Again, Riquer could be right, but we can now see that so wide and sensitive was Per Abad's experience of French verse that it is best to postulate his residence and study in France, and his learning of the epic art there by both reading and listening. Nor do I have the impression that Per Abad, as he composed, consulted French epic MSS. He does not follow one source slavishly or for long, but combines (as was seen in the study of Jimena's prayer in Chapter 4) and re-creates, taking hints and producing echoes, always his own man with his own story to tell. This suggests that he composed from the resources of a rich memory and of a poetic imagination in which French materials had been moulded anew and recombined before he ever set pen to parchment.

I deal here with episodes and features for which, I think, the poet took inspiration from identifiable French texts, reserving for the next chapter those motifs, formulae, etc. for which no single source, but rather a generality of experience in a number of texts, has to be postulated. It should be remembered that, while the Latin sources discussed above were and are relatively fixed in their textual tradition, this did not apply to French epic. There was often textual diversity in what remained the same poem but had been subject to copying idiosyncrasies or dialectal adjustments, and major reworkings existed too. We cannot say precisely what version of *Fierabras* Per Abad knew, and can quote as sources only what survives and is available in printed editions, without being sure that the version known to Per Abad coincided precisely with these. In one important instance, *Berte aus grans piés*, we have only the version of Adenet, the original of the late twelfth century being wholly lost. *Florence de Rome* survives in three MSS, none early enough to be that known to the poet. The task of seeking sources is, in this respect, inevitably one hedged about with uncertainty, as recent critics have not been slow to tell us; but enough can still be said to form a fairly clear idea of the poet's inspiration and methods of work. In what follows, I deal with items in their sequence within the *Poema*, abbreviating evidence which has been fully presented in print elsewhere.

As argued above, the poem may have begun with a brief passage in prose about the events which led to the Cid's banishment, based on the *Historia Roderici*. By a strange coincidence, *La Chevalerie d'Ogier* began in much the same way. Charlemagne has sent four knights to collect tribute from Gaufrois of Denmark; the Dane insults the emissaries, whereupon, on hearing of this, the Emperor swears vengeance on Gaufrois's son Ogier, a hostage at the Frankish court. The first laisse of *Ogier* is brief – twenty-seven lines – and gives the reason for the hostility between Charlemagne and Ogier which is the theme of the poem. Per Abad thus found, in a journey to collect tribute, an astonishing echo of the *Historia Roderici*'s episode (which is, so far as we know, historical) in a French epic, so that he could begin to compose his opening scene not only on the basis of the history of the Cid, but with a precedent in epic literature too. He probably took from *Ogier* one suggestion not present in the *Historia* (and hence presumably unhistorical). Gaufrois insulted the Emperor's knights by tonsuring them and shaving their faces, so that when they reappear at court:

Corones orent, s'ot cascuns res la barbe
E les grenons, le menton e la face   (ll. 13–14)

This Per Abad applied to the Cid's treatment of García Ordóñez at Cabra. The insult was presumably mentioned in the prose passage which preceded the verse text, being the reason – beyond mere capture and the taking of spoils – for the lasting enmity shown by García Ordóñez to the Cid, as provocatively recalled by the Cid in court (ll. 3282–90). The act consisted, in Spanish style, documented for us in *fueros* of the time, not of tonsuring and shaving but of the tearing of the beard (*mesar la barba*).

In the scene of the hero's departure from Vivar, the poet seems to have had in mind the departure of Ogier from Castel Fort (where, in a notable example of Gallic *verismo*, he has sustained – alone – a seven-year siege by Charlemagne's army). Some five points in or related to Per Abad's scene correspond to those in a ten-line passage of *Ogier*, with several close verbal similarities, such as 'tornava la cabeça y estava los catando' (l. 2) = 'Vers Castel Fort avoit son cief torné' (l. 8877; see further Smith, 1977b: 148–9). Other possible influences on this scene of departure from *Garin le Loheren* are indicated by Hook (1979b: 498–501), and I agree with him that both *Ogier* and *Garin* must be taken into account together with a long tradition of symbolic references and folkloric motifs in studying the subtlety with which the poet composed this strongly emotive passage. For the equally important scene of the Cid's arrival in Burgos, embarrassingly closed against him (ll. 15–32), Hook suggests that the poet took features from *Garin le Loheren* and *Doon de la Roche*, again combining the two in a convincing re-creation (1981).

Jimena's prayer is, as has long been recognised, present in the *Poema* because such 'narrative prayers' were featured in many *chansons de geste*. Once given a model, however, the poet not only made something highly attractive out of it, in terms of the moment and of characterisation, but further provided a number of thematic indications which prefigure elements to come in his plot (Gerli, 1980). No single model for the prayer, or series of models each partially exploited, is known to exist or need have existed, although some details are owed to specific texts. As shown in Chapter 4, the lines about the Crucifixion, 352–7, are substantially indebted to two prayers in *Fierabras*, combining elements from both together with details from *Parise*; as also noted earlier, Menéndez Pidal long ago perceived the relationship with *Fierabras* but was unable, because of illusory dating, to affirm a borrowing. The form of the name 'Longinos' (l. 352) was possibly taken from *Parise* (l. 813), as I proposed elsewhere (1977–8: 15), but might merely represent standard medieval Latin 'Longinus'. The poet's source for the names of the Magi (l. 337) is debated. Michael has shown that the names were known in Catalonia and Aragón before and during the twelfth century (note to this line in his edition), but there is no evidence for similar early knowledge of them in the central and western parts of the Peninsula. The poet probably took the names from the interpolation made in about 1178 in the *Historia ecclesiastica* of Petrus Comestor, for the forms of the three names correspond precisely to those in the *Poema*. The 'oro e tus e mirra' (l. 338) are probably drawn from Comestor also, or directly from Matthew 2.11, for *tus* is present in Comestor and the Vulgate but not elsewhere in the Hispanic tradition outside Catalonia, and the word is undocumented in Old French.[16] The best full study of Jimena's prayer is that of Russell (1978: 115–58). After discussion of the traditions behind it and of modern studies, he adopts the conclusion of Scheludko (1932, 1934): the prayer in the *Couronnement de Louis* – about 1125? – itself based on various liturgical and other Latin texts, provided a model for later developments in French epics, and from the latter the Spanish poet took his materials, although 'es evidente que introdujo en su modelo importantes modificaciones que afectaban tanto la función temática y situacional de la oración como no pocos detalles de contenido y vocabulario' (150). A few details, such as mention of St Sebastian, appear to have no parallel in French. Russell is right to insist on the poet's independence of spirit and the importance of his thematic innovations. The poet produced, from rather conventional materials, a most moving episode. That the prayer is uttered in the abbey church might, as Russell says (119), be simply a consequence of the action up to that point, and not be owed to one of the few French texts in which this is also the setting. The prayer is specially moving in the mouth of Jimena, which contrasts with its utterance generally by men in French poems (an exception, a prayer by a woman, occurs in *Amis et Amiles*, ll. 1277–1321, as Russell notes). But Per Abad could have found both aspects authorised in a poem not mentioned by Russell, for in *Raoul* Dame Aalais prays in the abbey church of Saint Geri (ll. 1138 ff.). The tender scene of the parting of Jimena from the Cid (ll. 368–75) more than vaguely resembles that in which Parise parts from her husband (*Parise* ll. 773 ff.; Smith, 1977–8: 17).

The appearance of the Archangel Gabriel to the Cid in a dream (ll. 405–12) has long been taken to be modelled on Gabriel's appearance in dreams of Charlemagne, for example in *Roland* 'O' (ll. 2525 ff., 2555 ff.). The correspondence, moreover, is directly with the *Roland* and not with other French texts in which the Archangel appears, as Horrent, usually so sceptical, is for once persuaded (1973: 372–3). This note of divine assurance, though common enough in epic, is somewhat out of key with the *Poema*, although thematically fitting at this point and presumably intended by the poet to indicate, to those aware of such things, the equation between the eventually patriarchal Cid and Charlemagne, patriarchal Emperor of the Franks. This is continuously suggested also by the motif of the Cid's flowing beard, and the equation was much developed later in the thirteenth century (Smith, 1976a: especially 529–31).

The conquest of Valencia was a fully historical achievement of the Cid, and the poet had the support of the *Historia Roderici* for some of the details of his narrative, analysed above. But as elsewhere in his work, he had the fine idea of associating the hero's womenfolk with the city soon after its capture. The audience first becomes aware of the full import of the Cid's achievement when, in two splendid lines (1606–7), he conducts his wife and daughters formally into their new 'heredad', and its magnitude is appreciated only when, from the top of the citadel, the women view the panorama of city, sea, and 'huerta' (ll. 1610–17). This passage has been justly admired for its poetic vision, and for its elegance of sentiment and diction. A strong suggestion came for it, I think, from the lost original of *Berte aus grans piés* (Smith, 1977b: 141–2). In the work of Adenet, lines 1959–75, Queen Blanchefleur of Hungary, newly arrived in Paris, contemplates from the height of Montmartre the city spread out beneath her. There is a general similarity in the way in which a panorama is presented through womanly eyes to which it is new and impressive, and in both scenes a personal domain is being viewed, that seen by Blanchefleur coming to her daughter by marriage. We do not know what changes Adenet wrought in the twelfth-century original of *Berte*, but there is no reason to doubt that the original contained such a scene, and it could well have impressed Per Abad. In Adenet, it is a fine passage indeed. Menéndez Pidal himself surprisingly indicated (1913 edition) that the scene in which Jimena and her daughters view, from the citadel of Valencia, the army from Morocco (ll. 1644–56), and express alarm before the Cid calms their fears, bears a likeness to an episode in *Florence de Rome* (ll. 1059–80): 'También Florence, asomada a una ventana, ve el ejército dispuesto a combatir, y temerosa, quiere evitar la batalla, pero su padre la tranquiliza.' Given the disparity of dates (on his terms), Pidal could do no more than note the similarity. The question of the dating of *Florence* has now come to the fore again, as will be mentioned shortly, but it still seems possible that in the present instance Per Abad could have taken a hint from this poem. The scene which he developed, however, is much superior to that of *Florence*.

It was Rajna who, in 1884, suggested that the lion in the *Poema* owed something to a notable lion episode in *Berte aus grans piés*, an idea against which Pidal argued in detail, even suggesting – such is the *historicista* instinct – that the Spanish scene may have had some basis in the life of the Cid.[17] There remains the difficulty that we have for comparison only Adenet's reworking of *Berte*, but the original probably contained such an episode, and it could well have put Per Abad in mind of the notable *coup de théâtre* with which he raises the curtain on his third act. If one concentrates on the similarities between the Spanish poet's scene and that of Adenet, instead of on the differences of context, outcome, and dramatic purpose, which are certainly there as Pidal said, one can see that there are enough for a link to be argued between them. Both scenes are set in court, with witnesses of quality present; in both, the lion is a domestic one which has escaped from its cage; and in both, two people flee from it (Charles Martel and his queen; the two Infantes). There are verbal parallels too: 'Au mengier sist li rois et sa gente maisnie' (l. 48) = 'En Valençia seye mio Çid   con todos sus vassallos' (l. 2278), with identical structure; 'Vers le lion s'en va' (l. 66) = 'e adeliño pora[l] leon' (l. 2297); and 'Chascuns i acorut la merveille esgarder' (l. 72) = 'A maravilla lo han   quantos que i son' (l. 2302). Per Abad took suggestions from *Berte*, no more, and he probably combined these with hints from the biblical source identified by Bandera Gómez and Hook. In a poem now well under way, which by its progress was defining the roles of the Cid and the Infantes, the poet was naturally going to adapt the episode of *Berte* to his own needs.

From *Ogier*, Per Abad may have taken suggestions for the Cid's dramatic pursuit of Búcar (ll. 2408–25). In *Ogier*, a thousand Franks with Charlemagne at their head chase the fleeing Dane (ll. 8932 ff.). The Emperor shouts to the fugitive 'Cha revenrés, cuvers . . .' (l. 8936), just as the Cid shouts to Búcar '¡Aca torna, Bucar . . . !' (l. 2409), while if Ogier is 'li Danois d'outre mer' (l. 8956), Búcar has come 'd'alent mar' (l. 2409). A further suggestion about the pursuit of Búcar and his escape in a boat, in the variant version of the *Poema* whose existence I surmised earlier, may have come ultimately from a narration of the escape of Algisus from Pavia in A.D. 774 (Smith, 1980b: note 7, c).

In an important paper, Walker indicated the strong possibility that for certain central aspects of the Corpes outrage, the poet found inspiration in the *Chanson de Florence de Rome* of about 1200 (1977). Since many critics were by then disposed to recognise that the Corpes scene is a poetic fiction, as are the first marriages and all that flows from them, the way was clearly open for the episode to be treated either as the product of the poet's imagination, or as one owed to a literary source or sources. *Florence* is a somewhat tedious poem, little read and neglected by critics; Walker was led to the French original only as a result of working on the fourteenth-century Spanish prose version of the story. His proposal is less startling when one recalls the similarity between a passage of *Florence* and the viewing of the Moroccan army in the *Poema*, observed by Pidal and noted above, together with other likely echoes of lines of *Florence* by Per Abad, discussed in the previous chapter. Very recently Deyermond and Hook (1981–2) have disputed Walker's chronology, showing that in its only form now known to us, *Florence* may have been composed somewhat later than Walker supposed, and hence may not have been available to a Spanish poet in 1207. Even so, their conclusions do not, as they recognise, wholly negate this availability, and there remains – as I think is well established for the lost early *Berte aus grans piés*, now known only in Adenet's reworking – the possibility that *Florence* had some earlier but now lost form, and that this was known to the Spanish poet.[18]

Two further suggestions for the elaboration of the Corpes scene may have come to the poet from *Parise la duchesse*. Parise was maltreated and tormented in a not dissimilar way to the Cid's daughters; among other details:

An pure sa chemise est li suens cors remés   (l. 647)

with the mention of the 'chemise' suggesting mention of the

same to Per Abad (l. 2721), for this is not present in *Florence*.
Earlier, in her distress, Parise has cried:

Quant serai relevée, si me copez le chié   (l. 628)

which may have put the Spanish poet on the way to his line:

¡cortandos las cabeças,   martires seremos nos!   (l. 2728)

Again, as will be seen, it is not solely a question of these isolated
lines, but of other borrowings from *Parise* by the poet. To all this
one must add, for a comprehensive view of how the poet drew on
widely disparate materials in constructing this episode, Curtius's
identification of the Corpes setting within the *locus amoenus*
tradition of Latin writing: not a matter of a specific source, but of
composition on the basis of materials and of a sensibility within
the poet's intellectual ambit, and, it should be added, within the
competence of at least a part of his potential public. Walsh's
sensitive analysis of this scene in terms of the tradition of
martyrdom both literary and iconographic must be borne in mind
too (1970–1), together with the proposal by Gifford (1977) that the
Corpes beatings may retain something of folkloric and other
traditions which go back to at least the ancient Roman Lupercalia.
Now Deyermond and Hook (1981–2) seek to show that the tale of
Philomela, Procne, and Tereus, in Book VI of Ovid's *Metamor-
phoses*, provides in some respects closer analogies with the
Corpes episode than does the French *Florence*. It is clear that
Walker's 1977 study has opened up inquiry into a large range of
possibilities which it would be premature to assess definitively;
and since the poet early in the episode put in what is perhaps a
deliberately mystifying allusion to the 'caños' and to 'Elpha' (l.
2695), he might almost be warning moderns that no such thing as
a 'definitive' study of this part of his work is to be contemplated.
That he knew the French sources indicated and used them as a
framework for his episode and for some details still seems to me
highly likely.

The scene in which the Cid dresses to go to the Cortes (ll.
3084–100) is a notable one, of larger dimensions than that of a
mere motif which might be repeated within one work. Although
it may have folk-analogies, the scene had, in the poet's intention,
the definite aim of equating his hero, by this act, in dignity and
splendour, with Charlemagne and Baligant as depicted in the
Roland. These leaders arm themselves for battle in lines 2987 ff.
and 3140 ff. Since the Cid dresses for a civic occasion, there is
here no more than an intended equation with the French scenes,

and no verbal parallels except that the formulaic line which introduces the scene in the *Roland*, 'Li amiralz ne se voelt demurer' (l. 3140), is echoed in the *Poema*, 'Nos detiene por nada el que en buen ora naçio' (l. 3084). For precise verbal indications, Per Abad probably had in view not the *Roland* but two scenes of *Girart de Roussillon* which include not only robing but also the wider setting, and a further note may have been adopted from *Amis et Amiles*, about mass heard at dawn and the 'ofrenda' (ll. 3060–2; see Smith, 1977*b*: 142–4).

The suggestion for the great Cortes scene probably came to the poet, in general terms, from the trial of Ganelon in the *Roland*, as mentioned earlier. But the development of it, rich and assured in dramatic terms, and dedicated to a profoundly ideological intention, was entirely the poet's own. As for the duels, it was shown earlier, following Lacarra, that they are very much part of the judicial process as envisaged by a reforming lawyer. Yet such duels were well known in literary tradition also, for the complement to the trial of Ganelon in the *Roland* is the duel between Pinabel and Tierri. To this Walsh adds the duel between Gui d'Alemaigne and Guillaume in the *Couronnement de Louis* (and the duels in the Spanish Zamora story, which did not, in vernacular epic form, with any certainty pre-date the *Poema*), and furnishes a useful analysis of the stages followed, perhaps conventionally, in such 'epic duels'.[19] The *Poema*, however, shows no verbal parallels with the French texts named, whereas some are to be noted in *Parise la duchesse*. In this, a judicial duel is fought between Béranger and Milon to resolve a matter touching the honour of the Duchess, this having a general air of similarity to some aspects of the duels in the *Poema*, and the following close parallels:

Il hurte le cheval des esperons dorez	(l. 521)
batien los cavallos con los espolones	(l. 3618)
Li gloz torne sa regne, s'a la sselle versé	(l. 579)
bolvio la rienda al cavallo por tornasse de cara	(l. 3659)
Les cengles sont ronpues qu'il avoit renoé	(l. 580)
quebraron le las çinchas, ninguna nol ovo pro	(l. 3639)

What is said in two instances in the *Poema* (ll. 3644–5, 3690–2) when a combatant, or a relative speaking for him, recognises defeat and has this confirmed as a verdict by the judges, is anticipated in *Parise*:

Et Miles li escrie: 'Merci, por amor Dé!
Je me rant recréus; gardez ne m'ociez!'
Quant les gardes l'oïrent, cele part sont alé   (ll. 589–91)

6. *Personages and names*

The creation of a large number of personages named in accordance with usages of the period is important for the *verismo* of the
Poema, and for the sense of the literary life as a 'richly-peopled
continuum'. However, apart from Jimena and her daughters
(poetically renamed), the King, García Ordóñez, and Jerónimo,
none of the rest can be shown independently to have had much to
do with the Cid of history after his exile in 1081, and in some
instances it is sure that they did not. Since the poetic associations
are for the most part non-historical, it is needless for traditionalists to argue that so many personal names had been accurately
preserved in a verse tradition continuous from the time of the Cid
down to the moment at which the poem is recorded for us. But
since so many of the personages can be shown to have had a real
existence in the Cid's time, there must be some explanation. The
poet was not simply inventing or guessing. Russell's remark that
the poet no doubt undertook 'a certain amount of historical
investigation' has turned out to be very fruitful. Since the
principal historical source, the *Historia Roderici*, gave the poet no
names of the Cid's associates, and we have no reason to suppose
their presence in some other chronicle source now lost, we turn to
the only other possible source, that of legal records. If the poet
was a lawyer, not only were numerous documents available to
him, but he would have had the instinct to go to them. Per Abad
sought names in diplomas of the time of the historical Cid
(defined for him, perhaps, by the date of the hero's death,
precisely stated by the *Historia Roderici*, and certainly known in
Cardeña). He needed names not only proper to the time, but also
sufficiently defined by class – if worthy to confirm diplomas, then
worthy to be the Cid's captains; while if some names were
defined in the records by territorial titles also, they were to be
useful both for *verismo* and for metrical convenience and epic ring
(as can be appreciated in verses where a roll of heroes is called, ll.
733–41, 1990–6, 3063–71). The process is not really extraordinary,
being akin to that followed by historical novelists, and, for a
non-literary motive, by Per Abad himself when he forged the
'Lecenio' diploma.

Russell thought that the poet went to diplomas in which the Cid figured as grantor or among the confirmers, since it could then be naturally assumed that other confirmers had been present with him. This may be too restrictive, for such documents – as they survive for us – are few and, moreover, scattered. It may have sufficed for the poet to study diplomas of the right period in archives accessible to him, that is in Burgos and at Cardeña. Those known to us in both places are quite numerous, but probably represent only a fraction of those held there in the poet's day. In some instances one can detect associations which led the poet to choose men as poetic companions of the Cid, or as his enemies, but these associations were fortuitous within each document, in no way guaranteeing associations of the kind postulated by Menéndez Pidal and others.[20]

It should first be noted that the poet seems to have disregarded what little the documentation told him about blood-relations of the Cid, preferring to establish a new series of poetical relationships in which that of uncle–nephew was, as in French epic, paramount. In 1971 I drew attention to the fact that the poet did not make Alvar Alvarez a *sobrino* of the Cid, even though Jimena's *carta de arras* of 1074 says that he – together with Alvar Fáñez – was a *sobrinus* of the hero; concluding from this that the poet did not know this document, even though it was presumably then (as now) in Burgos Cathedral archive. I would now prefer to say that the poet could well have known this *carta*, but chose not to use the information in question (he did in the case of Alvar Fáñez: not by mentioning a *tío–sobrino* kinship, but by having him call the Cid's daughters his 'primas', ll. 2858, 3438). It is also the case that on each occasion Alvar Alvarez is mentioned, his name occupies the first hemistich and another name fills the second (ll. 443, 739, 1719, 1994, 3067); that is, there was no space metrically for the poet to mention the kinship (hypothetically as *'so sobrino del Campeador', as of another knight in l. 741), or, to put the point differently, the poet did not need an epithet or line-filler here.[21] Since the poet's concern was with *verismo* rather than with historical accuracy, as has been shown repeatedly, any assessment of kinships in terms of history is a side-issue only.[22]

For the Cid's *mesnada* the poet took, then, from diplomas, the names of Alvar Alvarez (e.g. Burgos, 1074; mentioned in the *carta de arras*, and confirmed it), Pedro Bermúdez (e.g. Cardeña, 1085;

this diploma was also confirmed by Alvar Fáñez), Muño Gustioz (Cardeña, 1113; confirming a sale of land by Jimena to the Abbot of Cardeña), and Alvar Salvadórez (confirmed jointly with the Cid diplomas of 1066, 1069, 1070, 1080; made, with others, a donation to Cardeña in 1072; confirmed Jimena's *carta de arras* in 1074).

Other instances involve territorial titles and details which need different considerations. Per Abad knew of Alvar Fáñez in various ways already mentioned, but he wished to add a territorial title, of respect or for metrical reasons, defining Alvar as he 'que Çorita mando' (l. 735). He was indeed 'Alvar Fanez de Zorita' in a Silos diploma of 1097, and 'Alvar Faniz dominus de Zorita' in 1107 (Toledo), and the same, presumably, on some Burgos or Cardeña diploma not now extant. His honorific *Minaya* may not have been borne by the historical Alvar Fáñez, but it was used by others of the time and figured in legal documents; one cannot be sure what source the poet had for this usage.[23] Rather different is the case of Muño Gustioz, described in line 737 as 'que so criado fue' (of the Cid), and 'mio vassallo de pro' in line 2901, with the addition that '¡En buen ora te crie   a ti en la mi cort!' (l. 2902). The poet may have taken this idea from the fact that Muño Gustioz, fourteen years after the death of the Cid and hence presumably rather younger than him, confirmed Jimena's sale of land to the Abbot of Cardeña in 1113. It is noticeable that two of the phrases, in lines 737 and 2901, are second hemistichs of the kind that the poet often needed as fillers, but the whole line 2902 is both an echo of 737 and dramatically potent here, for the Cid needs a specially trustworthy, home-bred man to take the claim for redress to the King. It seems unlikely that the poet knew of Muño Gustioz's relationship to the Cid: he was the hero's brother-in-law, being married to Jimena's sister Orovita, and this equality of social status serves to disprove, as history, the poet's notion about his being the Cid's 'criado' ('person brought up in the household of . . .') or 'vassallo'.

The matter of Diego Téllez is problematic. Men of this name appear in the legal records of Old Castile from 1063 to 1106, variously married to ladies named Teresa and Paula. The one married to Paula made a donation to Silos in 1088, and the spouses had tombs in the monastery. Another, or possibly the same, was governor of Sepúlveda in 1086 (diploma of San Millán); and since Alvar Fáñez had taken a part in the settlement of Sepúlveda in 1076, there may have been some association which suggested to the poet that Diego Téllez was 'el que de Albar Fañez fue' (l. 2814), but in what form the poet could have acquired this information is not known. Equally, the line could be wholly an invention, to show that a man with special obligations to Alvar Fáñez, and hence indirectly to the Cid, was at hand to play his part in the rescue of the Cid's daughters.[24]

There remains Galín Garcíez, 'el que fue de Aragon' (l. 1996, and similar in 740, 1999, 3071). He was a historical person, lord of Estada and Liguerre in western Aragón and *majordomus* of the Aragonese monarch in a document of 1116 (also recorded in 1081, 1084). He would hardly have figured in any Castilian diploma, and it is not known how the poet could have picked up his name.[25] The same applies to Martín Muñoz, 'el que mando a Mont Mayor' in Portugal (l. 738, etc.). He was an important and well-documented man who was Count of Coimbra from 1091 to 1094. Perhaps, as a Leonese at a time when the kingdom was united with Castile, he figured, with territorial title, in some royal diploma known in Burgos or Cardeña, but no trace of this survives. He may or may not be the same as the 'Martinus Muniades' who figures in the *Historia Compostelana*, fighting alongside the Aragonese at Astorga in 1111, but this text does not give a territorial title.

In the band opposed to the Cid, we can assume that the Castilian leader of it, García Ordóñez, was given this role because he alone figured with it in the *Historia Roderici*, as 'comes'. His nickname 'Crespo' and his territorial title could have been taken by the poet from the *Chronica Najerensis* or from whatever source this had for its account of the battle of Uclés, for in it there appears 'Comes Garsias de Grannione, cognomento Crispus'. As a principal courtier, the Count was a frequent confirmer of diplomas from 1062 until his death at Uclés. He held Grañón from at least 1089, and was remembered by it still in an Aguilar de Campoo diploma of 1199 (well within the poet's time, then) by which land being sold was defined as 'que supradicta hereditas fuit de comite don Garcia de Grannon'. If Lacarra's thesis – to be discussed shortly – is correct, the poet was in any case well-informed about the Count and his family.

Just as some of the Cid's poetic *mesnada* entered it through fortuitous association on diplomas, two poetical enemies may have joined García Ordóñez in the same way. Alvar Díaz confirmed a donation to Cardeña in 1085, being mentioned immediately after García Ordóñez, and he appears often in the record from 1068 to 1111. In history he was García Ordóñez's brother-in-law, being married to the Count's sister Teresa; the poet might – on Lacarra's terms – have known of this, but he does not mention the kinship. Alvar Díaz appears once only in the poem, line 2042, where he is associated with García Ordóñez (Pidal added him in l. 3007b). Finally, there appears as an ally of Ordóñez and the Infantes one Gómez Peláyez (l. 3457). A Count of this name figures in the record from 1096 to 1135, and Pidal thinks there is reason to believe that he was indeed of the Beni-Gómez clan, on which the poet, as indicated above, may have had detailed genealogical information. Alternatively, the poet may simply have taken the name from the record of a donation made by Alfonso VI to Burgos Cathedral in 1096, for he there appears confirming jointly with Alvar Díaz and Diego González (one of the two poetic Infantes de Carrión).

New personages were needed by the poet for his court scene, it being notable that his *verista* instinct leads him to name initially four chief courtiers (ll. 3002, 3004), and to select two of these as judges to be mentioned several times together with others unnamed (l. 3136). The judges named are Enrique and Ramón, the Burgundian princes who had come to Spain to marry daughters of Alfonso VI. Enrique as Count ruled what is now northern Portugal from about 1095, and his son Alfonso took the title of King of Portugal in 1139. Ramón was the father of the 'Emperor' Alfonso VII (1126–57). Since both were of such importance in the ruling families of the Peninsula, it seems likely that the poet knew of them from a genealogical source; Ramón's fathering of Alfonso VII is specifically recalled in line 3003. Since each features in diplomas as 'gener regis' (1092, 1100, etc.), the poet could also have realised their importance from this source, and naturally gave them prominent positions at court. Another of the chief courtiers, Count Fruela (l. 3004), could have been known to the poet as a frequent confirmer of diplomas from 1077 to 1116. He was Count of León and Jimena's brother, no less, but the poet seems not to have known this or did not care to make use of the information. Count Beltrán (l. 3004) is either fictitious or, if a real person, anachronistic; there was no-one so called at the court of Alfonso VI, but a man of this name succeeded as Count of Carrión in 1117 and later married Alfonso VII's half-sister Elvira, being very prominent in his day and much mentioned in the legal record.[26]

The poet's *verista* need to name the Cid's legal expert, Mal Anda (l. 3070), is also notable, even though this man is given no further part in the proceedings. One might doubt if the appellation, being a nickname (alluding to lameness?) was dignified enough for it really to have been borne by a 'sabidor', but such a name was in formal use in Castile and figured in a diploma of 1144 as that of a man apparently then living (an Oña document, relating to land in Villahizán de Treviño, some 35 km north-west of Burgos). Since one Pedro Bermúdez, also apparently living, figures in the same diploma, it is possible that Per Abad's eye was caught by the coincidence and that he consequently adopted Mal Anda in a minor poetic role; but he is not likely to have known this Oña diploma. Pidal observes that the Cid held lands at Villahizán, which could enhance the possibility that some Cidian diploma not now extant connected Mal Anda with the hero, perhaps as tenant or successor by purchase, but the designation of such a man as 'sabidor' is probably fanciful on the poet's part. His name was not retained by Cardeña tradition.

Two members of the *mesnada* are not recorded in documents of the time. They may be wholly-invented names, but since so many others are accurately documented in or a little after the time of the historical Cid, and were known to the poet from his study of diplomas and histories, there is a presumption that these two had an existence in the Cid's day. Félez Muñoz and Martín Antolínez have entirely acceptable names. The former might have been a son of Muño Gustioz; he was the Cid's brother-in-law, and Félez is said to be a 'sobrino' of the hero and 'primo' of the Cid's daughters, although the poet does not mention any kinship between Muño Gustioz and Félez (as he might have been expected to do if it had existed). As for Martín Antolínez, he appears richly characterised soon after the start of the poem in the Burgos episodes, and as others have noted, he serves to keep the Burgos theme going throughout the poem, as 'el burgales de pro' and in similar epithets. He is the only *burgalés* to help the Cid at the lowest point of his fortunes, and thereby saves the honour of the city. If such a person did not exist, the *burgalés* Per Abad would have had to invent him. He may, indeed, have had a real existence, since as his putative father one Antolino Núñez, a Burgos man much present in the Cardeña diplomas, is recorded from 1061 to 1092; the name *Antolino* (*Antonino*, etc.) was not common at the time. It should also be noted that his baptismal name *Martín* is that of the Cid's own parish in the city, *San Martín*.

We do not know what source the poet had for the name of Jerónimo, Bishop of Valencia, but it was historically accurate, as was the statement that he came from France, 'de parte de orient' (l. 1288). The *Historia Roderici* records the conversion of a mosque in Valencia to a cathedral, its dedication and endowment, and the celebration of a first mass there (968.1–13); later, after the Cid's death, there is mention of the bishop of the city being sent to seek the aid of Alfonso (969.3), but again, the bishop is not named. The poet could have taken details of the dedication and endowment of the cathedral from the *Historia*, but he must have had another source for the name and origin of the bishop. Later in the Middle Ages Jerónimo was claimed for Cardeña,[27] but there is no evidence that such a claim was being made in the time of the poet, and, as far as we know, in history Jerónimo had no connection with Cardeña or Burgos. After the abandonment of Valencia he went to Salamanca as bishop, taking with him documents about the Cathedral of Valencia which are still extant; and, as argued above, he may have had charge of the Cid's whole archive, depositing this in Salamanca. The extraordinarily interesting diploma of 1098 by which the Cid endowed Valencia Cathedral (text: Menéndez Pidal, 1929: II, 866–9) naturally names Jerónimo, 'uenerabili pastori nostri Ieronime pontifici' (dative), etc., no fewer than five times. It also alludes to a donation made to Jerónimo 'ante quam ad pontificatus honorem ascenderet, eo adueniente de susanna', this last phrase meaning 'from higher up, from the north', that is, 'from France' (= 'de parte de orient' in Burgos usage?). It may be conjectured that this diploma was known to the poet, either in Salamanca, or in a copy, perhaps accompanying a text of the *Historia Roderici* sent to Burgos or Cardeña; or possibly the bishop's name was added as a marginal gloss to the MS of the *Historia* used by the poet.

The naming of the other ecclesiastic, Abbot Sancho of Cardeña, has always constituted a problem. It seems likely that the poet, so well informed in other ways, having access to Cardeña and Burgos documents, and concerned to use authentic names of the period whenever he could, would have known that the Abbot of Cardeña at the time of the Cid's exile was Sisebuto, who had a long and distinguished rule from 1056 to

1086, confirming many diplomas of the kind known to the poet. Had Per Abad been beholden in any way directly to Cardeña, it is likely that respect for the house would have imposed the name Sisebuto upon him. But although in close contact with the monastery, indebted to its archive, and proposing to give it a prominent place in his work, he still felt free to rename its famous abbot. I would not now maintain my earlier proposal that this happened because of a misreading. Rather, I think the reason was metrical, in that *Sisebuto* would not fit the system happily, and there are no *ú-o* rhymes in the poem (the abbot's name *Sancho* ends a first hemistich in line 237, but is a rhyme-word on four other occasions, lines 243, 246, 256, 1286). The reasoning here, then, is akin to that about 'don Elvira e doña Sol'. Later, Cardeña was in two minds: it wanted Sisebuto from its own tradition, but could not reject the Sancho propagated by the poem.[28]

Almost a person in his own right was Bavieca, the Cid's horse. History records nothing about any horse of the Cid. The origin of the name is literary, through a curiously mistaken interpretation which the poet made of *Bauçan*, the name of the horse of Guillaume d'Orange in French epic, as Riquer has shown (1953).

Among the Moslem personages, the fully historical Yúçef, Joseph, Emperor of the Almoravids (1059–1106), could have been known to the poet in the *Historia Roderici* ('Juzeph', 957.6, etc.), but doubtless figured in other historical records too. 'King Búcar' probably represents the Almoravid general Sir ben Abu-Beker, well-known in the Cid's time but not in connection with any attack on Valencia. If this is right, the poet in this instance acted in the same way as with many Christian personages, taking names for his poem from records contemporary with the Cid, but in this case we do not know from what source. It is likely to have been a Christian one, not Arabic.[29] The names of Tamín, King of Valencia, and of his generals Fáriz and Galve, are fictitious, though credible, being the kind of names for Moorish personages that might have occurred to any Spaniard at the time. Avengalvón, ruler of Molina, is best explained in terms of the survival of some local tradition known to the poet, perhaps in the way suggested by Lacarra and discussed below.

To trace sources for names in the historiographic and diplomatic record does not, of course, imply that in those sources the poet found the faintest hint for the character and actions which he attributes to personages in his work. For the most part, he freely invented these. But in two important instances, he had literary precedent in French also. It seems likely that Alvar Fáñez's role as deuteragonist of the Cid is owed to the Roland/ Oliver association in the *Roland*, supported, within Spain, by what was said in the *Poema de Almeria*, as argued earlier, while the literary *persona* of Jerónimo is very much that of Archbishop Turpin in the *Roland*. But since Alvar Fáñez's character and conduct in the *Poema* can scarcely be said to reflect those of Oliver, I offer – without analysing here – the possibility that Per Abad modelled his Alvar Fáñez more directly on Fouques in *Girart de Roussillon* – a poem which, on other grounds, Per Abad probably knew – for Fouques constantly acts as lieutenant, emissary, and adviser to Girart, in ways precisely similar to those of Alvar Fáñez in relation to the Cid.[30]

I have already suggested how the poet could have known the names and titles of García Ordóñez, and in a recent paper (1980a) I discussed his sources of information both diplomatic and genealogical for Diego and Fernando González as 'Infantes de Carrión' and members of the Beni-Gómez family. The historical role of Ordóñez as enemy of the Cid was also well-known to the poet. For what reason, however, did the poet select the Infantes as chief villains in his work? In history, there was no enmity between the Cid and the Beni-Gómez, not even a hint of difficulty or mistrust. One may readily allow that the poet envisaged from the start a plot in which, after the acquisition of wealth and power by the Cid and the restoration of his honour by reconciliation with the King, his daughters were to be married well and then abandoned, with resulting trial and duels. Since these marriages were fictitious, hypothetically any pair of young men, of high birth but credited with villainy of character, would have served the purpose, bearing fictitious names; and these could, after the breaking of the marriages and resulting enmity of the Cid, be associated with García Ordóñez as ally, already established in the public's mind as the Cid's permanent enemy. Yet this fictional creation would not serve, partly because the poet's instinct was to use authentic persons of the Cid's period, from the King right down to Diego Téllez and Mal Anda, to be mentioned only once; partly because the husbands were to be portrayed as members of a powerful family which was to be of nobler blood than the Cid and would give them support, and for this no wholly fictional group could be intruded into the history of the late eleventh century and at the same time convince a public of 1207 by no means ignorant of genealogies. The problem of trying to find out why the poet made his choice did not exist at all while Menéndez Pidal's view was – within his general insistence on the poem's fidelity to history – accepted: there had been in history at least 'tratos matrimoniales' involving the Cid's daughters and the Infantes de Carrión, that is, betrothals and plans for marriage, then broken off, and the poet, aware of this historical 'fact', had developed betrothals into full marriages for the purposes of his drama. With the dismantling of this belief, and removal of the date of the poem to long after 1140, there arises the need to explain the poet's motivation in selecting two members of the Beni-Gómez family for his purpose.

In 1980 (*a*) I proposed that the poet chose his villains as a result of a long-running ecclesiastical dispute. In 1142 the Abbey of Cardeña was ceded by Alfonso VII to Cluny, by an agreement with Peter the Venerable, Abbot of Cluny; in return, the Crown of Castile–León was relieved of its payment of a heavy annual tribute to the great Burgundian house. Cardeña, which under the arrangement would be reduced to the rank of a priory, claimed to be in no need of spiritual reform, and held that the Crown had no legal power to dispose of it in this way. It was, after all, a very proud foundation, and one of the chief monasteries of the realm. The Benedictines' resistance was ended in 1144 when the Cluniacs invaded it and drove them out. The Abbot of Cardeña, Martín I, went to Rome to protest, the Bishop of Burgos supported him, and after a delay of three years, the Pope ordered the Cluniacs to leave. This they did, stripping the abbey of all its treasures and, it seems, of almost everything movable, as was poignantly recorded in Cardeña tradition and long remembered (the eloquent passage from the *Cronicón de Cardeña* is quoted in my 1980*a* paper, 111). A later Bishop of Burgos took a contrary line, supporting the Cluniac claim, which was by no means surrendered for long after 1147. The Cardeña community did not feel safe until 1190, when a document of Alfonso VIII confirmed the monastery in all its rights and possessions without mention of the Cluniac claim.

The connection of all this with Carrión is that the invading Cluniacs had almost certainly come from the Cluniac monastery of San Zoil there. It was their chief house in Castile–León, and the residence of the Cluniacs' chief officer in Spain, the *camerarius*. Peter the Venerable had used it as his base in his Spanish itinerary of 1142, and it would have been natural for him there to make his plans and designate monks for the occupation of Cardeña. The monastery of San Zoil had been a foundation by the Beni-Gómez family, in about 1024. The remains of the saint had been brought from Córdoba by a member of the family in 1070. Its refoundation as a Cluniac house in 1076 owed much to Countess Teresa, and at that time the family declared itself secular patrons and protectors of the monastery; the monastic church contained the pantheon of the family.

Per Abad, as a lawyer of Burgos having close contacts with Cardeña, and possibly a professional obligation to the monastery, could well have come to share its feeling against the monks of San Zoil and their secular patrons, the Beni-Gómez family who provided successive Counts of Carrión. This feeling was a lively fear until perhaps 1190, and thereafter an enduring bitter memory. The expulsion of the monks in 1144 had been violent, the spoliation of the monastery total; possibly armed retainers of the Counts of Carrión had accompanied the Cluniacs. Per Abad, affectionately disposed towards Cardeña, took his villains from the family which was inseparable from the action of the Carrión monks in 1144. Any evil might appropriately be attributed to such a family, and would – an important point – be readily acceptable to a Burgos public of 1207, perhaps vaguely recalling the events of 1144 or still sharing in the prejudice without remembering the cause.

In her book (1980a: 140–59), Lacarra offers a different explanation. After quoting passages of Horrent, who in 1964 suggested the need for some such reasoning, Lacarra proceeds to a most interesting inquiry into twelfth-century noble genealogies and rivalries. A marriage in the early twelfth century between Gutierre Fernández de Castro, grandson of María Ansúrez who was sister to the famous Pedro Ansúrez, Count of Carrión (d. 1117), and Toda Díaz, granddaughter of Teresa Ordóñez (sister of García Ordóñez) and her husband Alvar Díaz, drew together all those who figure as enemies of the Cid in the *Poema*: the Beni-Gómez (Ansúrez) family, García Ordóñez, and Alvar Díaz. By another line, Beni-Gómez blood was joined in marriage to Rodrigo Fernández de Castro, and it is the Fernández de Castro family – Gutierre, Rodrigo – in the middle years of the twelfth century which represented the blood and power of the earlier Beni-Gómez. Throughout the twelfth century, at times in violent incidents, the Castros were opposed by the Laras. Increasingly, the Castros – as much Castilian as Leonese in reality, as the earlier Beni-Gómez had been – became identified with Leonese interests, while the Laras, with a strong base in and around Burgos, identified themselves with the interests of the Castilian Crown and Alfonso VIII. In 1195 Pedro Fernández de Castro fought alongside the Almohads at Alarcos, and in 1196 he was with the Leonese and Almohad forces which invaded Castile; in 1205 and 1206 he was at Alfonso VIII's court, but any reconciliation was short-lived, and he died a traitor in Morocco in 1214. Plainly, any Castilian from 1195 onward would have had every reason for considering him, and by implication the Castro clan, traitors to Castile; and any Castilian poet would have had every justification for assigning villainous roles to members of the clan retrospectively in a fiction.

According to Lacarra, there was more to the poet's motivation than this. A Navarrese great-granddaughter of the Cid, Sancha, married Pedro Manrique de Lara in 1173, dying before 1177 having given birth to a son, García. The Lara family of the poet's day could claim, then, to have the Cid's blood. Lacarra concludes:

Este parentesco explica, a mi juicio, los motivos que llevaron al autor del *Poema* a proyectar su propia realidad histórica sobre los personajes de su narración y a asignarles unos hechos que nunca llevaron a cabo. Indudablemente el autor debió ser hostil al bando de los Castro y favorable a la causa del rey y de los Lara. El *Poema* es, por tanto, una obra *de escarnho e de mal dizer*. El autor, al acusar a la familia Beni-Gómez de haber sido traidora al rey y a la familia del Cid, ya en el siglo XI, aumenta la magnitud e intensidad de su ataque y, por tanto, deforma conscientemente la realidad histórica de los acontecimientos que narra. El *Poema*, por consiguiente, no refleja la realidad histórica del siglo XI, sino la ideología del autor, quien al tomar partido en los conflictos de su época hace una obra de propaganda.   (1980*a*: 159)

This is an attractive and convincing thesis in some ways, but objections can be made to it (as I made them when reviewing Lacarra's book: 1981). First, the descent of the Castros in about 1200 from the Beni-Gómez family and from García Ordóñez was not very direct, and the family did not bear the title of lords of Carrión nor any of the personal names given by the poet as names of members of the family in the Cid's day. Second, nothing is said in the poem which would have helped a public of 1207 to associate the Beni-Gómez family of the Cid's day or García Ordóñez with the contemporary treachery of Pedro Fernández de Castro. Certainly it would not have been easy for the poet to inject any specific reference that was not overtly anachronistic, but he did make one allusion, to the parentage of Alfonso VII, in line 3003, a narratorial intrusion – as it were – made from a standpoint well outside the lifetime of the historical Cid and the action of the drama. From Alvar Fáñez's mouth there also comes, in the court scene, a reference to the earlier honourable history of the Beni-Gómez (ll. 3443–4, with 3445 adding a nearly contemporary hint). Third, the Cardeña tradition, the national chronicles, and later literature have nothing to say about this aspect and were oblivious to it. Finally, although I am inclined to think that Per Abad was well-informed in general, a frequenter of archives, even an expert genealogist, and although I am therefore inclined to concede that Per Abad could well have had the motivation and the knowledge which Lacarra indicates, it is hard to think that his audience was equally well informed about what is, after all, a quite complicated genealogical matter; and if the audience was not *au fait*, Lacarra's idea of the *Poema* as a work *de escarnho e de mal dizer* and of propaganda loses its point.

Much the same can be said about the Laras. Perhaps, around 1200, they claimed to descend from the Cid, and this was known in Burgos. We do not know. No such link could be guessed from the *Poema*. What can be said in relation to this, and against Lacarra, is that the poet makes nothing much of Alvar Salvadórez, present among the Cid's poetic captains, and in history the younger brother of Gonzalo, Conde de Lara, no less.

Yet Lacarra's thesis can by no means be dismissed. Perhaps her suggestion about a motive of *escarnho* based on genealogical factors is to be joined to mine about the long-standing prejudice in Burgos and Cardeña against Carrión and the Beni-Gómez family. Both could well have operated together in the poet's choice of villains. Genealogical matters in both France and Spain doubtless have a good deal to tell us about heroic traditions, and for Spain they, together with monastic links, were for long neglected, on principle, by traditionalist modes of inquiry.

Lacarra's insistence upon the descent of the Laras from the Cid has other attractive consequences in its favour. The part played by San Esteban de Gormaz in the rescue of the Cid's daughters, and the poet's eulogy of its inhabitants, may be owed to a memory of the hiding and protection there in 1163 of the infant Alfonso VIII by the Lara family, whose territory it was (Lacarra, 1980*a*: 182–6). More telling is the prominence given in the *Poema* to Avengalvón, last Moorish ruler of Molina before its conquest by the Christians (at a date unknown, but probably shortly before 1138). He did not coincide with the Cid of history, so the association between them in the poem is fictional. The Laras were lords of Molina in the later twelfth century, and it seems entirely likely that the poet knew of the historical Avengalvón through some connection with the Laras of Molina, and so gave him such a significant and sympathetic role in his work (Lacarra, 1980*a*: 195–201).

In starting this chapter I remarked that the *Poema* is not a historical work in verse, but a human drama. That it had an ideology there can be no doubt, nor that this amounts to, or is part of, a serious moral and exemplary purpose. It cannot however be true – as Lacarra at times implies – that the poet's main purpose was one of *escarnho* against the Castros or propaganda of what would be, on her terms, a rather crude kind. If her thesis is accepted – and I have made it clear that, despite some reservations, I think it should be – it is still relevant to only one facet of the poet's creation, and is not an 'explanation' of the whole. It is one feature – an important one – among many, among the mass of historical and literary materials which a man becomes acquainted with during perhaps half a working lifetime, and makes a part of himself, together with what enters into him from oral traditions, chance remarks by others about local and family affairs, mere impressions of how things were a century previously, and much that is simply the product of a lively imagination.

6   Linguistic and stylistic resources

The basis of the poet's language was that which was native to him as an inhabitant of Old Castile about 1200. There is no feature which obliges us to maintain Menéndez Pidal's view (arising from his still indispensable analysis) that the language is that of the frontier area of Medinaceli about 1140, nor to entertain Ubieto's notion of an original text in Aragonese. As we read the surviving text, allowance must be made for the disturbances and inconsistent modernisations of copyists, and also for the fact that the poet, composing in a dignified genre, may have used words and forms that were even in his day archaic, together with poetic variations of word-order, as mentioned above. The poet's basic vocabulary seems adequate for the expression of his themes, and extends without strain to mildly technical matters such as dress and warfare.

Yet the poet's daily *parole* took him only a short distance towards the creation of a rich linguistic instrument. We know nothing of his apprenticeship, but can make conjectures. His instructors were not grammarians or rhetoricians in the schools, who would have taught in and about Latin (and even though I have assumed above that the poet was trained in the Latin language as a working instrument, and in law), but the metrical patterns adduced in Chapter 4 and the literary texts cited in Chapter 5, most notably those of French epic, whose stylistic exemplars were to be paramount for him. The poet had a good ear in general, and remarkable powers of narration and of dramatic force in direct speech, together with an often subtle allusiveness which enriches situations and the interplay of personages. The great moments have been the subjects of excellent critical analyses, but more ordinary ones often demonstrate the poet's competence. Laisse 34, for example, begins by depicting the Cid's men in a desperate situation, besieged in Alcocer by the army from Valencia. The laisse starts with the leader's assessment of the position, with discussion of a plan and then preparations to put it into effect. By dawn all are armed; the Cid issues final orders; the gates are opened; the Moorish scouts return to their main body; the Valencian drums begin to beat and standards are raised. Then:

Las azes de los moros   yas mueven adelant   (l. 700)

The rhythm of the drums is now that of the two advancing lines of Moorish infantry, who step confidently, unhurried, full of menace ('ázes ... móros... muéven ... adelánt'), a menace enhanced by the poet's alliterations. The Cid's men wait, obeying orders but numb with apprehension, and so I have often waited with them, hypnotised into an admiring numbness by the words of this extraordinary poet. It is hard to see how his scene could have been better constructed or written. The poet selects the essential details, shifts his perspective rapidly, mixes narrative with direct speech, and tells all with fine economy. The scene has, moreover, no source in history or in fiction, and no special stylistic models guided the poet at this point. One may then usefully contrast this early part of the episode with what follows. The tension of waiting is shattered by the restless enthusiasm of Pedro Bermúdez, who charges the Moors in imitation of Caesar's standard-bearer. The following battle is recounted in largely formulaic terms derived from French epic, and includes the roll-call of captains which equally has literary precedents. All is moulded together in a competent narrative. The momentum of the action up to this point and of the personages carries the poet successfully on beyond it, indifferently whether he is inventing unaided or is guided by a source and a rhetorical tradition.

In presenting these aspects in my 1972 edition I remarked that the writer 'has a rich and assured instrument for a great diversity of tones and situations, which betokens long cultivation in the oral stage of the genre'. This, after much further ·work and reflection, I would not now maintain. The 'rich and assured instrument' is manifestly there, but now that we know so much more about the poet's sources for episodes, personages, and style, I find the supposition about the poet simply taking over much that had been fashioned in an oral tradition in Spanish both superfluous, on the one side, and unjust to Per Abad's creative talent, on the other. We still cannot assert that we know 'how he did it', as though some mystery of the detective-story kind had been resolved. The central mystery of poetic creation remains, as always, agreeably inviolate; but we can now indicate many of the guides which the poet had in forming his style.

To the poet's everyday *parole* can be added the specialist *parole* which was natural to him as a practising lawyer. The presence of specialist legal language in the poem has long been recognised, but has usually in the past been taken to be merely what a well-informed *juglar* used in his accurate representation of juridical subject-matter. As has been shown in Chapter 3, the emphasis is now different: the poem cannot be the work of any *juglar*, but is the highly-wrought product of a cultured man with special interests and competence in the law, and is itself a vehicle for statements of an exemplary intention and for a series of legalistic arguments, even – on Lacarra's terms – for a juridical reforming programme. Legalistic words and phraseology are both a natural part of the poet's *parole* and a proper expression of themes and aspects. Beyond this, one can see that the poet was concerned to get things technically right even at the cost of occasional slight pedantry. We are told that Martín Antolínez, when supplying the Cid in Burgos 'de pan e de vino' (l. 66):

non lo conpra,   ca el selo avie consigo   (l. 67)

a matter of some importance in the laws of the time. The detailed narration of the negotiations which led to the first marriages, and of the procedure in the Cortes, with much technical vocabulary, may have gone over the heads of groundlings in the audience (for whom, at intervals, the excitement of battles and duels was provided), but was likely to hold the attention of the cultured part of the public; yet technical parlance about more everyday matters may not have created much of a problem for anybody familiar with the 'publicising' of Latin legal documents in *ad hoc* Romance versions, in a process mentioned above. Such technical terms are scattered throughout the text: *apreçiadura* (ll. 3240, 3250), *condonar* (l. 887), *conloyar* (l. 3558), *enmendar* (l. 963), *entençion* (l. 3464), *manfestarse* (l. 3224), *natura* (l. 3275), *natural* (l. 1479, etc.), *ocasion* (l. 1365), *onor* 'fief, estate' (l. 289, etc.), *paria* (l. 109, etc.), *recudir* (ll. 3213, 3269), and others. Even if they occasionally produced difficulties for listeners, and reduced the dramatic impact of the work, these technicisms surely count as important *verista* elements in the way the poet handles them, and contribute to the human complexities of a situation. In rare instances the poet's strongly-felt need to insist on a legalistic detail overburdens a line or series of lines:

Esto mando mio Çid,   Minaya lo ovo conssejado:
que ningun omne de los sos ques le non spidies o nol besas la
   mano,
sil pudiessen prender o fuesse alcançado
tomassen le el aver e pusiessen le en un palo   (ll. 1251–4)
which the poet, on reflection and in writing that hypothetical
polished version, might have reformed. A less conscientious poet
might have put the point in simpler terms, or merely omitted it.
Sometimes the legalistic detail has dramatic force, as when the
penalties which the people of Burgos will face if they help the Cid
are stated in frightening terms (ll. 27–8, repeated by the girl in
ll. 45–6). These lines echo the penalty clauses of diplomas of the
period.[1]

Some of the legal phraseology is more than a technical overlay,
since it forms an integral part of the poet's rhetoric and has its
structural importance. The abundant binary phrases of the sort
which I have called 'inclusive pairs' reflect a habit of mind –
widespread and not.confined to medieval Spain – according to
which abstractions are made more concrete and generalities are
expressed by contrasting polarities (on this and what follows, see
Smith, 1977b: Chapter 7). Many of these phrases form natural
hemistichs or full lines. They often originate in, or imitate, binary
phrases of Latin, especially that of the law, and may in that
language have had structural importance too, giving rhythmic
and alliterative effects which were by no means disdained in
Latin prose. A good example is 'los grandes e los chicos' (l. 591),
'chicos e grandes' (l. 1990), that is 'everybody – young and old,
the powerful and the weak'. This goes back through such
formulae in the diplomas as 'de majoribus et minoribus' and the
'iuventutem complectitur et senectutem' of the Fuero Juzgo to the
ancient traditions of the Bible ('tam maiores quam minores', 1
Chronicles 24.31) and of Sallust ('nobiles et ignobiles', Catalina,
xx.7). In the same category come other phrases which express,
with other polarities, the idea 'all the people' (or, in the negative,
'nobody') in terms of race and religion ('moros e christianos',
frequent) or sex ('mugieres e varones', 'burgeses e burgesas', ll.
16b–17; 'mugier nin varon', l. 2709; 'nin cativos nin cativas', l. 517)
or rank ('A cavalleros e a peones', l. 848; also l. 807), etc. In the
Poema and other early texts a wide variety of similar phrases,
many of them with a tradition in the language of the law, is to be
found, amounting to a virtually complete range covering 'all
places', 'at all times', 'all the property', and so on. A different

kind of analysis would throw into relief the structural importance of this phraseology, some pairs being restricted to first hemistichs, others to second hemistichs because they provided easy rhymes, others being extensible to the full line. It is indeed a structural consideration which led to the 'moros' being regularly placed before the 'christianos', since rhythm and rhyme imposed this order. Once Per Abad had established this usage in the vernacular, the phrase – nearly always in this fixed form – became a cliché in later composition. A full study of this aspect brings to light many ramifications and emphasises the length of the tradition within literary and legal Latin. The habit of this phraseology which the poet had acquired as part of his lawyer's *parole* was reinforced, however, by the literary example of French, since such binary phrases (sometimes precisely equivalent to Per Abad's) abound in the *chansons de geste*. There they seem to have been adopted not directly from the language of the law but from the rhetoric of still older vernacular texts, since they abound, for example, in the *Vie de Saint Alexis*. Sometimes a pair-phrase in a particular context of the *Poema* may turn out to have a precise model in a French text, as Hook shows for the 'burgeses e burgesas' of line 17.[2] In a few cases Per Abad's direct dependence upon the tradition of legal language in Spain is clear, since the phrases seem to have no parallel in French epic: such are 'en yermo o en poblado' (l. 390) and 'las exidas e las entradas' (ll. 1163, 1572) (Smith, 1977*b*: 194–8).

Some pair-phrases seem to correspond to social formulae and the courtesies of ceremony (in which the poet may be assumed to have been a participant or at least an observer) rather than to legal usage in the strict sense. Examples are the address to the King 'commo a rey e a señor' (l. 2109), and the reference to the second marriages of the girls 'a ondra e a bendiçion' (l. 3400), in both of which set formulae have evolved from an earlier double reality. The poet's sense of ceremonial propriety leads him to mention hand-kissing in a variety of circumstances, and he would have known that Latin texts gave precedent for recording the act.[3]

Religious attitudes of the poet, and those attributed to the hero, have been discussed in Chapter 3. The phraseology of devotion, prayer, thanksgiving, and much else may be assumed to have been a natural part of the poet's *parole*, adapted to the verse medium. Local factors are borne in mind by the poet in mentions of the Virgin, to whom the Cathedral of Burgos is dedicated (as was, later, that of Valencia), in Jimena's prayer to St Peter, patron of Cardeña, and in the thanks which Alfonso offers both to God and to St Isidore, patron of León. A few phrases of religious import have precedents in French epic, just as the dream in which the Archangel visits the Cid was imitated by the poet from the *Roland*; but the poet's practice in this regard is largely independent.[4]

Other elements of vocabulary and phrasing – on the whole neglected by critics – cause us further to extend the concept of the poet's *parole*. These are elements which he had learned over the years as a cultivated and attentive layman from the Bible and the liturgy and general Latin usage of the Church. The word 'virtos' in the sense 'army, forces' (ll. 657, 1498, 1625) is a latinism, drawn from the Bible or from the *Chronica Adefonsi Imperatoris*, which in turn depended on biblical precedent (Smith, 1977b: 95, adding an example from the *Poema de Almeria*, l. 85). In an important but little-used study, Terlingen explained the poet's habit of reckoning certain times of day by reference to the *gallos* as derived from monastic usage, specifically the office of the *gallicantum* or *gallicinium* which preceded matins. Thus 'cantar los gallos' is used three times with reference to Cardeña (ll. 209 and 316, spoken by the Cid; l. 235, in narrative), and once outside any liturgical context but, Terlingen thinks, by extension of it (l. 169, spoken by Martín Antolínez). There is also the phrase 'a los mediados gallos' (ll. 324, 1701) signifying 'midway between the Night Office and *gallicantum*', perhaps about 3 a.m. That the poet, as a learned layman, could have picked up such usage – presumably from the vernacular of Cardeña monks – is demonstrated by the fact that he puts it into the mouth of lay persons (the Cid and Martín Antolínez), and does not confine it to the narrative voice. Moreover, the poet expects the phrases to be understood by his public, and later vernacular texts bear him out. Half-learned words such as 'miraclos' (l. 344; read by Michael as 'miraculos', since the *l* bears a possible mark of abbreviation), 'sinava' (l. 411), and 'sieglo' (ll. 1295, 1445, 3726, with a special sense developed from Latin *saeculum* by the Church) show similar progress from learned origin towards general currency.

The greatest concentration of latinisms is naturally in Jimena's prayer. Attention is drawn to them in Russell's recent study, against the tendency of so many to pass in silence over a feature that defies explanation in oralist or traditionalist terms. Some of

the latinisms could have come either from the Bible or from
Comestor, for they are present in both (e.g. 'adorar', 'glorificar',
'laudare', 'monumento'). Others, such as 'encarnaçion', were in
the tradition of the Church Fathers (in whose writings *incarnatio*
first appears). While the notion that 'Susanna' (l. 342) of the Old
Testament was 'Santa' is obviously non-biblical and is not found
in Comestor, and probably reached the poet from a French epic,[5]
the word for 'slander' used in connection with her, 'falso
criminal', seems to represent the standard Roman-law term
crimen falsi rather than to echo the 'falsum testimonium' used in
the story of Susanna in the Book of Daniel (three times) and by
Comestor. 'Vocaçion' (l. 1669) is a further instance of the
adoption of a learned form from the Church, in a specifically
ecclesiastical gloss of some importance; 'vigilia' (l. 3049) is
another.[6] In the same category may be placed the seven examples
of a vernacular version of the Latin 'ablative absolute' construction (ll. 147, 213, 320, 366, 1308, 1703, 3678), an extraordinary
feature – especially in direct speech, as in two instances – on
which most critics have not cared to comment. This could have
been adopted by the poet from his general knowledge of Latin,
but one or two examples may have specific sources.[7]

The poet's *parole* included also a number of French and
Provençal words. They are scattered in his text and in some
instances repeated, being used as a natural part of the lexis. This
aspect is, again, not adequately studied as yet. Among such
words are 'ardido', 'ardiment', 'barnax', 'cosiment', 'gentil',
'mensaje', 'solaz', '(h)usaje', and 'vergel'. One cannot say
whether they were present in the poet's language because they
were already current in parts of northern Spain as a result of the
influx of trans-Pyrenean pilgrims, merchants, soldiers, and
settlers (including those of the *barrio de francos* of Burgos itself),[8]
or whether the poet had assimilated them when travelling or
studying in some area of French or Provençal speech, as
conjectured earlier. Some of the words seem to belong to literary
style rather than to everyday usage, such as 'barnax' and 'vergel'.
All were evidently expected to be intelligible to the audience of
the poem.

The poet's natural *parole*, however rich in such special features
as those analysed above, would still not have sufficed for him to
compose the *Poema*. As I tried to show earlier, he probably had no
full-scale epic work or literary language in the vernaculars of

Spain to guide him in his experiment, and he had to forge for himself the rhetoric he needed. That his metrical system depended in some way on that or those of French has been argued in Chapter 4, and his adaptation of episodes, and adoption of hints for episodes, from that source has been demonstrated in Chapter 5. For metrical patterns and for episodes, sources and models in French texts have been adduced. When we investigate the way in which the poet created his rhetoric, we cannot usually – in the nature of the case – be so specific, and the perils of trying to do so have rightly been pointed out to me. A great deal of the poet's rhetoric is adapted from that of French epic, or takes up in new ways suggestions offered by that epic, and in recent comparative studies large numbers of French texts have been gathered in order that a comprehensive range of possibilities should be made available for study. In my view this corpus should be limited by several considerations. It should include only those French poems which can be shown with some confidence to pre-date 1200, thus being notionally available to the Spanish poet. It could usefully be limited to those texts which we know, from survival of MSS or wealth of references at the time, enjoyed a certain circulation (although losses, such as that of the original of *Berte aus grans piés*, have to be borne in mind too). If it can be shown, as in my Chapter 5 and in the work of others, that the Spanish poet drew upon specific French texts for episodes and suggestions, it is obviously likely that he learned his rhetoric also in those texts. What remains still makes a large corpus, which would allow us (as oralist critics prefer) to consider this rhetoric on generic terms. I have allowed for this concept of the 'generic' above (Chapter 4, notes 9 and 11), but should say here that the concept is hardly valid. Per Abad did not know an undifferentiated 'genus', but a series of perfectly specific texts, perhaps both from reading and from hearing them, and if we fall back on the notion of the 'genus' it is only because in the uncertain state of our knowledge (and these investigations are still very new) we do not know precisely from which specific texts Per Abad took his materials or how he combined and further adapted these. It is also, of course, true that since so many French epic texts are of somewhat unsure date, and since so few texts survive for us in the form in which they might have been known to Per Abad, the 'state of our knowledge' will never reach total certainties; but that it will steadily improve is shown by scholars who have, in recent publications, corrected and refined conclusions reached by others (including myself) earlier.

That the style of French epic should be imitated by the first man to write an epic in a related Romance language, Castilian, seems on all grounds logical. De Chasca and most other oralists, believing that the *Poema* represents no more than a first written record of an age-old native Spanish oral tradition, do not seem to consider this possibility despite the ease with which similarities between the style of the Spanish poem and that of French poems can be demonstrated, and even when one noted oralist, Duggan, has studied both in invaluable contributions. Work of Herslund (1974) and of Adams (1978–9, and 1980) now provides a mass of comparative material on which I shall rely, even though it is clear that in using it I am perverting its oralist intentions.

That the style of the *Poema* is to a considerable extent formulaic is obvious. I do not wish to propose a definition of a 'formula' beyond that which de Chasca and others have suggested, and I think the concept tolerably precise already. Nor do I wish to define that 'considerable extent' over which the oralists have agonised as, seized with statisticosis and the urge to be scientific, they have nourished their computers with data. The one statement I must make is that formulaic composition by no means guarantees that a text was orally improvised, for formulaic systems are just as useful to a poet in a written medium, and natural enough to a poet who was closely acquainted with the formulaic character of legal documents, as argued earlier. Certainly, if the poem was to be memorised and recited to an audience, the ease with which duly rhyming formulae could be produced would be a comfort to a forgetful presenter; but one has known cases of actors who, in a momentary lapse, could improvise passably Shakespearian blank verse. Beyond that it does not seem necessary to make concessions to the oralists. Other features which they adduce are undeniably part of Per Abad's system: parataxis, the absence of enjambement, composition by motif (a small descriptive unit) and by theme (a recurrent episode, built up from motifs, of the kind furnished by battles, journeys, meetings, gifts, prayers, etc.). The oralists' analysis of these features is often useful, and it would be churlish not to adopt their terminology.

The course of the debate on the indebtedness of the *Poema* to French example has been outlined already. It is proper to add a

word about it here concerning the contribution of von Richthofen, in a number of studies conducted with a thoroughly
independent criterion.[9] It is Herslund's extensive analysis which,
to my mind, puts the question of the debt beyond doubt:

Après examen, il paraît que la rhétorique du jongleur, auteur du *Cid* . . .
est la même que celle qu'on trouve dans la chanson de geste. Et la
conclusion à en tirer . . . est que le jongleur espagnol (ou plutôt ses
devanciers espagnols . . .) a *appris son métier* par des jongleurs français.
Son métier, ce sont essentiellement les schèmes abstraits dont je viens de
parler, seulement adaptés à une langue étrangère avec des conséquences
importantes pour le vocabulaire, et pour la versification. Il ne s'agit pas
de trouver des formules traduites en espagnol, mais seulement de
montrer que là même où il ne se trouve pas de modèle immédiat dans
l'épopée française, l'architecture des expressions du poème espagnol a
son parallèle exact dans les chansons françaises. Evidemment, le *Cantar
de mio Cid* n'est pas une traduction, mais une création tout à fait originale
par un poète espagnol qui employait la technique que lui avaient apprise
des jongleurs français (peut-être indirectement, voir ci-dessus).

(1974: 71–2)

Herslund envisages, then, a Spaniard (a *jongleur*, but also,
revealingly, perhaps a *poète*) who learned his craft by listening to
French performers, and of course one can by no means dismiss
this possibility. To accept it, one does not have to follow the
standard oralist belief that all, teachers and learners, were
illiterate. Herslund's belief in possible Spanish *devanciers* need
not be retained in the same way.[10]

   Herslund's analysis is organised in six sections. Reference has
already been made to his second, on laisse structures, and to his
sixth, on lexical items. His first section concerns the performer's
relations with his audience, ranging from the exclamatory
'Afevos . . .' (l. 262, etc.) = French 'as vos . . . ', 'Ez vos . . .',
through 'veriedes . . .' (l. 726, etc.) = 'La veïssez . . .', 'commo
odredes contar' (l. 684) = 'com vos orrez', to the full-line narrative
formula 'dexare vos las posadas, non las quiero contar' (l.
1310) = 'De lor jornees ne sai que vos contasse' of the *Couronnement de Louis* (four times). The third section studies the motifs
which build up into themes: general descriptions of battle; the
attack with the lance; sword-blows; knights under arms; journeys; joy and grief, a sub-section which continues none too
logically into matters of praying, arming, the assembly of troops,
descriptions of wealth and horses, and the priest's address before
battle. Section four studies formulae which in most instances do

not build up into motifs and whole themes of the kind analysed earlier: formulae which express hastening ('non lo quiso detardar', l. 1693, = 'ne se volt atargier'), time (nightfall, daybreak, the season), relations of the lord and his vassals or the general and his army, social courtesies, standing up in an assembly, shouting, and finally similes. Within this section Herslund includes a note on binary phrases which, while certainly formulaic and a part of the poet's rhetoric, I isolated above for separate discussion. His fifth section concerns 'Les syntagmes', taken to include epithets for persons, cities, countries, horses, weapons, etc.

This summary does little justice to the amount of material convincingly assembled by Herslund, nor to the quality of his often very useful comments. Improvements in his demonstration, as he would probably agree, can readily be made by turning to French texts other than those he selected, particularly by going to those poems which we can now see probably served as sources for episodes or provided suggestions for Per Abad's work. Such improvements in the comparisons may also help us to see more clearly what were the poet's working methods.

Herslund's view of the matter should be given priority. In concluding, he discusses as an example line 1826, 'Passando van las sierras   e los montes e las aguas', agreeing with Menéndez Pidal in rejecting line 861 of the *Voyage de Charlemagne*, 'ils passent les païs, les estranges regnez' as a model for it: 'Non, bien sûr, le vers 861 du *Voyage* n'est pas, ne peut pas être le modèle du vers 1826 du *Cid* (comment le serait-il?)' (119). He continues:

Mais il ne s'agit pas de trouver des vers bien délimités, individuels qui soient les modèles d'autres vers d'autres chansons; de telles recherches seraient absurdes, car de tels vers n'existent certainement pas. Ce qui importe, c'est le schème abstrait, sous-jacent à la création épique, l'art du poète épique par lequel il bâtit ses motifs à partir des formules (les hémistiches), l'art de construire une chanson par ces motifs, *sans l'aide de l'écriture*. Le poète du *Cid*, version conservée, n'a pas emprunté quelques vers ça et là dans quelques chansons françaises (et cela serait la 'imitación superficial' dont parle Menéndez Pidal dans son édition du poème), il en a appris la technique.   (119–20)

If, in accordance with my whole approach, we discard the words 'sans l'aide de l'écriture' (italicised by Herslund), we can readily agree: Per Abad, as he began to write, had his head full of that 'schème abstrait', patterns, hemistichs, lines containing standard motifs. He did not consciously translate, but allowed Spanish half-lines and lines to form themselves and come to his pen as a result of auditions and private reading of French epics, which had instilled their patterns into him. A good deal of Per Abad's formulaic style was formed in this way, and I have no doubt that *in part* the process was that sketched by Herslund with line 1826 as an example.

Yet the matter goes, in many instances, beyond this acceptable notion of a 'schème abstrait', for it is possible to indicate formulae and half-lines in the *Poema* which imitate perfectly specific French half-lines or lines, in texts moreover which we can show on other grounds were probably known to the Spaniard. These are 'vers bien délimités, individuels', and it is hard to see why Herslund should think there is anything 'absurd' about a quest for them. I do not propose to review the whole of Herslund's evidence and add refinements; this would be pointless, and a few examples must suffice.

As parallels for the line 'Fablava mio Çid   commo odredes contar' (l. 684) Herslund cites 'com voz orrez' from the *Couronnement* (ll. 313, 1377, etc.), and from *Raoul* (l. 1134), in all cases first hemistichs, and plainly this is sufficient within Herslund's idea of the 'schème abstrait', since a French first-hemistich cliché has been transferred to a Spanish second hemistich, and Spanish adds 'contar'. But a more direct equivalent can be produced, one already used in a metrical demonstration in Chapter 4. In one of the texts studied by Herslund, *Raoul*, one finds 'c'est Herchanbaus, si l'ai oït conter' (l. 6381), of which Per Abad's line, 'aqueste era el rey Bucar,   sil oyestes contar' (l. 2314) is surely a direct echo. A similar case involves 'sabet', 'sepades', no more than a single-word formula, but one which seems to have a specific model in *Raoul* (as indicated in Chapter 4) because of the structure of the lines in which it occurs. It is proper to note that Herslund, after citing marginally relevant examples of 'sachiez' etc. in *Amis* and *Floovant*, had remarked justly that 'Sans doute, on le trouverait aussi dans d'autres chansons de geste', which, with *Raoul* in view, turns out to be so. One is concerned with the precision of the echo rather than with any quantity. At times the problem is complicated by the fact that Per Abad was echoing and combining more than one French text. In earlier work (and above) I suggested that the line '¡Firid los, cavalleros,   todos sines dubdança!' (l. 597) imitated two lines of *Girart de Roussillon* (ll. 1287, 1300), which share a first hemistich 'Firaz les, chevaler', and in another paper, that a closer parallel was offered by a line in

Raoul because the second hemistich of this conveys the same sense as that of the Spanish line, 'Ferez, baron, n'alez mais atargant!' (l. 2758). Yet the 'chevaler' of *Girart* as well as the second hemistich of *Raoul* are equally relevant. There is more to it than this, however, because Per Abad used this spirited cry again in another battle description:

> A grandes vozes lama   el que en buen ora na[çi]o:
> '¡Ferid los, cavalleros,   por amor de caridad!
> ¡Yo so Roy Diaz el Çid   Campeador de Bivar!'
>
> (ll. 719–21; again, 1138–40)

The new element here is the crying of the hero's place of origin as an encouragement to his men, for which there were precedents in *Raoul*: 'Mort le trebuche, "Cambrai!" va escriant' (l. 2699), '"Cambrai!" escrie, hautement, en oiant' (l. 2757), and, most pertinently of all, this cry associated with the formulaic 'Charge them, men!' in the line ' "Cambrai!" escrie, "ferez i chevalier!" ' (l. 2733). Of this I would conclude, provisionally, that Per Abad was combining elements from both *Girart* and from *Raoul*, and echoing specific texts even when combining the results, in a process which is still far from that proposed by Herslund in his 'schème abstrait'. That word 'provisionally' implies that some yet closer source for the poet's usage might yet appear.

Herslund's section 3.1, 'Description de la bataille', and the more detailed ones that follow, 3.2, 'Attaque à la lance', and 3.3, 'Coup d'épée', usefully assemble materials already analysed in part by Bello, Hinard, Milá, von Richthofen, etc., and within French, by Rychner and others. The sequence of motifs tends to be the same in all texts, and many half-line formulae can be readily identified: 'C'est peut-être ici que les ressemblances sautent le plus aux yeux: le schème rhétorique, sous-jacent à la création poétique, semble bien être le même pour le jongleur espagnol et ses collègues français' (88). The clear impression one has is that Per Abad knew in detail some French epics and, in spirited and convincing fashion, adapted the rhetoric of their battle-scenes to this work. His battles remain exclusively *literary*, on the consecrated model of French, and – except in the account of the defeat of the Count of Barcelona – have in them no element from the historical reality of battles as they would have been observed on Spanish soil. I have already noted the poet's unwillingness to describe in any detail what might have been the high moment of the siege of Valencia. He had no precedent in

French epics known to him for such a description, and does not mention the siege-towers and other standard equipment which the Cid of history must have had (the *Historia Roderici* mentions the *machinamenta* which the Cid used in the siege of Murviedro, 964.9).[11] Similarly, in pitched battles, the archers, spearmen, and slingers used in the time of the Cid and throughout the twelfth century do not appear, having no literary precedent in French as known to the poet. As in French, the actions of knights viewed as individuals – hero and captains – armed with sword and lance, together with many details about the horses, armour, and the blows struck, are alone sufficient. In this respect the poet's *verismo* is much modified, even suspended. A wholly unrealistic detail may, because of Latin and French authority, find its way impressively into the text of the otherwise rational and moderate *Poema*. The Cid cleaves Búcar from helm to waist (l. 2424; earlier, l. 751), imitating a blow first struck in the *Fragment of The Hague*, repeated in the *Roland* and the *Historia Turpini*, and often mentioned in later French poems. The striking of jewels from the helmet of an adversary is another example of a purely literary imitation (*Poema*, ll. 766, 2422; *Roland*, l. 1326, and many other instances).

Within the general imitation of a French theme and its constituent motifs, such as that of battle, one can sometimes distinguish an item which is likely, because of textual similarity, to have had a source in a specific poem. The line 'veriedes . . ./tantas cabeças con yelmos   que por el campo caen' (l. 2405) surely echoes that of *Girart de Roussillon*, 'Viraz . . ./Tante teste ob elme caoir ensens!' (l. 2522). This poem was, on other grounds, probably known to the Spaniard. Further, despite the similarity of the *Poema*'s battle-scenes to many in French, a similarity which justifies Herslund's idea of the 'schème abstrait', I have the impression that one battle in a French text provides the closest parallel in general structure and in many details and formulae: that in *Parise la duchesse* (again, a work very probably known, in other respects, to the poet), lines 1924 ff.

Further work on other aspects may show up conclusions of importance. There can be no doubt that the phraseology of the itinerary theme, studied by Herslund and others, and by Russell (1978: 189–94), is imitated from French. The places mentioned by the poet are in logical sequence, and Per Abad's means of knowing of them have been mentioned above, but nothing said by the poet to have happened at them need have done so in history. The itineraries, like the battles, are yet another bookish element in a work of the imagination, in a poem made largely from other poems and literary texts.

In taking so much from the French formulaic system, Per Abad retained his critical faculty. There are many clichés in French which he did not adopt, either because he had no need of them, or because they struck him as superfluous and inappropriate. Such, illustrated from *Raoul* but common to many texts, are: 'ne vos mentirai ja' (l. 2420), 'a celer nel vous quier' (l. 1347); 'Tout a vostre commant' (l. 3259); 'destriers d'Orqenie' (l. 2364); 'Au vis cler' (l. 115), 'a la clere façon' (l. 962); 'le sens quida changier' (l. 2617); 'Par cele foi qe je doi S. Denis' (l. 2643), 'Por Dieu te pri qi en la crois fu mis' (l. 2651); 'N'ot plus bel hom de ci q'en Oriant' (l. 2687); and many others. Even in this group, however, it might be argued that some French formulae have correspondences (but not echoes) in Spanish, since to 'Tout a vostre commant', a regular second-hemistich formula of assent, there corresponds in the *Poema* the direct-speech second hemistich 'D'amor e de voluntad!' (l. 1692; with variations in ll. 1282, 1698, etc., and perhaps also in ll. 1390, 1447, 1487, 2227, etc.). Equally, to 'N'ot plus bel hom de ci q'en Oriant' there correspond both Alfonso's eulogy of the Cid, 'juro . . . / que en todas nuestras tierras   non ha tan buen varon!' (l. 3510), and the Cid's praise of his horse, 'en moros ni en christianos   otro tal non ha oy' (l. 3514, this perhaps an echo of 'I. des mellors que l'an poïst trover / N'en paienime n'en la crestiënté, *Prise de Cordres*, ll. 561–2).

The epic epithets of the *Poema*, together with related appositional phrases, laudatory formulae of address, and so on, are a special part of the formulaic system, and have been much studied. Many epithets owe both their form and the manner of their usage to French examples, as shown by Herslund and others, but it has been demonstrated in one notable study that the poet's practice in handling epithets for persons was thoughtful and sensitive and in no way automatic (Hamilton, 1962; also Hathaway, 1974). These epithets, remote from the usages of daily speech, are essential in producing the authentic epic resonance. The same may be said of the poet's epithets for cities, those relating to Valencia having a fine evocative quality.[12] Among epithets for persons, those of astrological import attached to the hero are frequent second-hemistich formulae: 'el que en buen ora çinxo espada' (l. 58), 'el que en buen ora fue nado' (l. 507), the latter with variants for different rhymes. Both have a wide range of grammatical functions, including the exclamatory and laudatory in direct address, and as periphrases. Herslund (112) excluded them from his analysis, dubbing them 'honorifiques' and remarking on their abundance, the exclusion being caused, presumably, by the absence of analogues in the French texts he had in view. They are certainly original creations of Per Abad, though perhaps ultimately depending on such French clichés as 'buer soit de l'ore que tu fus honques né[s]!' (Prise de Cordres, l. 1688; also ll. 185, 2133), 'Benéoite soit l'oure que il fu engenrez!' (Parise, l. 681). Both French poems seem on other grounds likely to have been known to Per Abad. It is noticeable that the exclamatory form of phrases in the Poema is closest to their form in French, and that on their first appearance in the Poema, both are exclamatory (ll. 41, 71); it may be that after first using them in the French way as an experiment, the poet was pleased enough with the results to extend them afterwards to other functions, eventually, as his confidence grew, going well beyond any precedent in French.

One epic epithet was almost certainly adopted by the poet from a Latin source. In the Poema de Almeria Count Poncio is described as 'nobilis hasta', an appositional phrase which ends line 163. Of Alvar Fáñez the poem says that 'nullaque sub coelo melior fuit hasta sereno' (l. 219). Per Abad imitates the synecdoche and in part the appositional function, applying the phrase 'ardida lança' in formulaic second hemistichs to Martín Antolínez (l. 79), Galín Garcíez (l. 443b), and Alvar Fáñez (l. 489). Presumably his attention was first caught by the phrase in Almeria applied to Alvar Fáñez, but the other phrase applied to Count Poncio is structurally closer to his vernacular version of it. [13] The other laudatory phrase applied to Alvar Fáñez in direct address by the Cid, each time as a complete second hemistich, is 'vos sodes el mio diestro braço!' (l. 753; also l. 810, and varied for a different rhyme in l. 3063). This is plainly imitated from line 597 of the Roland 'O', in which, in narrative, Roland is 'le destre braz del cors' of the Emperor (again, l. 1195). Herslund seems not to mention this, but Horrent, in general reluctant to recognise such dependence, accepts it as a borrowing from French (1973: 371–2, adding a comment on the reason why Pidal rejected the idea of an imitation). Per Abad perhaps wished to do more than fill a line with a vivid metaphor. The phrase is reserved for Alvar Fáñez, is repeated, and as Horrent says, is applied to the man who bore the same nephew–uncle relation to the hero as Roland had to Charlemagne, a very special one in epic. One might go further and suggest that here, as perhaps in other instances, Per Abad was deliberately hoping to awaken, in the few members of his public who could be expected to know, a memory of the great French poem together with thoughts of the equivalence of the Cid in some respects to Charlemagne.

The enumeration of captains in strongly formulaic terms in a variety of contexts, the 'dénombrement épique', is another feature which Per Abad in all likelihood imitated from French epic, specifically from the *Roland*, in which it is frequent.[14] The enumeration occurs first in the middle of the battle outside Alcocer (ll. 735–41), is repeated in the description of the host which accompanies the Cid to his meeting with the King (ll. 1991–6), and is used again as the Cid names those who are to go with him into the Toledan court. This feature is not listed by Herslund.

Herslund's comparative work has been followed up on syntactical and grammatical aspects by Adams, also basing himself on oralist principles, in two important recent papers. In the first, answering a brief and inadequate suggestion of mine, Adams shows that the varied use of *pensar de* + infinitive is a calque on the widespread periphrastic and possibly line-filling use of *penser de* + infinitive in French epic. As an oralist, Adams naturally assumes that Per Abad did not invent his rhetoric but simply adopted what was already current in a long-established Spanish epic genre, the latter having adopted features generically from French. However, since Adams cannot deny some learned features in the *Poema*, he concludes in terms of a compromise:

I am aware that Smith believes in a considerable degree of specific line-for-line borrowing in the *Poema* – and it is hard to dispute the direct learnedness of some of his (and R. M. Walker's) sources – but the general utilisation of devices such as *pensar de* in its various structures also suggests that cultured intervention could be a late layer on an earlier formulaic model.   (1978–9: 11)

In his other paper, Adams shows conclusively that the *Poema*'s use of the historic present is similarly a calque on the very general usage of French epic. In its dimensions, the feature is an important one: 'I find some 675 cases of such usage in the *Poema*: since there are very few instances of two occurrences in the same verse, this means that about eighteen per cent of all lines contain the feature, and a considerably larger proportion of the purely narrative sections contain it' (1980: 781). Spanish usage often echoes French precisely in respect of the verbs used, the contextual phrasing, grammatical inversions, and so on: 'The historic present and associated usages are not only fundamental features of the diction of the *Poema* but . . . provide us with one of the most blatant imitations of the *chansons de geste*' (796). Adams uses materials from some thirty French poems, including some which, I think, are known to have been composed after 1200, and many of which cannot be shown on other grounds to have been probably known to the Spanish poet. In his introductory remarks Adams justifies this as a working method: 'The large selection of French examples suggests a generic rather than specific source for *Poema de mio Cid* usage, since so many of the verbs appear in most or all of the poems' (783). Clearly, Adams is on strong ground here, but I would still hold, bearing my earlier definition in mind, that Per Abad could not borrow anything 'generically', but did so in several, perhaps many, specific texts; but in this instance – the use of the historic present – we have no means of identifying these, in the nature of the case.

Somewhere between the formulaic elements discussed up to this point and the items treated in Chapter 5, there comes a mass of materials which are less easy to categorise. At their simplest they involve a single line or detail for which the poet received a hint from a text in Latin or French, as when the duration of the siege of Valencia by the Cid is said, unhistorically, to have been ten months (ll. 1209–10), this being the duration of a major heroic siege *en règle* as indicated by accounts of Charlemagne's siege of Pavia, mentioned in various Carolingian annals (Smith, 1977b: 149–50). When the suggestion has come to the poet from Latin it is not to be expected that there should be precise verbal equivalence. The prose of the *Chronica Adefonsi Imperatoris*, 'et vidit quia nullo modo poterat ire in terram suam sine bello' (13), was transformed by the poet into:

> Essora lo connosçe mio Çid el de Bivar
> que a menos de batalla nos pueden den quitar   (ll. 983–4)

while in the same text 'Domus autem regis Aragonensis, semper erat decrescens; domus regis Legionis, gratias Deo, de die in diem semper augebatur' (19; in turn based on a biblical sentence, 2 Samuel 3.1) was neatly abbreviated as:

> la conpaña del Çid creçe e la del rey mengo   (l. 2165)

and another phrase from this *Chronica*, 'non remanserunt ex eis nisi pauci, qui fugerunt pedibus equorum' suggested to the poet his vivid line:

de pies de cavallo los ques pudieron escapar   (l. 1151)

Sometimes the poet seems to have gone through a slightly more complicated process. He had observed that several times, in patriarchal pensiveness, 'Li empereres en tint sun chef enclin' in the *Roland* (l. 139, etc.). It was proper that both Alfonso and the Cid should do the same in his own work, but not in a line which directly echoes the French. The closer parallel was provided by the *Chronica Adefonsi Imperatoris*, which says of its imperial subject 'Imperator, hoc audiens, considerabat dicta eorum et fere dimidia ora tacitus, respondit . . .' (146). The poet made his own full-line formula from this:

Una grant ora el rey pensso e comidio
(l. 1889; also ll. 1932, 2828, 2953).

Similarly formulaic, or potentially so, is the relatively unimportant second hemistich 'e quantos con el son' (l. 2428), 'e a quantos aqui son' (l. 2561), a version of what was already formulaic in Latin prose: there is 'omnes qui cum eo erant' in the *Chronica Adefonsi Imperatoris* (155, and often elsewhere), 'omnes qui cum illo erant' in the *Historia Roderici*, 935.21, and behind these lie biblical precedents. Even so seemingly minor a matter, noted in West's thesis (446–7: e.g. 1 Kings 30.4, 2 Kings 1.11, 2.32), may be significant in the study of the poet's stylistic formation. His half-line 'assi parientes commo son' (l. 2988) seems to be a variant of his own devising, keeping the same rhyme.

A number of motifs, or in the older terminology 'topics', *topoi*, seem to have been imitated by the poet from the twelfth-century Hispano-Latin texts, and have a useful effect in dignifying the epic narration. They include consultation, the secret taking of counsel, proclamations, pitching camp, two topics connected with sieges, booty and captives, the joyful reception of a leader into a city, and what one might call the formal or diplomatic smile which precedes a meeting or introduces a discourse (Smith, 1971b: 14–17). The poet's phraseology in these items does not usually echo that of the Latin prose, but it occasionally does so. In the *Chronica Adefonsi Imperatoris* (32) there is an account of an expedition of Alfonso VII into Andalusia: 'ex altera parte dimiserunt Cordubam et Carmonam a sinistra, Sibiliam vero, quam antiqui vocabant Hispalim, relinquentes a dextera'. The poet adapted this for his account of the Infantes' journey towards Corpes:

> a ssiniestro dexan a Griza   que Alamos poblo
> – alli son caños do a Elpha ençerro –
> a diestro dexan a Sant Estevan,   mas cae aluen   (ll. 2694–6)

in which it is noticeable that even the asides correspond (though the Latin gives no hint of what the poet may have intended in his mysterious line 2695). Some of these topics naturally have models also in French epic, but here the poet may have found that Latin texts written in and about his own country provided a better guide. In some cases there must be doubt whether Per Abad was following suggestions from the *Chronica Adefonsi Imperatoris*, which is heavily indebted to biblical phraseology, or used the Bible itself. For example, his lines about the Cid's siege of Valencia:

> bien la çerca mio Çid,   que non i avia hart,
> viedales exir e viedales entrar   (ll. 1204–5)

echo precisely words of the *Chronica*: 'Et circumdedit rex castellum in circuito muro magno et vallo, ita ut nullus poterat ingredi vel egredi' (24; also 107, 117), or, a little less precisely, those of the *Historia Roderici*, 'atque eisdem egressum a castello et ingressum ad castellum omnino prohibuit' (964.11). Behind both there lie such biblical models as 'muro circumdabat Rama, ut nullus posset egredi et ingredi de regno Asa' (2 Chronicles 16.1), 'Qui autem erant in arce Ierusalem, prohibebantur egredi et ingredi regionem' (1 Maccabees 13.49). While the poet's use of verbs – *exir, entrar* – is closer to that of the *Chronica* and the Bible, he may have been attracted to the topic because in the *Historia Roderici* it is used of the Cid in the description of the siege of Murviedro, and, as shown in Chapter 5, he used other details from that in his work. Even when biblical precedents, including quite close ones, can be adduced for the poet's usage, I still think it likelier that he depended more immediately upon the topics and phraseology of such works as the *Chronica Adefonsi Imperatoris* and the *Historia Roderici*, simply because the latter were closer to him in time, were of Hispanic origin and dealt with persons and events of the Peninsula, and, of course, in the case of the *Historia*, because this was a direct source of information about his hero. However, as with details of the gifts of the Magi which might have been taken from Matthew's Gospel or from Comestor, the poet's source cannot absolutely be determined. The same may now be said of the usage 'o dizen Castejon' (l. 435, and other instances), which was attributed above to the recurrent phrase of the legal diplomas of the poet's day and profession, 'ubi vocitant Villanova', etc. This is also common usage of the twelfth-century Latin texts, e.g. 'in loco quod dicitur Vallis Tamaris' (*Chronica Adefonsi Imperatoris*, 12), and beyond that, of the Bible, e.g. 'in civitate quae vocatur Nazareth' (Matthew 2.23).[15] A variant of the siege-topic cliché in which verbal *exir/entrar* is stated by nouns is used by the poet in lines 1163 and 1572, 'las exidas e las entradas', whose immediate model lay, as mentioned earlier, in the frequent phrase of the legal diplomas by which the totality of a property was designated as 'con entrada e con exida', first documented in Romance at Burgos in 1197 (Pattison, 1967: 449); but this followed a long tradition of use in the legal Latin of Spain and elsewhere which seems to go back ultimately to biblical 'egredi et ingredi'.

Similar materials, that is, lying roughly between the episodic and the formulaic, were taken in quantity by the poet from French. Scholars had centred their study of this chiefly upon the *Roland*, and their findings were reviewed by Horrent who in almost all instances denied any imitation of French by the Spaniard (1973: 343–74). But Horrent wrote at a moment (his original publication was in 1956) when the early date of the *Poema* was maintained and before recent inquiry had begun to reveal the nature and extent of the poet's knowledge of French. I think, therefore, that his conclusions must be rectified throughout, and of course the field is not now restricted to borrowings from the *Roland* but takes in the large number of French epics available to the poet at the later date now ascribed to his work. Space does not allow a recapitulation of all the evidence presented in recent publications, and nothing less than a new edition of the *Poema* with a detailed commentary about sources, suggestions, and adaptations, will do justice to the matter. A few examples must suffice here, in addition to those presented for another purpose in Chapter 4. With regard to the *Roland*, it seems to me that, against Horrent's denial, the line:

¡Dios, que buen vassalo! ¡Si oviesse buen señor!   (l. 20)

is manifestly a calque on that of the *Roland*:

Deus, quel baron, s'oüst chrestïentét!   (l. 3164)

It is true that we cannot be sure how the Spanish line should be construed grammatically and hence punctuated, and it is sure that the poet's thought has nothing to do with that of 'Turoldus' about Baligant. Exactly what Per Abad implied by his line is much debated. But it is plainly a key line in terms of the poet's plot and characterisation, the only line spoken in unison by the people of Burgos, and Per Abad took an equally impressive French line as a model, structurally, for his. A more complicated relation (one also rejected by Horrent) is to be discerned in:

los montes son altos, las ramas pujan con las nues   (l. 2698)

in which a setting full of potential menace is created as the Infantes' party enters the oak-forest of Corpes. This is another key line, within one of the poet's finest passages. He had probably been impressed – as who would not be? – by lines of the *Roland* in which the dark menace of the Pyrenean defiles is expressed:

Halt sunt li pui, e li val tenebrus   (l. 814)

Halt sunt li pui e mult halt les arbres   (l. 2271)

but of more immediate concern to him contextually was the line from *Florence* adduced earlier, 'La forest fu parfonde, li bois haus et foilluz' (l. 3776; also 4019), for this – even if itself ultimately dependent on the lines of *Roland* – concerned the forest setting of the outrage on Florence from which he probably took elements for his Corpes scene. A similar process of contextual suggestion must be envisaged for the poet's lines 1087–93, in which the Cid's conquests are listed at the start of Cantar II. This passage, almost a *topos*, was probably suggested by Roland's brief listing of his conquests (ll. 197–200). Sometimes, a French line offered Per Abad a detail whose significance he independently expands. When the Count of Barcelona gives up his fast, 'Alegre es el conde e pidio agua a las manos' (l. 1049). This turns out not to have the single source in *Raoul* I suggested earlier, 'L'aigue demande[n]t li chevalier vaillant' (l. 358), since as Hook has shown,[16] the same occurs when knights sit down to meat in several other French epics. What is then notable is that an unemphatic, near-formulaic line in French, applied to 'chevalier vaillant' or their equivalents, is adapted by Per Abad to suggest an extravagantly fastidious action on the part of the starving Count, in harmony with his general portrayal of this personage.

In some instances an element as small as a hemistich or even a single word may be involved. The relative rarity of a word may cause one to suggest a link between Spanish and French lines. It was suggested above that 'vistios el sobregonel' (l. 1587) is a calque on 'vestue ot sa gonnele' of *Raoul*, line 1757; since *sobregonel* is otherwise unrecorded in Spanish and *gonel* or *gonela* is rare, it seems likely that Per Abad borrowed both garment (with the addition of *sobre-*) and phrasing from French. As also indicated above, the 'ofrenda' and other details of lines 3060–2 lead us beyond passages of *Girart de Roussillon* to the 'offrande' and accompanying details of *Amis et Amiles* (ll. 232–5). In the connection which I noted elsewhere between the fine line 'miran la huerta espessa es e grand' (l. 1615) and the equally impressive French line 'Et la forest fu large, espesse et longue et lee (*Florence*, l. 3676), there is nothing more in question than the one word *espessa/espesse*, and the suggestion of a borrowing may seem unwarranted. It does to Deyermond and Hook (1981–2: 28), who say that the word is 'quite commonly encountered in French epic in descriptions of landscapes' and give line-references for five instances in *Girart de Roussillon* and one in *Floovant*. It is a pity that they do not quote the actual lines so that readers could judge the matter: it would then be seen that in *Girart* the word ends a line in each case, and is the penultimate word in *Floovant*, whereas in *Florence* alone 'espesse' impressively begins a second hemistich as in the *Poema* (and is there used to make an agreeable vowel-harmony with 'huerta' (*é-a, é-a*). It is on this structural ground that I would maintain the link with *Florence*. In line 1615 we have no automatic borrowing, nor was Per Abad here merely filling a line with a cliché or convenient word (as he sometimes was), despite the fact that 'longue et lee' was a cliché of French epic and that in the *Poema* a formulaic second hemistich consisting of adjective + 'grand' is found several times (ll. 422, 427, 554, etc., this in turn imitating 'merveillose et grant' of the *Roland*, etc.: Smith, 1977b: 173). As with so much else, what the poet had heard or read in French – and in Latin – entered the storehouse of his memory and imagination and was brought out again, newly polished and full of poetic sense, when he composed, and particularly when the tensions of his drama called forth special emotive effects. It will be realised that, since he had never seen Valencia, the splendid panoramic view of it had to be painted from imaginative and literary elements, without, of course, flying in the face of geographical fact.

I remarked earlier that we could not add, to conjectures about the poet's training in Latin and in the law, a notional education in formal rhetoric, that is in Latin, which he would then have applied in his vernacular composition. That is an informed impression. The contrast with such a self-consciously rhetorical work as the *Libro de Alexandre*, in which the author displays his wares and names them in a proudly erudite fashion, is strong. However extensive and learned were Per Abad's sources for materials and style, he does not wish his public to know of them or to pay him tribute because of them.

However, just as Chiri and Curtius and others have analysed aspects of the rhetoric of the *Roland* in terms of classical and medieval school rhetoric, so a few have attempted to do the same with the *Poema*. Thus, for example, Garci-Gómez, after quoting Dámaso Alonso ('Quien escribía así venía, sin duda, detrás de una larga tradición, de una escuela literaria'), defines his approach: 'En estos estudios me propongo contribuir a examinar y aclarar, precisamente, esa técnica, creyéndola el producto de una preparación cultural, escolástica, retórica' (1975: note 13 to p. 49). Garci-Gómez therefore takes line 7 of the *Poema*, 'Ffablo mio Çid bien e tan mesurado', as a kind of programmatic statement, 'con peculiar función proemial': the poet is telling his public that his work will be composed in a 'lenguaje artístico, guiado por las recomen- daciones de la retórica o *scientia bene dicendi* . . . según la definición tradicional de los manuales del estilo'. Much of Garci-Gómez's book then proceeds on this assumption, and concludes with a long chapter on 'El arte de la amplificación en *Mio Cid*', *amplificatio* embracing, indeed, many fundamental aspects of style as medievals envisaged this. The analysis is expertly and sensitively conducted and much of the poet's style is brought under review in terms of medieval rhetoric. Some items considered by Garci- Gómez to result from the poet's rhetorical training have been dealt with in this book under other headings, for example alliteration, amplification by epithet, and various kinds of binary phraseology. Others not so far considered (and they are many) include periphrasis, litotes, enumeration, anaphora, *interpretatio*, *derivatio*, etc. To them one could notionally add techniques of antithesis and *oppositum*, the use of the *sententia*, *descriptio*, *admiratio*, *comparatio*, and doubtless many others, and for all, excellent examples in Per Abad's lines together with definitions and examples in the manuals of rhetoric can be adduced. But Garci-Gómez's approach seems to me, despite his skilful hand- ling of detail, misconceived. Since rhetorical manuals simply codify the most telling techniques observable in almost any successful composition (with variation according to the tastes of diverse periods and genres), one can rarely be sure how much formal instruction and deliberate self-conscious application of studied rhetoric has gone into any composition, unless an author (such as the *Alexandre*-poet) chooses to declare himself. One can readily analyse a set of nursery-rhymes or instructions on car-maintenance in terms of formal rhetoric, with results which would be hilarious and might rapidly disprove Garci-Gómez's case. The latter is further weakened by the fact that the writer makes no conjectures, as I have ventured to make them earlier, about the poet's cultural background, education, residence outside Spain, and related matters.

Further, I think that to accept Garci-Gómez's case (as would be by no means forced or hard for me to do, given my insistence upon, and demonstration of, Per Abad's learned formation and sources) would be to view the whole composition of the *Poema* as something too technically laboured for it to have any great virtues of human drama, vivid emotion, imagination, and power of words. The *Alexandre* is, after all, a rather dull 'school' poem. Yet Garci-Gómez's evidence is not to be dismissed as irrelevant. The techniques are visibly there. How were they acquired?

My view of the process is that, as the poet read and listened in French and Latin, he simply absorbed rhetorical techniques (without specially identifying them as such) as he did all the other metrical and linguistic and episodic materials I have studied. Moreover – and here we return to the notion of a professional *parole* – many of the techniques were already employed in the Latin of the diplomas and *fueros* among which the poet spent his working life. This may be true of something so seemingly artificial as the *sententia*, 'Qui a buen señor sirve   siempre bive en deliçio' (l. 850), in view of the formulaic opening of a typical royal diploma: 'Regie dignitati conuenit uasallos suos, et eos maxime qui sibi fideliter seruiunt, donationibus suis et dignis retributionibus honorare' (23 July 1167, in González, 1960: ii, 167). But the formative role of rhetorical materials already moulded in literature must have been much greater. A phrase in the *Chronica Adefonsi Imperatoris* or a line in French epic was charged with literary electricity, already impressive, and if in verse it may have had metrical or structural convenience which made its transfer to the poet's own work a simple matter, as has been repeatedly shown. My conception is therefore much closer to that of

Herslund than to that of Garci-Gómez. If we select the phraseology of *admiratio*, wonderment, as an example, this can be easily
illustrated. The Latin term is merely that: a term, a definition, and
one may use it without implying that the poet learned its
technique in any manual. Herslund does not trouble to use the
term, but in his first section he has a useful series of quotations
from French epic (including the *Roland* and *Raoul*) of lines which
begin 'Ki dunc veïst . . . ?', recalled and imitated by Per Abad in
'¿quien vio por Castiella   tanta mula preçiada . . . ?' (l. 1966). In
second hemistichs the poet asks '¿qui los podrie contar?' (l. 699;
also ll. 1214, 1218). This seems to have no direct models in French,
but is perhaps a vernacular version of such phrases as 'Et erat
numerus militum fere triginta milia et peditum et ballistorum non
erat numerus' in the *Chronica Adefonsi Imperatoris* (115), which are
frequent in this text as are its biblical models (e.g. 'Ecce populus
multus, cuius non erat numerus', 1 Maccabees 5.30). The
interrogative form of the Spanish phrase then repeats that of
'¿quien vio . . . ?' or that of other biblical *admiratio* phrases which
have question form. In any case, not all the poet's *admiratio*
expressions have this form, since another group is in plain
narrative, e.g. 'atantos mata de moros   que non fueron contados'
(l. 1723; also ll. 799, 1795, 1983, 2491). One can even catch the
admiratio phraseology of Latin in its first passage into other
vernacular texts roughly of the time of Per Abad: in the Navarrese
Linaje, 'et ovo y XIIII reyes, et la otra gent no avía cuenta' (34), and
in the *Fazienda de ultramar*, 'e l'otra gent non avia cuento' (127). In
another kind of exclamatory *admiratio* involving '¡Dios!' (e.g. ll.
457, 789), the poet has absorbed a simple usage of French epic, as
Herslund has shown. A similar approach could be easily extended to most, perhaps all, of the techniques thought by
Garci-Gómez to result in the *Poema* from the training of its author
in formal school rhetoric.

Hence it may be preferable to refer to the poet's system of
expression as partaking of a sort of 'common rhetoric' of its
period, a concept kept deliberately vague, which I offered a few
years ago (Smith, 1977b: 210–12). It was a rhetoric employed for
many kinds of written text, including the legal and historiographic as well as the literary, and within the latter, common to
both verse and prose. When the first vernacular texts appear in
France and later in Spain, we find it already formed (though still
naturally capable of much development), and conclude that

much of it was simply transferred from Latin when men began to write the vernacular. Within Latin, the tradition was both entirely alive and very ancient, for its elements stretch back through the language of the law (national laws, informed by canon law, the language of papal diplomatic, etc.) and of many literary texts both medieval and classical, to the Vulgate, Sallust, and others of whom a knowledge was never lost, early Roman law, and so on. This tradition in respect of one constituent element, that of binary phraseology, I began (no more) to study some years ago. Its ramifications are impressive, and so hard to disentangle that the notion of a 'common rhetoric' as we find it in the twelfth and thirteenth centuries seems the only safe refuge. The same turned out to be true of the 'physical phrases' ('llorar de los ojos', etc.) which I tried to analyse at the same time. This 'common rhetoric' was simply the basic method of composition of the time, and whatever further learned overlays writers might add to it, from 'school' and other sources, it was absorbed without effort rather than resulting from deliberate study of rhetorical models and manuals, at least in the form in which we find it in the *Poema*. I notice that a similar conclusion is reached in a recent study of rhetoric in the *chansons de geste*.[17] Clearly, a full study along these lines, taking in a wide variety of texts in Latin, French, and Spanish, and perhaps other vernaculars, could be undertaken; but the task would be enormous. What has been said suffices, I hope, for a sane and moderate view to be taken of Per Abad's attitude and practice.

7   'El romanz es leido, dat nos del vino'

So the presenter of the poem to his audience, at some date in the later fourteenth century. He was presumably a professional, for he goes on to ask not only for a draught of wine but also for money. This presenter's explicit is written, in perhaps five short lines of verse, after the author's explicit in lines 3731–3, which conclude the poem proper. The presenter's lines demonstrate that, for whatever purpose the surviving MS of the *Poema* was made, it was used at least a century and a half after the composition of the work for a public reading, probably in or near Burgos (since the MS long survived in Vivar). Moreover, the poet's name was attached to his work still, and was made known at the end of the reading: 'Per Abbat le escrivio . . .' It was recalled still, perhaps, in that 'Cabeça de Per Abat' adjacent to the 'Cabeça del Çid' mentioned in the *Libro de la montería* of roughly similar date. But when, in the early 1950s, a set of statues was erected, in a quite impressive modern-Romanic style, along the principal bridge of Burgos (itself the line of the 'Vía Cidiana'), to represent the hero and his chief associates in history and literature, no place was provided for the poet.[1] Over a century of modern scholarship up to that time had achieved the unthinkable: to make one of Spain's greatest poets, and incontrovertibly one of her earliest, a non-person, a mere wraith dimly perceived in the mists of anonymity and in the marching ranks of the undifferentiated *autor-legión*. More recently, oralist studies will presumably have served to postpone yet again the moment of recognition, when Per Abad (portrayed as fancifully as the Cid, Sisebuto, Martín Antolínez, and the rest, in their present statues, for no-one knows what they looked like) will take his rightful place on the 'Vía Cidiana' of Burgos. He not only wrote the great *Poema*, but initiated the Spanish epic genre, and it is probable that without him there would not have been a cult at Cardeña, the massive presence of the Cid in the vernacular chronicles, much of the later literature, nor the status of national hero which the Cid came to enjoy. One should not, however, spoil a good case by overstating it. As I have made clear, I think the *Poema* an experimental work which never received from its author the final polish it needed, both in metrical forms and in other ways. To consider its defects briefly is to show a little more of the poet's working methods and, I hope, to strengthen my case for its being an experimental work.

On the whole the structure of the *Poema* seems to me masterly: in its tripartite division, in the placing of climaxes, in the rhythm of the fall-rise-fall-rise of the Cid, in the progress of the hero's relationship with the King, in the cunning placement of humorous episodes, even (despite Russell) in its quiet and rather abrupt ending. Moreover, the motivation of personages is both logical and subtle. The mere passage of time might not have persuaded Alfonso to pardon the Cid (even if, in the interests of justice, he had become uneasy about the role of those 'malos mestureros' in securing the banishment): it is the hero's new power after his conquest of Valencia which makes the pardon a necessity of statecraft. The Infantes, too, are first attracted by the notion of marrying the hero's daughters when he has enriched himself by that conquest ('pora huebos de pro', l. 1374), and it is the deep psychological wound of their loss of face in Valencia which leads them to plan the Corpes outrage. But within the structure, one might wish better balance in one respect. The minor but detailed episodes of Castejón and Alcocer outweigh, in prominence, the episode of the taking of Valencia. We can now say what the reason was: that the poet had good classical sources for what he says about the two former places, but only the account of the *Historia Roderici* on which to base his Valencian story, and this text, while strong on politics and diplomacy, does not say much about the siege operations, French epic sources also failing the poet here. On reconsideration, the poet might have found some way of redressing this imbalance, not, I hasten to say, in the interests of historical accuracy (the importance of Valencia), but in those of the structural equilibrium of his literary work. The justification offered by Hook in his 1973 paper is well argued, but I still see a defect here.

Among the narrative lapses of a minor kind to which attention has been drawn, several may be mentioned. In line 1333, Alvar Fáñez reports that the Cid has won 'çinco lides campales' in the Levante, but the poet has narrated only two (see Michael's note to this line in his edition). In line 1681, Alvar Salvadórez is captured by the Moors, but in line 1994 he reappears among the Christian captains although nothing has been said about his release. In lines 1994 and 1996 Alvar Salvadórez and Galín Garcíez are among those named as members of the host which is to accompany the Cid to the meeting with the King, but in line 1999 the two are placed in command of the garrison left to guard Valencia in the hero's absence. The poet had carelessly repeated the line 'Alvar Alvarez e Alvar Sa[l]vadorez' (l. 1994; earlier, 739, and later, 3067) within the formulaic roll of captains, and the same for Galín Garcíez, forgetting that he had a different duty in mind for these two. In lines 1789–90 the Cid says he will send the captured tent of Emperor Yúçef to Alfonso, but nothing is said later about its delivery. In line 3115 the King invites the Cid to sit 'en aqueste escaño quem diestes vos en don', the poet having omitted to say earlier how this 'escaño' – eventually famous – was won by the hero from one of the Moorish leaders and was sent to Alfonso. It is also arguable that Jimena's line 1596, on joining her husband in Valencia, 'Sacada me avedes de muchas verguenças malas', needs justification by some allusion to these 'verguenças' at an earlier stage. Even if we can now see that the line is there because the *Historia Roderici* tells of the King harshly imprisoning Jimena and her family, this does not justify a textual inadequacy within the poem. Of all these lapses Per Abad might well have responded as Cervantes did (*Don Quijote*, ii.3) to those who had criticised shortcomings in Part i.

Of greater moment are defects observable within episodes that are fully narrated. Russell draws attention to the 'extraordinaria extensión' of the tale of the chests of sand, and to the fact that in it, the Jews are presented as 'improbablemente crédulos', while no fewer than 'cinco escuderos' each fully laden are needed to transport the modest weight of 600 marks (1978: 104–5). Illogical and unsatisfactory features in the Alcocer episode are also noted by Russell (1978: 51–5). My defence of the poet here would dwell on the fact that for both scenes he was following a literary source and did not succeed fully in adapting this to a credible or *verista* situation of Spain in the Cid's time. He was, then, working too hastily in these early parts of his composition, on what was intended as a first draft only but has remained as the only version known to us. In both episodes, his enthusiastic adaptation of a literary source (with much expansion for comic purposes, and for characterisation, in the tale of the chests) has caused him to overlook the needs of total realistic credibility.

With regard to some of these features and to others, Russell suggests an interesting practical cause, of importance because it may affect our view of the authorship of the poem. We know that later, pretended relics of the Cid were displayed in Cardeña: the *escaño*, at least one of the *arcas*, and much else that does not figure in the poem; that a sort of sub-cult of the hero's horse, Bavieca, existed around his pretended burial in the courtyard of the monastery; and that Jerónimo as Bishop of Valencia was in various ways claimed for the monastery. Could the mention in the poem of the *escaño*, the 'extraordinaria extensión' of the tale of the *arcas*, the strangely late introduction of Bavieca (l. 1573, with the Cid's recent acquisition of him explained in a rather unhappy afterthought or gloss), and the prominence accorded to Jerónimo, all be owed to the fact that Per Abad was influenced by objects, sub-cult, and wishful pseudohistory already (by 1207) established in Cardeña? Russell agrees that these matters are not documented in the monastery until a later date, except for the document supposedly issued by Jerónimo in 1103, but this, as I have shown above, is spurious. I would not, however, rest my case against Russell's proposal entirely on the lateness of the Cardeña documentation, nor would I dismiss that proposal entirely. We know already that Per Abad as secular lawyer had a close association with the monastery and gave it an honourable place in his work. Evidence might one day appear which would define or strengthen that association. For the moment, I persist in thinking that in 1207 there was no cult of the Cid at Cardeña, and no objects on which to found one, except, of course, the tombs of the hero and his wife. The cult grew in the thirteenth century as a consequence of the diffusion of the *Poema*, reaching its height in 1272, and objects to be associated with the Cid, which were many, together with the pretended burial of Bavieca, the claim upon Jerónimo, and much else, simply materialised out of the *Poema* (for dates and details, see my forthcoming paper 'Leyendas de Cardeña'). This they did elsewhere in Spain out of other literary texts, and of course widely in France and in other countries. Within the *Poema*, the explanation for the slightly puzzling features to which Russell draws attention is literary in each case. The *escaño* is needed at the moment in the Cortes when the King specially honours the Cid by inviting the hero to sit with him. Perhaps the poet envisaged a small bench of richly-wrought ivory, a royal possession which should notionally have figured among the spoils of Valencia. The *arcas* are those of the tale in the *Disciplina clericalis* used by the poet as a source; the description (ll. 87–8) is detailed because that in the source was, but corresponds naturally to that of real chests of the poet's day.[2] Bavieca is of literary origin, probably equivalent to the steed of Guillaume d'Orange, his Spanish name being an erroneous translation as Riquer showed.[3] The presence and *persona* of Jerónimo in the poem are owed to those of Turpin in the Roland story, but as argued earlier, the poet had a further source of information of a non-literary kind, very likely in Salamanca, for his name and perhaps some details. One can imagine that, if Russell were right, some aside or gloss would have appeared in the text of the *Poema* in order to associate one or all of these items with the monastery; for example, for Jerónimo, a line after the actual 1289, *'aquel que en San Pero   tres años ha morado', equivalent in form and intention to the existing line 3003; but it does not.

We do not know how the poet, having resolved that his experimental work should be about the Cid, determined where to begin it. Since he was writing a drama and not a rhymed chronicle, his choice was free. To begin his work with the Cid's first (and poetically, only) exile was surely a sound decision. As hinted earlier, this may have been influenced in part by the fact that *Ogier* began with the mission to collect tribute, and with the offence to honour which motivates the whole course of the epic, just as the same mission by the Cid (narrated by the *Historia Roderici*) leads directly to the Cid's exile while at the same time involving the offence to honour which made a permanent enemy of García Ordóñez. The diverse sources discussed in Chapter 5, convincingly strung along the line indicated by historical fact, allowed the poet to carry his plot forward to the point at which Valencia is conquered, the Cid's power and wealth and eventually (by reconciliation with the King) his honour are restored, indeed enhanced. But long before that, the poet had formed a clear idea of what the rest of his work, the true core of his human drama, should be: the Infantes, with their marriage plan, are introduced from line 1372, and this matter is thereafter delicately carried forward by stages. Even if we accept Lacarra's thesis that the *Poema* is, in one important respect, a work of *escarnho e mal dizer*, directed against the descendants of the Beni-Gómez family and of García Ordóñez, this does not explain why the poet made marriages the core of his drama. *Escarnho*, after all, could have taken many different forms all leading up to a trial scene and to duels (for which good literary precedents were, as I have suggested, available to the poet). We can, however, conjecture why it was in terms of marriage that Per Abad chose to work out the rest of his plot, in two ways. In the first, the poet could see that the emotions involved in the most intimate bond of marriage would provide fine literary material, especially when the brides are 'de dias pequeñas' (l. 2083), in their father's tender words, and the grooms are devious, secretive, of superior social status and, as eventually shown, cowardly, envious, and perhaps sexually inadequate or deviant (on the psychology of the Infantes, see Hart, 1956; Leo, 1959; and Walker, 1977). External circumstances conspire – or was the lion deliberately released by the Cid's men? – to play upon innate defects of character in the Infantes, and even though the Cid does what he can for the Infantes in difficult situations, by ordering the public humiliation of them to cease and relieving them of the duty to go into battle, the final disaster of Corpes comes irresistibly forward, as the Cid's auguries had foretold (ll. 2615–17). The pathos of the Corpes outrage – enhanced, I think, by the fact that the marriages were consummated only the night before (Smith, 1977*b*: note to p. 84) – and its aftermath then give the poet one of his best moments, and their details go echoing on in the Cortes (ll. 3260–7). In this first respect, the poet could not have made a sounder choice for the core of his plot. The second manner of reasoning starts from the assumption that Per Abad, as a lawyer, had been professionally concerned with marriage at a high level, and knew that he could make good drama out of its technical details, not only those relating to the preparation of a marriage, but also those resulting from its breaking, about which argument takes place in the Cortes. The most relevant real-life occurrence of the poet's day in this regard was the marriage of Berenguela, daughter of Alfonso VIII of Castile, to Alfonso IX of León, in 1197, which was dissolved in 1204, as mentioned earlier. Legal dispute about the return of the dowry and other matters went on for some time, and might have concerned a civil lawyer such as Per Abad in Burgos (Smith, 1977*b*: 83–4; also above, Chapter 3, note 26). Even more dramatic had been the marriage of Philippe Auguste of France to Ingeburga of Denmark, at Amiens in August 1193:

Philippe's instant repudiation of his wife, supported by the perjured evidence of bishops and nobles, produced a scandal whose legal reverberations went on for many years. In February– March 1200 Queen Eleanor of Aquitaine was in Burgos to arrange the marriage of Blanca, another daughter of Alfonso VIII, to the same Philippe Auguste (Blanca being Eleanor's granddaughter), as mentioned earlier in a cultural connection. Another marriage at top level which might have interested the poet was that of Berengaria of Navarre, a descendant of the Cid, to Richard I of England and Aquitaine in 1191; the spouses lived together but little, Berengaria surviving her husband in retirement in France. Nearer home the poet had examples of the betrothal of princesses 'de dias pequeñas'. Berenguela, daughter of Alfonso VIII, was aged eight when betrothed to Konrad von Hohenstaufen, at Cortes in Carrión in 1188; this did not lead on to a marriage. The Queen of Castile in the poet's day, Eleanor (Leonor), daughter of Henry II Plantagenet, born in 1160, was married to Alfonso VIII in 1170, probably in Burgos; thereafter the King subscribed his documents 'cum uxore', but the marriage was not consummated until 1176–7.[4] Of some of these marriages, or of aspects of them, it is surely possible to conjecture that the poet–lawyer was aware, and that they furnished him with a central idea for his plot and perhaps with some of the details. So convincingly did he tell his fictional tale, his *verismo* being taken as historical truth, that nearly four hundred years were to pass before scholars began to query it.[5]

All critics have recognised this *verismo* as a major feature of the poet's art, and I have repeatedly alluded to it. Yet, in view of much that has been offered in this book about the poet's sources and methods of composition, the concept should now be understood with certain limitations. Geographical *verismo*, for example, is modified by imitation of the itinerary theme in its phraseology from French epic, and the very sources of these itineraries may be those suggested by Russell and not the journeys of the lawyer I earlier proposed, none necessarily corresponding to journeys made by the Cid of history. The setting of Corpes is *verista* in a way, its menace exaggerated for dramatic reasons, and such a place doubtless existed in the poet's time; but the literary analysis of the poet's scene must include suggestions that came to him from non-Hispanic traditions, including Curtius's *locus amoenus*, the Pyrenean setting of the

Roland, the forest of *Florence*, perhaps a much wider tradition
even embracing Ovid, as recently proposed by Deyermond and
Hook. To what has already been moulded in the poet's imagination over the years are added the threat of the 'bestias fieras' (l.
2699) from contemporary reality, together with the dark menace
of 'alli son caños do a Elpha ençerro' (l. 2695), which presumably
meant something to a public of the time. Even such a constant
feature as the Cid's noble beard, so rich in symbolic connotation
and providing so many opportunities for eloquent gesture by a
presenter, and so well represented in later iconography, has a
literary origin in the noble beard of Charlemagne rather than in
any *verista* memory of the historical Cid (for knights of the time
seem to have been clean-shaven, or had very small beards). Such
is the poet's skill in his depiction, however, that a modern reader
is no more conscious of any artificiality here than an audience of
1207 would have been.

Sometimes the poet's *verismo* has been praised by critics who
thought it contrasted with a general lack of this quality in French
epic. This contrast could certainly be pointed out all the while the
only element considered on the French side was the *Chanson de
Roland* in its 'Oxford' version: this is not only consistently
elevated in tone, so that the grosser details of daily life are absent
from it, but also stretches credulity in some ways (the peers long
resist the onslaught of thousands of the enemy; Roland's horn is
heard through the Pyrenean passes, etc.) and makes Charlemagne the object of divine favour in the form of a biblical miracle
(the sun is stopped in its course). But the contrast loses much of its
sharpness when French epics of the later twelfth century are
taken into account. Although some of these have romantic and
erotic elements (Saracen princesses, etc.), a rather cloying
religiosity, series of unlikely coincidences, incredibly vast armies,
and so on, they also have to some degree the kind of *verista* detail
which is natural to Per Abad. I mentioned examples of this
earlier, from *Girart de Roussillon*, in discussing the motivation of
personages. Mentions of booty and monetary evaluations are
made there. The case is not unique. In *Raoul*, the description of
blows and resulting wounds has a clinical zest, king and knights
exchange coarse insults, and there is a bedroom scene involving a
very liberated 'damoisele' ('Veés mon cors com est amanevis'). In
Aliscans, Rainoars gets drunk after dinner, goes to sleep in the
kitchen, and is sobered up next day when riding through the

cold water of a ford up to his belly (ll. 3499–538). In the same poem, the detail:

Leur chevaus ont torchiés et abrevés,
Fuerre et avaine leur donnent a plentés   (ll. 3478–9)

may be set against the detail which is sometimes mentioned to illustrate Per Abad's special *verismo*, in lines 420 and 827, in which horses are fed. The poet's frequent concern with amounts and kinds of money is not owed solely to his legal professionalism, but is authorised by literary precedent of his day: ·vint mille mars d'argent' are an annual tribute in *Florence* (l. 1225), and a sale is made for 'cent mars d'argent' in *Amis et Amiles* (l. 2651). Occasional humorous scenes, involving realistic detail and low-class personages, also figure in these poems and in others of the period, so that it is erroneous to think that Per Abad's work may be less than epical, within the tastes of its time, because it includes the humorous, non-noble episode of the moneylenders, though the Spaniard's development of this scene as a miniature drama (farce?) is surely distinctive too. The poet's *verismo* is still to be applauded, then (especially as this quality is much less present in the other Castilian epics, so far as we can judge), but with reservations about its nature and without emphasis on any contrast with French. If discussion of *verismo* is made to centre not on any realistic daily detail, and still less on the supposedly accurate representation of historical fact, but on the evolution of the plot and the motivation of the personages (whose psychology and interaction are full of subtleties), then we can identify truly distinctive aspects of the poet's art, for here he far outshone the epic poets of late twelfth-century France. The latter often seem to be writing for the equivalent of not over-bright modern teen-agers, readily contented with accounts of Superman presented in strip-cartoon form, perhaps with dashes of James Bond here and there (indeed, the comparison might be worth making).

One final aspect of the poet's technique calls for comment. His handling of direct speech of all kinds has rightly been regarded as masterly, and the proportion of such direct speech to narrative is a high one. It is so too in French epic, from the *Roland* onward, perhaps reaching its greatest extent in *Raoul* and other poems of the late twelfth century. In this respect of proportion, the Spanish poem is thus typical rather than distinguished. In naturalness and conviction Per Abad certainly did well, and by his frequent omission of the introductory *verbum dicendi* he at times almost silences the narrative voice and allows the personages to function autonomously as in a true drama. In this particular he certainly seems to have exceeded his French counterparts (Alonso, 1969; on direct speech in general in French epic, Wilmotte, 1939: 93).

It would be pointless to review here all aspects of the poet's artistic achievement. Other poets (Dámaso Alonso, Salinas) in the 1940s began to say much that was admirably perceptive, and scholars and critics have done the same more recently. Among the many critical items that might be mentioned, I draw attention to the excellence of de Chasca's rapid survey of the poet's art in the concluding chapter of his 1976 book, and I do so in part because I wholly disagree with de Chasca's oralist approach. Our human and aesthetic valuations, our capacity to be moved by the poet, are more or less at one and are not affected by radical differences of theory. There is, I think, a slight danger that modern methods of analysis may perceive subtleties which were not willed by the poet in his generally very plain and direct manner, subtleties perhaps of structural patterning or symbolic suggestion or numerological import (this last being a special enthusiasm of de Chasca's); yet I am impressed by, for example, the study which Deyermond made of 'Structural and Stylistic Patterns' (1973), and that of Deyermond and Hook on 'image-patterns' involving cloaks and doors (1979). Oralist critics who, like de Chasca, rightly analyse the poem in terms of high art and structural sophistication should, I think, ponder an awesome logical impasse: can all this complex composition *really* have been improvised by a chanting illiterate? Within the terms of my very different approach I have tried to avoid tumbling into another logical pit. In affirming that Per Abad wrote the first Castilian epic and that it was naturally an experimental work, I cannot at the same time claim that this work was one of infinite subtlety and complexity, good though I believe it to be in general. To some extent I think I am saved from that pit by my analysis of the poet's working methods, by conjectures about his training, and especially by discussion of his models and sources, for these show on the one hand that he had a professional, linguistic, and literary education which gave him an adequate confidence, and on the other that he was able to start with an epic art already available to him in a sister language. He could take over much of that and then build an original creation upon it.

The portrait of Per Abad which has emerged by conjecture

contains no element which should surprise medievalists. He had the moderate learning, the general knowledge, and the tastes of a cultivated lawyer of Burgos, capital of Old Castile and important international centre, in the years around 1200. To a professional training in Roman law and in Latin, probably in France, he added a sound knowledge of a small number of classical texts, perhaps known only in excerpts, and of Latin writings composed in Spain in the twelfth century, most notably the *Chronica Adefonsi Imperatoris* and the *Historia Roderici*; and he knew parts of the Bible. His professional association with Cardeña furnished some of the texts he needed, both literary and diplomatic, and it was there that he could have picked up details from Petrus Comestor and a few habits of speech. He honoured the association by giving Cardeña a place in his work, as he naturally honoured Burgos. In Burgos or much more probably during a period of study and residence in France, he acquired a love and a wide knowledge of French *chansons de geste*, the dominant vernacular literary mode of the time, and in varying degrees he paid the tribute of imitation to some version of the *Roland* and to perhaps a dozen epics composed in the last decades of the twelfth century.[6] These more than amply sufficed to train the poet in the whole art of epic as this was practised in France in his time. More than this: at some point, French example combined in Per Abad's mind with a powerful vision of his hero and of a possible plot to fire him with the bold notion of composing an epic in Castilian. 'Das *Poema de mio Cid* ist eine von einen spanischen *juglar* verfasste Nachamung einer a.fr. *chanson de geste*' (F. Körbs in 1893, quoted indignantly by Menéndez Pidal in his 1913 edition of the poem). This is true only in the most basic and impoverished sense, for Per Abad produced not a mere imitation but a powerfully original work of revolutionary outlook, and moreover, I think, one whose literary qualities much exceed those of the French poems of its period.

We cannot know what that Burgos audience at some moment late in the fourteenth century retained from their audition of the *Poema*. Perhaps the wine with which they rewarded the presenter was suitably *añejo*, for the poem must have appeared honourably archaic to them, not only in words and phrases, but in some of its concepts too. In any case, much else concerning the Cid had been produced in the previous century and a half, and they would have known of it: the Cardeña pseudohistory of the Cid, extravagantly pious, and all the elements of the cult at Cardeña and elsewhere; the massive genealogical fabrications; the poem or poems of the *Mocedades*, whose brash and youthful hero charged romantically about an unreal world; the hero's very substantial presence in the national chronicles; and much else. Yet if the presenter was skilled in voice and gesture, the qualities which still impress us would have commanded the attention of that fourteenth-century audience. Even if the exemplary, archaically dignified hero, or the juridical programme of the poet–lawyer, no longer meant anything in practical terms, the public might still have taken pride in the expression of the heroic virtues of Burgos. Even if the forest of Corpes was by then a distant memory, the poet's evocation of it would still send a shiver down the spine. As the people retired in darkness to their homes, they would recall details, perhaps most strongly those in which a visual impression, especially of light, is called forth in words of peculiar power: the bright dawn at Castejón, which heralds the Cid's victory; the sweep of the sea at Valencia; the sudden unnatural flash of colour as the girls' blood splashes over silken garments, in Corpes; the glint of the Cid's two swords as the King draws them from their scabbards in the court at Toledo, before returning them to the hero. The presenter has earned his wine. And the poet . . . his statue.

Notes

1. The twelfth-century background

1 I notice a tendency among specialists to put this date rather later now. See, for example, H.-E. Keller, 'The *Song of Roland* and its Audience', *Olifant*, 6 (1978–9), 259–74: 'I contend that the "omega" version, from which the English model of the Oxford manuscript (Segre's "alpha") derived, was composed around 1150 at the Abbey of Saint-Denis for the cause of the Capetians, under the inspiration of Suger' (269).

2 Even the necessary basic texts must have been scarce in Spain. We know that Einhard's *Vita Karoli* was known and used in Spain in the twelfth and thirteenth centuries, but no MSS seem now to survive there. An even more dramatic indication of Christian cultural impoverishment in the eighth century is that when, late in the century, MSS 'L' and 'M' of Bede's *Historia ecclesiastica* reached the Carolingian court and were there copied and diffused, no hint of any knowledge of Bede emerged in northern Spain for a very long time. There are dozens of MSS in Britain, France, Germany, Austria, and several in Italy, but none of this work now in Spain. The Mozarabs may actually have been better off than the Christians of the north: in 882 the Cathedral of Córdoba had MSS of 4 classical writers and 22 Christian authors, including *Libros Storie eglesiastice*, which might conceivably be Bede's work.

3 On French penetration, there is much of value in Defourneaux (1949) and Sholod (1966). On cultural matters generally in Castile and León, see González (1960: 1, 626–35; and 1944: 447–64). Knowledge of the French historiographic tradition in Spain is examined by Horrent (1973–4).

4 Lomax (1969). A strong indication of continued laxity and ignorance came when, on his visitation to the Peninsula, Cardinal John of Abbeville held a provincial council at Lérida in 1229. In promulgating the sixth *constitutio*, concerned with the establishment of new schools, the Cardinal began: 'Nos attendentes quod in partibus Hispaniae, ex defectu studiorum et litteraturae, multa et intolerabilia detrimenta provenient . . .' See further Beltrán de Heredia (1946: 340). Even Toledo's reputation was, although high, a peculiar one about 1200: the

219

ex-goliard Cistercian Hélinand de Froidmont (1160–1230?) remarked that 'Ecce quaerunt clerici Parisius artes liberales, Aurelianis auctores, Bononiae codices, Salerni pyxides, Toleti daemones, et nusquam mores' (*Patrologia Latina*, ccxii, 603).

5   There is an excellent survey by Rico (1969). For the Ripoll school and for what little we have of non-lyric Latin verse elsewhere in the Peninsula, see García-Villoslada (1975).

6   Nobody has the right arbitrarily to rename a text, and it would be confusing for all if unrecognisable new names were introduced. Here I vary accepted names slightly in accordance with the principle that Latin texts should have Latin names (*Historia Seminensis, Najerensis*, etc.; earlier, the *Poema de Almeria* – without accent on the place-name – is to be understood as Latin, 'poem concerning Almería'). Equally, Romance texts should have Romance names, hence *Cronicón villarense* is to be preferred to *Liber regum*.

7   The identity of this *Seminensis* monastery has been much discussed. The chronicle's more generally known name, *Silense* 'of Silos', is certainly not right. M. C. Díaz y Díaz suggests very reasonably that perhaps a miscopying of abbreviated *domus sci innis* (referring to the monastery of San Juan de León) produced *domus seminis* in an archetype.

8   On the circumstances, see Lapesa (1948: 103–4).

9   Tilander (1967: 452). Not only judges: long after Lateran IV and the further educational effort mentioned above, and even in what had been the learned Cathedral Chapter of Palencia, one finds that in 1293 four canons, the *maestrescuela*, and the Abbot of Hermida, could not write (Beltrán de Heredia, 1946: 337). In other countries such instances led to apologetic comment. At the great Abbey of St Edmund in Suffolk, in the mid-twelfth century, 'Abbot Ording was illiterate, and yet he was a good abbot and ruled this house wisely' (*Chronicle* of Jocelin of Brakelond, in Lane's translation of 1907, 17). On what follows, see Lomax (1971).

10   I draw attention to Dr P. Such's unpublished dissertation, 'The Origin and Use of School Rhetoric in the *Libro de Alexandre*' (Cambridge, 1978), in which much is said about this aspect of Berceo.

11   Aspects of the accepted canon are brought under critical review in recent studies by R. Hitchcock, with grave implications (e.g. 1980). See also the shattering paper by Jones (1981–2), together with the report of the 'Forum' on the same matter attended by Jones and Hitchcock in 1981 and reported in La Corónica, 10 (1981–2), 71–5.

12   Sánchez-Albornoz (1955); Linaje Conde (1976: 485). Lomax shows that the *Najerensis* 'fue escrita después, y quizá bastante después, del año 1174' (1974–9: 405–6). The interest shown by the *Najerensis* in the monarchs of Castile–León who had been such strong supporters of the Cluniac cause may mean that the

chronicle was written at a time when La Rioja, including Nájera, was under Castilian and not Navarrese rule: this was so from 1135 to 1162, and again from 1176, so the work was probably composed after this date. My references to the text are from the edition of Ubieto Arteta (1966).

13   Martínez (1971). He prudently expresses a reservation about sources of all these in epic, saying of *Sancho el fuerte* that 'Salvo la interpolación del milagro de San Hugo, y acaso el rapto de la esposa, todo lo demás procede de un cantar épico, mientras que para otros temas de la misma crónica, como por ejemplo la *Condesa traidora* o *Covadonga*, pudiera admitirse una fuente prosístico-novelesca' (1971: 153–4).

14   In his unpublished doctoral dissertation, 'History as Celebration: Castilian and Hispano-Latin Epics and Histories, 1080–1210 A.D.' (London, 1975), from which Dr West has kindly given me permission to quote. Sánchez-Albornoz is firm and amusingly ironical in dismissing Menéndez Pidal's claims about all the supposed early epic *cantares*.

15   Cirot (1928). Several of the poems in question could, on the evidence presented elsewhere in this book, have been known in Spain by about 1200. Chalon (1976: 447) denies the possibility of such French influence on this early stage of the Fernán González legend: 'Il ne semble pas cependant qu'aucun de ces poèmes français, même dans une version archaïque aujourd'hui perdue, ait pu influencer la *Najerense*.' This, presumably, is because on a dating of about 1160 for the *Najerensis*, the French epics in question had not been composed; on the later dating of the chronicle towards 1200, many things fall into place. On another point relating to the *Poema de Fernán González*, the first section of Chapter 3 of Cotrait's book (1977: 64–9) is an object-lesson about the confusion induced into literary history by Menéndez Pidal's 'passion patriotique'.

16   According to the *Primera Crónica General* (427.b.9), García Fernández went on a pilgrimage to 'Santa Maria de Rocamador', which moderns assume is the French shrine. It does not seem to have been noticed that there was a Spanish shrine of Rocamador, at the monastery of Santa María de Hornillos to the west of Burgos on the *camino francés*, which contained a famous image of the Virgin (Santa María de Rocamador). This monastery was founded in 1156; it had connections with Saint-Denis at Paris, and from 1181 with Saint-Martin de Tulle (diocese of Limoges), its prior and monks being French. A 'Cofradía de Rocamador' was founded in 1191 in the church of San Román in Burgos. To judge by Berganza's account (1719–21: II, 231), Cardeña always had a close interest in the Hornillos shrine and house, and took it over completely in the fifteenth century. As for the name *Argentina*, if it was not taken from French romance, it could have been suggested to a monk of Cardeña by the name of Santa Argentea, martyred in Córdoba in 931. Her

story is told in an appendix to Cardeña's *Pasionario* (now British Library MS 25,600). Details of this and other Cordobese saints could have reached Cardeña 'hacia el año 1097 cuando los monjes de Cardeña fueron a Córdoba para tratar del rescate y traer el cuerpo del gran bienhechor del monasterio caradignense el [conde] García Fernández' (Fábrega Grau, 1953–5: I, 31); the connection between Argentea and García Fernández is especially to be noted.

17   In the *Primera Crónica General* (429.a.16) he is associated with the rebuilding of the monastery following its supposed destruction and the slaughter of 300 monks by the Moors, but it is possible that the royal chroniclers misinterpreted a note sent from Cardeña. See my study 'Leyendas de Cardeña', forthcoming.

18   Alfonso VI figured in another dramatic miracle-story recorded by Peter the Venerable in Estella, from an old monk of Nájera, during Peter's visit to the Peninsula in 1142: Alfonso told how he had been saved after a time from the flames of hell by Cluniac prayers. See Peter's *Liber de miraculis* in *Patrologia Latina*, CLXXXIX, 904–7.

19   Reig (1947); Fraker (1974); Deyermond (1976: 290 and note 30). Rico (1969: 83) thinks it certain that the *Najerensis* depended upon the Latin *Carmen*, and knew a vernacular poem too. West (1975) holds that the existence of a vernacular poem on Sancho II cannot be proved from the *Najerensis*.

20   The number '14' may be conventional. It is common in such contexts in French epic, having perhaps been adopted for metrical convenience, e.g. 'Plus de .xiiij. en i fist trebuchier' (*Raoul de Cambrai*, 2545).

21   Dozy (1881: II, 235–6) recounts an anecdote from the *Sirâdj al-molouc* by Ibn abî-Randaca Tortôchî who was born in 1059, lived in Saragossa and Seville, left Spain in 1083–4, and lived eventually in Syria, writing his book in 1122. It concerns Almanzor on campaign. He asks his general Ibn al-Moçhafî how many brave men might be found in the army. After victory in single combat by an apparently unprepossessing Moorish champion, '''Voilà un vrai brave'', dit alors Ibn al-Moçhafî, ''et c'est dans ce sens que j'entendais la bravoure, lorsque je vous disais que votre armée ne comptait ni mille, ni cinq cents, ni cent, ne cinquante, ni vingt, ni même dix vaillants guerriers''.' The numbers here are nearly the same as those in the *Najerensis*, the setting not wholly dissimilar. One can hardly conjecture that the Arabic work of 1122 (from Syria) was known in Oña or perhaps in Nájera, but the story could well have circulated within the Peninsula in some other form.

22   Von Richthofen (1954: 130–3, reproducing a study first published in 1944). Deyermond's objection to von Richthofen's idea (1976; 290, note 33) on the grounds of date can now be disregarded.

23   This passage was erased in one of the MSS ('M') and hence did

not appear in Cirot's edition. Presumably a scribe thought it improper, and it is unsure whether it would have figured in the heroic verses of the *Carmen*. In the MS used by Ubieto in his edition, the phrase appears intact.

24   One cannot, unfortunately, find out much about this. To the losses suffered by Spanish monastic libraries for all too typical reasons must be added, in Oña's case, a sacking by troops of the Black Prince and sufferings in the Napoleonic invasion. Yepes was not able to say much about literary products in his lengthy account of the house (*Biblioteca de Autores Españoles*, cxxiv, 419 ff.), though he does quote epitaphs – in fifteenth-century Romance, which might have replaced original Latin texts – on a number of important royal and noble tombs.

25   On the Lara family, more is said in Chapter 5 in connection with Lacarra's work. The matter is surveyed by Cotrait (1977: 173–5). Menéndez Pidal recognised the debt of the *Infantes de Lara* story to the epic of *Renaud de Montauban*, naturally – on his terms – at a date long before that of the surviving texts (1969).

26   In Yepes's day both San Millán de la Cogolla and San Pedro de Arlanza claimed to have the tombs of the Siete Infantes. In 1600 the Abbot of San Millán opened his tombs, finding seven headless bodies. Since in 1597 seven bodyless heads had appeared in the parish church of Salas 'de los Infantes', Yepes (*Biblioteca de Autores Españoles*, cxxiii, 81–2) regarded the matter as neatly resolved. Whether Arlanza found some way of maintaining its claim is not recorded. See also Russell (1958: 57–8).

27   For a hostile view of the minimal differences between the two, see Siciliano (1968: 48 ff.). For a full exposition, one should study the first two chapters of Menéndez Pidal's 1959 book on the *Roland*.

28   For example, Dámaso Alonso's claim: 'Aquí [in Menéndez Pidal's book *L'Epopée castillane* of 1910] por primera vez se expone de una manera compendiosa, basándose en los poemas en torno al Cid, la tradicionalidad épica a lo largo de la literatura española: de los cantares de gesta pasa la materia épica a las crónicas; de unos y otras al romancero; de ahí, al teatro del Siglo de Oro, para renacer de nuevo, a veces, en el romanticismo, y, en fin, vivir otra vez con el conocimiento científico, tan bien representado por el propio Menéndez Pidal; y gracias a él y a su escuela obtener aún una relativa popularización en nuestra época' (*Obras completas*, ii, 172, with similar sentiments from earlier years in the same volume, 99 and 150).

29   This important aspect is discussed, but hardly explored, in a number of obituary essays about Menéndez Pidal. A hostile analysis, in language stronger than one cares for, with much that is relevant to the basis of Pidal's literary ideas in nationalism, the emphasis on Castile, and 1898 Generation thought, is provided by Cotrait (1977: e.g. 69–70, 73, and passim).

2 The Cid in legend and literature of the twelfth century, and the date and authorship of the *Poema*

1   Juan Ruiz de Ulibarri copied the MS in Vivar in 1596; his version is in the Biblioteca Nacional, Madrid (MS 6328). Other copying work of his is known. He was in the service of Gil Ramírez de Arellano, member of a powerful family and later a minister of Philip III, whose chief interest was to secure materials of genealogical importance. It was Ramírez de Arellano who found Jimena's *carta de arras* in Burgos Cathedral, as Sandoval recorded in 1601. He had in his library a copy of the forged will of Prince Ramiro of Navarre, 'of 1110'; Ramiro had married the Cid's daughter Cristina, and much is made of Cidian connections in the spurious will. If there had been other Cid documents extant around 1600, one suspects that Ramírez de Arellano or his man Ruiz de Ulibarri would have scented them out. See Smith, 1980c: 52–7.

2   There is not much reason to believe with Russell (1978: 86) of the Cardeña tomb that 'Junto a la tumba del Cid había otra que se decía que era la de Jimena, pero es casi seguro que no lo era.' Russell's doubt might be founded on an impression that the monks of Cardeña were capable of any *fraus* whether *pia* or not, which is true. He was probably thinking more specifically of the alternative tomb of Jimena at San Juan de la Peña in Aragón, but this is an obvious forgery (and a late one at that) in a house of noted improvers upon the historical record (Smith, 1980c: 51–2). Good logic requires us to think that Jimena would have been buried beside her husband, in Cardeña. The doubt is not so much about the tomb there, but the remains inside it. Sandoval recorded (1615: 62) of Jimena that 'En Cardeña se muestra, no solamente su sepultura, mas los huessos desta señora, aunque son tan grandes, que espantan, y parecen mas de hombre que de muger.' The tombs of the Cid and Jimena had been moved several times by Sandoval's day (1272, 1447, twice in 1541 . . .), and presumably disturbance of the remains had occurred.

3   For a summary of this, see Smith, 1980c: 44–7, with bibliography. As I observe there, the recently-discovered *Libro de memorias y aniversarios* of Cardeña does not give any proof that there existed a tomb-cult of the Cid in the monastery in the twelfth century. Entries for the Cid and Jimena in the *Libro*, which some have thought to be of mid-twelfth century date, seem to me to belong to the middle of the thirteenth century. They are in the vernacular and in language typical of that time, not earlier; though it is just possible that they represent new vernacular versions of older entries in some lost Latin original.

4   An excellent recent study, with text and English translation, is that of Wright (1979). He emphasises that the form of the *Carmen* gives the hero exceptional dignity: 'Rhythmic sapphics

are commonly used for hymns within both the Carolingian and Mozarabic Spanish traditions' . . . 'The title that this poem gives itself of *Carmen* (line 18) may imply that it is meant to be seen as a kind of hymn' (221).

5   For bibliography, see Wright (1979). Wright maintains, with detailed arguments, the very early dating. He also thinks that the lost continuation was not extensive, probably taking in only the Almenar battle and a formulaic conclusion.

6   Wright (1979: 229–31) discusses the relationship between the *Carmen* and the *Historia Roderici*, concluding that the author of the latter knew the former 'but only used it occasionally, preferring material of more obvious documentary authenticity when it was available'. On Wright's dating, this is naturally the only way to view the matter; but if the *Carmen* is later, it might be the *Carmen* which depended to some extent upon the *Historia*.

7   The best text of this, with a study, is that of Menéndez Pidal (1929: II, 904–70), from which I quote here. References are to pages and lines. A full new study of the text is badly needed.

8   According to the *Historia* (923.8–14) the Cid, to avenge a Moorish raid on Gormaz, gathered an army and made an incursion into the kingdom of Toledo, 'depredans et deuastans', bringing back 'inter uiros et mulieres numero .VII. milia', with great booty. But the Cid's force, even though described as an 'exercitus', must have been small, and it is hard to see how such a large number of captives could have been taken and transported (nor, indeed, why captives should have been taken at all; booty was, of course, another matter). This episode could have had a purely literary origin. Various of the Frankish annals record that in 795 Charlemagne raided deep into Saxon lands, 'et exinde adduxit obsides 7070' (e.g. *Annales Alamannici*, in *MGH Scriptores*, I, 47). In Spain, Sampiro as absorbed into the *Seminensis*, 24, tells how Ramiro II of León raided Talavera in 950, 'et asportauit septem milia captiuorum'.

9   At least one of these is of doubtful authenticity. In 1089 Alfonso VI gave the Cid hereditary rights over all lands and castles he might take from the Saracens, and the author of the *Historia* implies that he had seen the original privilege, 'sigillo scriptam et confirmatam' (931.12). This does not seem to be merely formulaic. Russell doubted whether Alfonso VI (or the Cid) had or used a seal, references to sealed documents in the *Poema* being non-historical and indicating that the *Poema* could not have been composed before the middle of the twelfth century (when the practice of sealing became more frequent). Neither Russell (1952) nor Lomax (1977: 77–8) in discussing Russell's view mentions the reference in the *Historia Roderici*.

10   Dr B. Powell in his doctoral dissertation (Cambridge, 1977; about to be published) notes that the omission of aspects of the Cid's life by the *Historia*, listed by Menéndez Pidal, is strange if the work really is to be taken as historiography. 'The mixed

nature of the text and the lack of historical support for events which fit so well into the poetic, legendary tradition, at least persuades one of a likely manipulation of history by imaginative minds, if not of the complete fabrication of stories' (18). Little can be deduced about the origins of the *Historia* from the MSS. The more important of the two extant, 'I', was written about 1200 and found in the library of the monastery of San Isidoro in León late in the eighteenth century. It and MS 'S' had a common prototype, already rather full of errors. The work was well known to the Alphonsine chroniclers.

11 Oña had important Navarrese tombs. J. del Alamo, in his introduction (1950), describes it as standing at the crossroads of Navarre and Castile.

12 I quote from the edition in L. Sánchez Belda (1950: 165–86, with translation following). It is also edited by Martínez (1975: 22–51). Martínez's admirable study takes in all aspects of interest here, including, for example, the significance of the reference to Roland and Oliver (298–313). Later citations of the *Chronica* are by page numbers.

13 Allusions in the chronicles use verbs equivalent to 'say' or 'tell': e.g. in the *Crónica de veinte reyes*: 'Algunos dizen en sus cantares que ...', 'assi como la cuentan los joglares'. The most direct reference is in the *Partidas*, and seems to imply recital: '... que los juglares non dixiesen ant'ellos [*caballeros*, at meals] otros cantares sinon de gesta o que fablasen de fecho d'armas' (II, xxi, 20).

14 Likely imitation by Per Abad of topics and stylistic features of the prose *Chronica Adefonsi Imperatoris* is proposed in a paper of mine (1971b). The metrical aspect is discussed below, in Chapter 4, the topics and stylistic features in Chapter 6.

15 The author of the *Poema de Almeria* shows in the prose *Chronica* a strong interest in vernacular nomenclature: e.g. 'Fortissimae turres, quae lingua nostra dicuntur *alcazares*' (102). References may be traced in the 'Vocabulario' to the 1950 edition.

16 To the non-oralist, it is extraordinary to find that in a worthy and wide-ranging book such as de Chasca's 1976 book on the *Poema*, the question of date is relegated to a sixteen-line footnote (163, note 15); but oralist theory perhaps leads inevitably to such neglect. At the end of the note, de Chasca appears to accept Pattison's findings in respect of certain parts of the poem.

17 The most sympathetic comment is that of Michael in concluding the note to line 3732 of the *Poema* in his edition of it: 'A todas luces, solamente Smith ha aducido a un Per Abbat relacionado con la leyenda del Cid.' See also Deyermond (1977: 22).

18 Further details are given in my 1973 paper (3–5), and the question is surveyed by Cañas Murillo (1978: 13–19).

19 Stanza 1799 states, impenetrably, the date of the composition. In 1965 Ware tried to solve the conundrum and came up with

the date 1204, but this is unconvincing (Cañas Murillo, 1978: 24). In any case, it is certain that Berceo, the *Alexandre*-poet and others writing in *cuaderna vía* adopted and adapted much of the rhetoric devised by Per Abad in the *Poema de mio Cid* (for samples, see Smith, 1980b: 422–5; the whole question needs now to be reopened).

Now in his *Obras completas*, II, 419–39. The historians are Argote de Molina (d. 1598), who wrote the comment on a MS of the *Repartimiento de Sevilla* in his collections, and Ortiz de Zúñiga, Argote's son-in-law and author of *Anales* of the city (1677), who drew details from a MS in Seville Cathedral.

Professor Seniff's paper was given at the Louisiana Conference on Hispanic Languages and Literatures at Tulane University in February 1981, and is printed. I am most grateful to him for a letter and a text of his paper in advance of publication.

Cotrait (1977: 340–4, etc.). The doubt was first raised by Monteverdi (1934); there is a reply by Menéndez Pidal (1951: lxix–lxx). The doubt is much strengthened by Pattison (1979), who further discusses a paper by Cummins (1976) on the same matter. In his very important essay, which prefaces the reissue of Menéndez Pidal's *Reliquias* (Madrid, 1980), Catalán makes the doubt a virtual certainty (xxxviii–xli). It is highly significant that Catalán, an expert traditionalist in ballad studies and the best living authority on the chronicles, should take such a sagely rational view of claims about epic *refundiciones*.

For example, the purely monastic origin of the personage Martín Peláyez and of episodes about him introduced into later chronicle versions of the Cid story can be readily demonstrated; and the motive of the monastery – Cardeña – is clear too (Smith, 1980c: 43).

3. The poet, his ethos and ambience

Various papers by Waltman fall into this category; see, for example, his 1973 publication. Of interest also is that of Myers (1977).

Russell (1958), translated in his 1978 book, at 97–103. After citing lines 3726–30, Russell refers to 'la brusquedad y la pobreza tanto técnica como poética de estos versos finales'. They are not great verse, but elsewhere I have defended the ending as brilliantly bathetic.

For example, that the man who was abbot in the Cid's day, the famous Sisebuto, appears in the poem as 'Sancho' (for reasons that have been much discussed but are still unclear; I suggest a metrical one, below, p. 173); that there is no mention of the burial in the monastery of the Cid and Jimena. See further Chapter 7. Russell's 1958 study and several of mine discuss these and related matters. See further Barceló (1967–8: 15–19) and Lacarra (1977). Moreover, monks could not be lawyers. At the Council of Valladolid in 1143, under Alfonso VII and for Castile–León, monks and regular canons were prohibited from studying law and medicine, and from practising either.

4   But see remarks of Armistead quoted (with a rejoinder) in a paper of mine (1977a: note to p. 176; translated in Smith, 1977b: note to p. 66). A useful comment is made by Hook (1980: note to p. 50).

5   On 'Turoldus' as a jurist, see Aebischer (1972: 272–3; quoted by Smith, 1977b: 78). Of great interest is Bloch (1977: especially 100 ff.).

6   Essential documentation about legal aspects of the poem is provided by Hinojosa (1899, 1915), García Gallo (1955), and García González (1961). Entwistle's two studies (1929, 1947–8) provide more. Zahareas sensitively analyses legal and other aspects of the Cortes scene (1964), and Dunn has perceptive remarks on this theme (1970: 114–15). All these scholars maintain the traditionally accepted view of the nature of the poet, but it requires only a small step, and a logical one, for them to be enlisted as precursors or supporters of my belief. Deyermond was clear in thinking that the poet 'certainly had a legal and notarial training' (1971: 45), though some reviewers took exception to this. My thesis receives support from Ter Horst (1972–3: especially 228), and in several recent publications such as those of Hook and Walker. For a useful survey, without new proposals, see Kirby (1979–80).

7   Further very detailed and entirely convincing evidence, with an important general conclusion, is provided by Hook (1980). I have preferred not to merge this excellent material with my own; it is an essential concomitant study.

8   For example, the line in which the origin of Bishop Jerónimo is stated is very curiously phrased: 'de parte de orient vino un coronado' (1288). Why should the poet not say simply 'de Francia'? Menéndez Pidal thought that the poet could have adopted the phrase 'ex orientis partibus' used in Latin documents of León and Castile in the eleventh century to indicate the origin of men who came from beyond the Ebro (Navarre and France) to take posts in the Church; though he does not explain how, on his view of the authorship of the *Poema*, the *juglar* might have adopted this and other latinisms. In Castilian, Per Abad must have been the first to use the word (also in line 1091). I would not reject Pidal's proposal by any means, but it needs to be supported by a reference to a continuing tradition of the use of *oriens* in the Latin of lawyers when defining the bounds of a property, e.g. 'Termini harum domorum sunt isti: *a parte orientis* sunt quedam domus . . . ' (document no. 735 of 14 April 1203, in González (1960), III, 292).

9   Hinojosa (1899), supplemented by García González (1961). The latter notes (541–2) that the Cid, contrary to established practice, fails (in the poem) to consult Jimena about the

marriages, suggesting reasons for the omission, and observing that the redactors of the *Primera Crónica General* repaired this (600.a.31). One can only suppose an oversight by the otherwise expert poet.

10   Ubieto (1972: 10) records an amusing case: 'En el pleito existente entre el monasterio de Leire [in Navarre] y el obispado de Pamplona, sustanciado ante la Santa Sede, los jueces pontificios declararon falsa una bula proviniente de la cancillería papal, mientras que consideraban auténtica una bula falsificada por los monjes legarenses en su monasterio para alcanzar la inmunidad eclesiástica.' The patently forged will of Prince Ramiro of Navarre was taken seriously by the judges of the Audiencia of Valladolid in 1554–5 (Smith, 1980c: 53 and 57).

11   García González (1961) discusses the fact that in court the Cid reclaims the girls' *axuvar* and his swords, but not the *arras* (estates in Carrión): 'También se podría interpretar la renuncia a las arras como una negativa de las hijas del Cid a querer reconocer que habían tenido relaciones íntimas con los infantes' (note 61 to p. 555).

12   Dutton (1980). This thoughtful study is one of the fundamental few in which questions are asked not only about what was transmitted from Latin to the vernacular, but also, in human terms, *how*. Dutton's study reinforces the view that 'the author of the *Poema de mio Cid* and Berceo were professionals or paraprofessionals in law and court procedures' (26).

13   Smith (1977b: 81–2). I was too specific there in suggesting that Per Abad was one of the royal notaries whose travels are so documented. Hook rightly takes me to task (1980a: note 9 to p. 34).

14   To the poet's line 'de siniestro Sant Estevan – una buena çipdad' (397) there correspond in *Parise la duchesse* the lines 'Vienent à Valancines, une bone cité' (787) and 'Il vindrent à Coloigne, une bone cité' (793). San Esteban, now a small place, was important enough in the late twelfth century to be often a host to royalty; for example, the court assembled there in 1187 to receive the ambassador of the German Emperor, when negotiations were opened about the betrothal of his son to Princess Berenguela. See also Chapter 5 for Lacarra's view of why San Esteban was specially mentioned in the *Poema*.

15   Russell (1978: 161–205). He thinks that the poet, following the model of itineraries present in some French epics, may have used rough route-maps as a basis for his poetic presentation. If this is right, it would remove any need for the poet to have travelled and acquired direct knowledge of the routes, and could also explain his deficiencies in this regard.

16   For example, Eleanor, daughter of Henry II Plantagenet, married Alfonso VIII, probably in Burgos Cathedral, in September 1170, with great pomp. The literary consequences of this, mainly for lyric, are discussed by Menéndez Pidal (1957:

115–20). In February–March 1200 Queen Eleanor of Aquitaine was at the court in Burgos to negotiate the marriage of Blanca, daughter of Alfonso VIII, to Philippe Auguste of France.

17   Montpellier had law studies from the time of the arrival of Placentinus as a refugee from Bologna and Mantua, about 1166. Orléans, though better known for studies of grammar and *dictamen*, probably had a school of law in the later decades of the twelfth century. The Sorbonne had well-established schools of civil law (from about 1140) and canon law (from about 1177). Toulouse University was founded in 1229; lawyers in the city began to introduce Roman-law principles into their work in the late twelfth century, but it is not certain if formal law studies existed before the foundation of the university.

18   It should be noted that Lacarra signed her preface in April 1977, the book appearing in early 1980. Her bibliography has a three-page appendix of work published in 1976–9 of which, she explains, she had been unable to take account because of personal circumstances. This, rather than regrettable, is a strength; many of the studies published in the intervening years greatly strengthen Lacarra's case, but her work has the merit of its largely independent nature.

19   But Guglielmi, to whom Lacarra refers at this point, distinguishes these *sabidores* as experts in the old custom-law of Castile. Guglielmi was writing, of course, at a time (1955) when Menéndez Pidal's ideas about the nature of the poem and its date absolutely dominated. Guglielmi does recognise the later advent of *jurisperitos* at the 'curia regia', and in her view it is these who are the Roman-law experts whose 'función requería un tecnicismo desconocido anteriormente'. If the *Poema* is dated 1207, Lacarra is surely right. See Guglielmi (1955: 148); also Procter (1980: 91–2).

20   For example, the Cid's victorious duel with the Navarrese knight Jimeno Garcés, recorded in the *Historia Roderici* (921.3) and by the *Carmen Campidoctoris* (25); also, according to the *Historia*, another with a Moor in Medinaceli (921.5). But these were not under royal supervision, or at least, the texts do not mention this final formalisation.

21   It should further be added to Lacarra's exposition that, as often, the poet had not merely a juridical motive but a literary precedent, that of French. See Bloch (1977: 119 ff.). The source which may have been used by Per Abad is discussed in my Chapter 5. The latest survey of the whole *judicium Dei* in law and literature is that of Van Emden (1980).

22   In traditionalist terms but with considerable prescience, Dunn perceived much the same: 'King and hero together stand for an order in which the right and honour of a free man are protected by the Crown, and in which the Crown is to become a public authority' . . . 'The whole last quarter of the *Poema* is not only a vindication of the Cid; it is also an encomium of the King as the fount of justice' (1970: 114–15).

23   'But the likeness of *Sancho* to the *Poema de mio Cid* could perhaps
      be pushed further . . . Could it be that the abstract view of
      kingship in the *Poema* is somehow of a piece with the premium
      the work places on law and legality? . . . The *Cantar de Sancho* is a
      rational jurist's poem and expresses his adverse judgement on
      archaic laws . . . The viewpoint, the critique, one might say, is
      that of a devotee, perhaps a practitioner of rational legal
      procedure' (1974: 484–5).

24   Guglielmi (1963–5: 64). Lacarra also has much on the laws
      concerning booty. A novel view of formal gifts intended to
      encourage reciprocity ('don y contradonación') in the *Poema*,
      against a background of ancient and widespread practice, is
      presented by Gifford (1980).

25   Two seemingly unimpeachable royal reports on the battle are
      published by González (1960). Alfonso VIII wrote to the Pope
      (no. 897; III, 571) that 'Occubuerunt autem in bello ex parte sua
      centum millia armatorum et amplius secundum estimationem
      saracenorum quos postea cepimus . . . et quod incredibile est,
      nisi quia miraculum est, uix uiginti quinque Christiani aut
      triginta de toto nostro exercitu occubuerunt. O quanta letitia! O
      quot gratiarum actiones! nisi de hoc dolendum sit: quod tam
      pauci martyres de tanto exercitu ad Christum martyrio
      peruenerunt.' Queen Berenguela wrote to her sister Blanca in
      France (no. 898; III, 573) that 'Aestimati sunt autem numerus
      occisorum usque LXX millia uirorum, feminarum uero XV
      millia. Ex nostris autem circiter CC reperti sunt occubuisse.'

26   Lomax (1977: 80). But the dissolution of the marriage of Alfonso
      IX and Berenguela, added as a possible cause of Castilian
      resentment by Lomax, may not be relevant. The couple were
      said to be very much in love and already had four children, and
      it was only by the Pope's ruling that they were put asunder
      apparently against the earnest wish of the spouses.

27   Menéndez Pidal (1929: II, 606). The section is headed 'El Cid,
      héroe español'; also in the concluding section of the introduc-
      tion, 'Valor nacional del poema', in his widely-used edition in
      Clásicos Castellanos. At a moment of political passion, E.
      Giménez Caballero saluted the appearance of *La España del Cid*
      by referring to Menéndez Pidal as the 'creador de nuestra épica
      nacionalista': 'Carta a un compañero de la joven España' (*La
      Gaceta Literaria* (Madrid), no. 52, 15 February 1929). Pidal would
      probably have been appalled at such a misuse of his work.
      Much more alarming is the use made of Pidal's analysis of the
      ethos of the Cid and the *Poema* by the Spanish military
      establishment in Franco's time, as documented by Lacarra
      (1980b).

4. Metrical structures

1   For publications up to about 1970, see Magnotta (1976: Chapter
      7). Much of the present chapter is based on my paper of 1979.

2   On the filling of putative lacunae, see opinions of Powell and von Richthofen quoted by me in 1979: 35. The activities of the chroniclers in this regard are discussed by Catalán, Horrent, and others: see Appendix II to my edition of the *Poema*.

3   This is not, of course, to be confused with the process by which the Zorraquín song was written into the prose of the *Crónica de la población de Avila*, or that by which long sections of the *Infantes de Lara* poem were entered with little change into the prose of the *Crónica de 1344*.

4   Our only possible text, the Zorraquín song, seems properly to have 'Olivero' (the more archaic form) in full rhyme with 'cavallero', conforming with the other two full rhymes in *-án*. 'Oliveros', present in the later version of *Zorraquín* and regularly in the ballads, gives an assonantal rhyme.

5   See Magnotta (1976: 152–4, etc.). On this matter, my 1972 edition of the *Poema* was attacked by one reviewer because due attention was paid in it to the fine qualities of the work done by Andrés Bello in London from 1810 to 1829. I was glad to have the opportunity to do justice to Bello at greater length in a paper, 'Los trabajos de Bello sobre el *Poema de mio Cid*', presented to the 'Bello y Chile' Congress (Caracas, 1980), which will be printed. Even Menéndez Pidal was at one time less hostile to the idea of French influence on Spanish epic metrics than one might expect (1908–11: I, 101–2, and III, 1174–5).

6   In the introduction to his edition and translation of the poem (1955), Kohler held (xxii-v) that both assonance and line-structure were imitated from French: 'L'assonance est certaine-ment empruntée à l'épopée française ... L'ametrie de sa versification est une imperfection de la primitive épopée espagnole en regard de la chanson de geste de la même époque.' In this simple form the argument was somewhat easily refuted by Horrent in his review (1959: 449–50). See also Magnotta (1976: 157 and note).

7   See Michael (1978: 21–2), with references to Bédier and White-head. Restori in his 'Osservazioni' (1887: 32–3) was disposed to accept some irregular assonances. Within French, there is a good discussion of irregular line-lengths by Windelberg (1978–9).

8   The rhyme-words 'laudare' (l. 335) and 'Trinidade' (l. 2370) are not in this class, both being Church latinisms in which a final *-e* was normal. Menéndez Pidal thought 'entrava' (l. 15) in the MS was a miscopying of original **entrove*, that is a preterite with paragogic *-ve*.

9   These will be mentioned in detail in Chapters 5 and 6. Even if the list is further extended by new revelations about Per Abad's sources, we shall not be able to say more about metrical patterns, since what follows here gives ample materials. If, as Adams thinks, much of the poet's imitation of French was generic rather than of specific texts, the picture does not greatly change, but its details are rather confirmed many times over.

10   I realise that we cannot know how Per Abad would have counted his syllables (in the event that he did count them). Here I reckon them with synalepha or elision, since it seems to me that in this 'public' verse one should apply the norms of ordinary speech. But I count a final stressed syllable as two, in accord with Spanish practice. The French texts used are listed in my earlier paper (1979: note 30 to p. 46). Abbreviations here are, I hope, readily intelligible.

11   Further similar French phrases for this formula in the motif of the pursuit are adduced by Adams (1980: 788). Here we meet a problem which will concern me in following chapters also. Adams's idea of 'generic' borrowings, certainly applicable to Per Abad's adoption of commonly repeated formulae from French, leads him to include at this point lines or half-lines from the *Chançun de Willame* and *Orson de Beauvais*, which there is no evidence (on other grounds) that the poet knew. In citing lines from the *Roland* and *Parise*, I am on firmer ground because there *is* other textual evidence that Per Abad probably knew these poems. There is one line cited by Adams, *Girart de Roussillon*, 7297, which I would agree must be taken into account, precisely because it is likely that Per Abad drew elements from this poem (as shown in Chapter 5) and also because the formula occurs in Girart's line as a second hemistich, just as we see it in the *Poema*. Much the same might be argued in defence of my association (above) of Per Abad's 'adtores mudados' (l. 5) with a source in the *Roland*. Hook (1981) thinks this source less certain in view of the presence of a similar phrase in other French poems, such as *Doon de la Roche*; again, it can be shown conclusively that Per Abad knew a version of the *Roland*, while his acquaintance with *Doon* is probable – as shown by Hook in the same paper – but limited. The balance of any authority would seem to lie with the *Roland* and not with the much less well known *Doon*. Hook does, however, add the point that other French epics mention a pair of birds in such contexts, e.g. 'Faucons . . . ostors', and this is certainly to be retained, for the Spanish poet in his line 4 does the same.

12   The chief purpose of Deyermond and Hook in their 1981–2 paper was to discredit *Florence* as a source for Per Abad. In a particular detail such as this they could of course be right, but they too readily dismiss (note 45) the fact that only in *Florence* (among texts they cite) is 'Que donc veïst' associated with this motif as 'i veriedes' is in Per Abad's line.

13   *Raoul* provides much the closest parallel in this instance. Herslund (1974: 77) remarks on the rarity of the *sachiez* phrases in the epics he studied (which included *Raoul*, where Herslund must have overlooked the usage); he found 'sachiez de voir', etc., several times in *Amis*, a poem possibly known to Per Abad, and once in *Floovant*.

14   A convincing example is line 2958, '¡si quier el casamiento fecho non fuesse oy!' One observes that the poet needed an

assonance in *ó*, possibly placing an anticipatory stress on a word that would not normally carry one, 'non', which is emphatic here. The line then has alliterations of *k-k*, *f-f*, and stresses on probably no fewer than four *e*'s.

15   Magnotta (1976: 151–2). Amador de los Ríos (1861, etc.) deserves more credit here than he is likely to receive from most modern scholars. His opinions (II, Chapters 14 and 15) are highly relevant, and the Latin texts gathered in 'Ilustraciones' 1, 3, and 4 to his volume II often have great interest.

16   Wright (1979: 219) does however note that the copying of the sole surviving MS of this poem at Ripoll came at a moment of crusading fervour, about 1200, of which renewed enthusiasm for the Cid was a part. The *Carmen* has many instances of internal rhyming of the kind shortly to be discussed, e.g. 'Fama pervénit in curiam régis' (l. 69), 'Nimis irátus iungit equitátus' (l. 73; full rhyme, enriched by extra *-i-*). Such rhyming is a feature of the first lines of some strophes (ll. 57, 69, 73, 81, 109, 121). On leonine structures in Spain see also Rico (1969: 35–6).

17   See the survey of García-Villoslada (1975: 26–7 and notes), and the extraordinary couplet quoted on p. 68. Epitaphs are collected by Flórez in *España sagrada*, XXVII (1772), col. 266, and from various monasteries by Yepes in *Biblioteca de Autores Españoles*, CXXIII-V, passim.

18   I am much indebted to Mr R. H. P. Wright for a text of this paper, 'Spanish Verse, 600–1200', which was read to the Oxford meeting of the Association of Hispanists of Great Britain and Ireland in March 1981. Wright's approach involves the surely sound belief that a Latin verse tradition was continuous in Spain from late Gothic times and was not (except in Catalonia) affected by the Carolingian reform of 'medieval Latin' pronunciation. In this Hispanic tradition, such Latin was pronounced – recited or sung – in accord with the Old Spanish phonetics of the time. This closing of the gap between Latin and vernacular literary productions and pronunciations, and hence of metrical modes, is of the utmost relevance to my arguments here. With his permission, I quote a key paragraph of Wright's in slightly adjusted form: 'There is a documented tradition of Spanish verse, which by about 1000 includes, on the one hand, the artificial "rhythmic" style, based not on rhythm but on counting written vowels, and on the other hand another vernacular style which *is* based on rhythm, usually having two or three stresses per hemistich. The latter can be dimly perceived continuing in the twelfth century in the brief jingle about Zorraquín Sancho; and as is well known, it can be seen in the *Poema de mio Cid* and the Roncesvalles fragment. Whatever else the author of the surviving *Poema de mio Cid* did, he did not have to invent the metre. There is direct evidence from Spain of precedents for anisosyllabic lines, for lines of approximately

fifteen or sixteen syllables, for lines with two or three stresses per hemistich, which is the *Cid's* general pattern. What probably *is* original in this *Poema* is its exceptional length.' This argument will be much expanded in Wright's forthcoming book, *Late Latin and Early Romance.*

19   Adams's excellent analysis (1980*b*) takes him towards illogical conclusions concerning the composition of the *Poema.* He remarks of the internal rhymes that they 'seem to be a strong pointer towards oral composition at some point in the poem's genesis' (453; again, 466). This can be instantly invalidated by an awareness that such techniques are an important element in the work of such manifestly learned – and also phonetically *virtuoso* – poets as Mena, Luis de León, Góngora, and Lorca (Smith, 1963).

20   The often surprising tense-usages of the poet have puzzled some and given rise to elaborate investigations by others. A simpler approach might show that seemingly aberrant usages obey not only the need to secure end-rhymes (as is obvious), but also to make rhythms and vowel-harmonies.

21   I cannot be alone in being impressed by line 399, 'passo por Alcobiella que de Castiella fin es ya', whose sound-effects both within itself and in the context of a six-line passage I analysed in an earlier study (1976*b*: 231, with a note associating the end of the line with the last line of the *Conde Arnaldos* ballad).

5. Historical, literary, and other sources and motives

1   On the poet's viewpoint, there are judicious remarks by Chalon (1976: 211 ff.), and in Spitzer's famous essay (1948). On the authorial mentality in general, there is a valuable study by Nichols (1969), of which I quote a section in my edition of the poem (p. xxii). An amusing jolt to dourly *historicista* scholars was delivered by Wilmotte: 'L'erreur des critiques ... ça'a été, de quelque parti qu'ils fussent, de vouloir imposer à la fantaisie des auteurs de chansons, plus ou moins ignorante, le respect d'une chronologie quelconque. La façon plus qu'arbitraire dont les grands poètes romantiques ont traité l'histoire de leur pays est un avertissement, dont auraient dû bénéficier plus largement les humbles créateurs de narrations des XIe et XIIe siècles. On sait ce que V. Hugo a fait de l'histoire de l'Espagne dans *Ruy-Blas.* Pourquoi exiger plus de rigueur de nos chanteurs de gestes?' (1939: 174–5).

2   'Aun cabe añadir que, dada la historicidad general del *Poema*, es muy arriesgado el declarar totalmente fabulosa la acción central del mismo': Menéndez Pidal, with reference to the marriages of the Cid's daughters to the Infantes, in the introduction to his 1913 edition of the *Poema.*

3   For example, Deyermond suggests that since the Burgos leper-house was sited near the 'glera' of the river, the fact that

the Cid camps there when rejected by most of the people (ll. 56, 59) would be highly significant (1973: 59).

4 Chalon (1976: 177–81) assesses the relation between the two with regard to the Count of Barcelona episode(s), and seems to deny any connection. Michael (1978: 38) mentions the 'Historia Roderici, obra tal vez conocida por el poeta', and in a note (1978: 42), on the Conde de Barcelona, judges that 'Hay aquí suficientes razones para pensar que el poeta estaba enterado de este relato, encontró impropio del carácter del Cid el trato descortés dado al Conde, y alteró adrede la narración inventando la escena en que el conde se niega a comer con el Cid.' Concerning the details of the Valencian campaign, Russell (1978: 177, and note 24) shows qualified support for the proposition that the poet knew the Historia.

5 'Tévar' is probably represented by 'Iber' in the Historia, 942.2, as indicated by Pidal in his index. If there was miscopying involving (T)iber, (T)ivar in the text as it has come down to us, one might suggest that the poet knew an earlier and better MS, and took Tévar correctly from it. The context shows how a miscopying could have occurred: 'in loco qui dicitur Iber', with some abbreviation of dicitur giving rise to confusion.

6 Menéndez Pidal thought that the Historia and the Poema had used here, independently, a 'canto noticiero que podía ser latino o romance'. I mentioned this in a note to my 1972 edition, but I now think such a supposition unnecessary. The author of the Historia knew a good deal about Catalonia and the Cid's relations with the Count, and found the texts of the letters, perhaps with related documents, in the Cidian archive deposited at Salamanca. This material, with rhetorical development, sufficed for his narration, and Per Abad then developed the Historia's account in a dramatic and imaginative way.

7 This aspect would be well worth a full study. Even though the Historia contains most names taken up by the poet, by no means all that are in common have the same form. One might need to suppose that the poet had a further source of information, such as a list of places which were tributary to the Cid.

8 'The poet has adapted history in such a way as to enhance the stature of his hero and do justice to his achievement in conquering Valencia, without thereby placing such emphasis upon it as would exaggerate its importance in the artistic scheme of the [poem] as a whole' (Hook, 1973: 126).

9 Apart from the associations already mentioned, there was also a Valencian connection between the two, for Alvar Fáñez went there to establish Alcadir, dispossessed ruler of Toledo, at Alfonso's behest (1086?). But this detail is not in the Historia Roderici, and the poet may not have known of it. Aubrun speculated about the role of descendants of Alvar in promoting the composition of the Poema (for Aubrun, of 1143) and the Poema de Almeria (1972).

10   Hook: (1979a) gives a summary of the contents of a Peñiscola
      MS of the fourteenth century which is probably just such a
      collection of excerpts. It includes some from Sallust's *Bellum
      Jugurthinum* and from Caesar, but is not of specifically military
      interest as a whole. To the few details about texts of Frontinus
      given in my 1975 paper, it may be added that according to an
      inventory of the rich library of the Bishop-elect of Cuenca in
      1273 he possessed, bound in one volume, 'Paladio *de agricul-
      tura*; Vegecio *de re militari; Strategematon*'; and that an Escorial
      MS of early thirteenth-century date containing Vegetius with
      the *Strategemata* is documented as present in Castile from the
      early fourteenth century. Several MSS of Frontinus together
      with Castilian and Aragonese translations are known in the
      Peninsula in the fifteenth century.

11   In his 1978 book, Russell reproduces a 1957 study of the Alcocer
      problem, and adds to it some 'Nuevas reflexiones . . .' (45–69),
      in which all proposals for a siting are reviewed. Scholars might
      in future be guided by the approach of Torrente Ballester to the
      location of Castroforte del Baralla in *La saga/fuga de J.B.* (1972),
      e.g. p. 46.

12   The initially promising discussion of biblical influence by Edery
      (1977) turns out to lack critical rigour. Two biblical passages
      might be adduced as analogues to the poet's account of the
      Cid's capture of Alcocer. In Joshua 8.2–25 there is a long
      account of the capture of Ai by ruse, and in Judges 20.29–33 the
      story of the Israelites' capture of Gabaa, which was imitated by
      the *Chronica Adefonsi Imperatoris* (106: the attack on Coria). But
      neither provides the detailed series of events in sequence which
      enables us to link the poet's Alcocer episode specifically with
      the passage(s) of Frontinus.

13   Milá y Fontanals concluded his discussion in 1874 as follows:
      'Hemos procurado exponer con imparcialidad los datos del
      problema sin resolver lo que nos parece irresoluble, y sin ceder
      al temor de pasar por tibios patriotas al admitir la realidad o
      posibilidad de influencias francesas en nuestra poesía épica'
      (1959: 581). Menéndez y Pelayo had to forestall the same kind of
      attack. After dismissing the possibility of Arabic influence on
      Spanish epic, he goes on: 'No sucede lo mismo con el poderoso
      influjo de la epopeya francesa, cuya difusión y prestigio en
      España, como en Alemania, en Italia y en toda Europa, es un
      hecho fundamental en la historia de los tiempos medios, que no
      puede negar el más ciego e intolerante patriotismo, pero que en
      nada contradice a la originalidad de nuestra epopeya' (1903–28:
      XI, 70–1). Both Milá and Menéndez y Pelayo were sensitive on
      this score because in volumes II and III of his history of
      literature, Amador de los Ríos had reacted in stridently patriotic
      terms to the indications of Damas Hinard in his edition of the
      Poema (1858) that it owed a good deal to French example (e.g.
      Amador, II, 290–1, and III, 215, note).

14   1976: 90–106. On p. 157, in discussing metrical questions,

Magnotta refers to 'la amenazadora tesis de la imitación francesa', though it is hard to see who could feel 'threatened' by a proposal about a text seven centuries removed in time from us.

15   1953: 144. When this paper was reprinted in Riquer's 1968 book, its final four pages – containing discussion of French influences and the passage quoted – were not reproduced; not, the author told me, to avoid wounding susceptibilities, but merely for reasons of space.

16   Smith, 1977–8: 16, with further details. It should be noted that the Cardeña library had a MS of Comestor's work, or at least had one in 1835 when its collection was transferred to Madrid. Much was lost or dispersed on the way, but the Comestor MS and a few others got there safely; this item is now Códice 70 in the Real Academia de la Historia. It is a handsome vellum codex, well written in a hand of about 1200, and it contains Comestor's text in the interpolated version.

17   'En fin, en la realidad misma podían repetirse algunas de las circunstancias del episodio del *Poema*, dada la costumbre de mantener fieras enjauladas en los palacios de los grandes' (introduction to the 1913 edition). For Adenet's text, see Smith, 1977b: 137–40.

18   The important paper of Deyermond and Hook arrived (late February 1982) when my typescript was almost ready for the press. It seems proper to take brief cognisance of it in this way, while regretting that at this stage and in this place no fully reasoned assessment of it can be made. I venture one comment, however. In their wish to remove *Florence de Rome* from among the French texts that may have been known to Per Abad, Deyermond and Hook (29) deny that the poet's line 'mantos e pielles   e buenos çendales d'Andria?' (1971) could depend specifically on the line of *Florence*, 'De pennes et de drais, de riches cendaus d'Andre!' (451). My parallel was drawn above, p. 115. But Deyermond and Hook adopt an argumentation which is distinctly facile. In the first place, mention of *Andre* is not 'formulaic' as they seem to think, for references to it are uncommon in French epic and the line of *Florence* is individual and distinctive. In the second place, they cite only the second hemistich of the French line and of the Spanish line, completely neglecting the point that there is much *structural* similarity between the complete lines and a near-total coincidence of first hemistichs too. In this particular case, I stand firm: it is surely extremely likely that Per Abad was here quite precisely echoing the line in *Florence*. If this commands assent, it remains likely that Per Abad drew upon *Florence* for other materials, including some with which he created his Corpes episode.

19   Walsh, 1976–7. This was not the main theme of Walsh's paper, which was rather to point out the transformation in the character of the Infantes in the duels, when they fight bravely. On such duels in literature, see now Van Emden (1980).

20   The source-material is assembled by Menéndez Pidal: 1908–11: II, passim, and 1929, passim, but especially in the 'Cartulario cidiano' in II, 825–75. The material is reviewed, with a few additions, by Rubio García (1972), and aspects of it are discussed in my 1971a paper.

21   Important aspects of the placing of proper names in the poet's metrical system are analysed by Aguirre (1980–1).

22   Since the historical Cid had no siblings (so far as we know), and since relationships on Jimena's side appear to have been disregarded or at least not retained, the way was plainly open for literary men, chroniclers, genealogists, and others, to invent; and the opportunity was, over the centuries, taken with enthusiasm. Rubio García thinks that the names of Alvar Alvarez and Alvar Fáñez may have been interpolated in the carta de arras, but Pidal assures us that the carta still extant in Burgos is the original.

23   The motive mentioned by Bello, as recorded on p. 164 of my edition of the poem, cannot now be sustained, for the reference is to a text now known to be spurious.

24   One might conjecture that Diego Téllez owed his place in the Poema to a hint from Cardeña: García Téllez was abbot of the monastery from 1098 to 1106, that is, at the time of the Cid's burial there (1102); could Diego and García have been related, perhaps brothers? It is presumably no more than coincidental that in Florence de Rome, the 'chatelain' who rescues Florence from the forest is named Thieris (l. 4149), Thierriz (l. 4188), Tierris (l. 5921, etc.).

25   Menéndez Pidal's explanation is that Galín Garcíez was one of forty Aragonese knights who fought as auxiliaries of the Cid in the early stages of the Valencian campaign (1929: I, 413–14).

26   'Beltran' is clear in the MS, but is not in even approximate rhyme with the laisse in ó(-e). The reading 'Fruella' in the same line is dubious also. Both names are discussed by editors of the poem.

27   Berganza (I, 463–4) says that Jerónimo had come to Spain with Bernardo, Archbishop of Toledo, and lived in Cardeña (a Cluniac house since the days of Sancho el Mayor, in Berganza's entirely wishful opinion) as Jimena's confessor during the Cid's exile, going to Valencia as bishop after the Cid's conquest. Berganza gives (I, 569) a Spanish translation of a Latin document 'of 1103' in which Jerónimo as Bishop of Salamanca asks to be buried beside 'el cuerpo del Venerable Rodrigo Diaz' in Cardeña, and assigns the Salamancan church of San Bartolomé to Cardeña. Since the monks of Cardeña had long shown a tomb in their Cid-pantheon as that of Jerónimo, while it was known that the bishop was actually interred in Salamanca, Berganza in accepting the authenticity of the '1103' text elegantly concedes that the bishop's wish for a Cardeña burial was genuine but that the Cardeña tomb 'despues se quedò por Cenotafio'. Russell discusses the matter in his 1978 book

(106–7), using the text of the Latin original 'of 1103' published by Ruiz de Vergara in the eighteenth century; the original is now apparently lost. Pidal thought it genuine, and even Russell hesitates to condemn it totally. It is a manifest forgery, most obviously in that word 'Venerabilis' applied to the Cid, and the forgery need not be a specially early one as Russell thinks. What is of interest (beyond the Cardeña claim to Jerónimo) is the possibility that the monastery was trying to inject into the record a legal right over the Salamancan church of San Bartolomé; if the monks had, or thought they had, such rights, some collaboration between Cardeña and Salamanca in the composition or at least the transmission of the *Historia Roderici* might be postulated.

28   In the great corpus of fabrications of the later thirteenth century, Sisebuto became a saint, as described in my 'Leyendas de Cardeña' paper. There was no space in the abbatial record for a Sancho, but the monks adopted him from the *Poema* and made him prior in the time of the Cid. In the forged will of Prince Ramiro, son-in-law of the Cid, dated '1110', he appears as 'Domino Santio Priore', twice, and as present in the year the will was made (Smith, 1980c: 53, 54, and note 17).

29   Late in the thirteenth century there was composed, probably in Cardeña, a work on North African rulers. The *Crónica de Castilla* took details about Búcar from it, acknowledging the source. This might show that Per Abad in 1207 took from some source or tradition already in the monastery at least the name of Búcar. See Catalán (1963–4).

30   It is possible that there existed in the twelfth century some link between descendants of the Cid and those of Alvar Fáñez, which might explain further the poet's interest. Alvar Fáñez's father could well have been the Han Hanniz who figures in diplomas from 1049 to 1080; he was probably, but not certainly, a Burgos man. According to Martínez, Alvar's grandson married the widow of the King of Navarre, which might explain a Navarrese interest in him; but again, the Navarrese *Linaje* of the Cid makes no allusion to this.

6.   Linguistic and stylistic resources

1   Although Alfonso's *carta* is fictitious, the poet is clearly depicting a real enough situation. Presumably, since the girl knows the terms of the *carta*, she has been told them by her parents and drilled in what she is to say. By implication, then, the parents have heard the *carta* – redacted in Latin – read out in Romance in the public square; an example, within the text of the *Poema* or as an extension of it, of the process mentioned in Chapter 3.

2   Hook, 1979b: 500, with further discussion and new materials from *Doon de la Roche* in his 1981 study. The lines in question are from *Garin le Loheren*, 11,598–9: 'Tot li borjoiz du chastel de

Belin / et les borjoises sunt as fenestres mis.' It is then to be noted that Per Abad, on taking up the suggestion from *Garin*, has reorganised the lines structurally so as to produce one of his regular pair-phrases.

3   In the *Historia Roderici*, the phrase 'rogans, tuas osculando manus, ut . . .' (936.10) is to be related to line 1275 of the *Poema*. In confirming the *fueros* of Guipuzcoa on 28 October 1200, Alfonso VIII recorded that 'quando in prefato rivo una cum fortitudine vestra superavi eum, et osculati estis meam manum in conspectu meorum optimorum et episcoporum regni mei, . . .' (González, 1960: III, 224).

4   The line 'Yo ruego a Dois e al Padre spirital' (300) may echo similar usage in French epics, where it is common; for example, in a poem which Per Abad probably knew, 'Damedieu reclama, le Pere espirital', line 723 of *Berte* in Adenet's later version. But the Spaniard did not adopt such clichés as 'Dieu qui ne menti' (e.g. *Raoul*, l. 981), 'Dieu qui tot a a jugier' (e.g. *Raoul*, l. 1740), nor the practice of invoking a wide range of saints variously named for rhyming purposes. The poet's attitude and language in religious matters, compared with those of French epic, would now repay further study.

5   That part of the study of Bustos Tovar on learned words in the *Poema* (1974: 138–55) is disappointing in its failure to discuss in detail the poet's possible sources for them. He adopts the traditionalist view that the poem was composed in about 1140 by a *juglar*, but is frank at one point about the logical difficulty in which this adherence to the orthodoxy of the times places him: 'Por otro lado es muy difícil establecer nexos entre el oficio de juglar, y el de conocedor de fuentes latinas' (144).

6   'Vocaçion' in the poet's usage almost certainly refers to the dedication of the new Cathedral of Valencia, as first perceived by Bello and accepted (after discussion of other possibilities) by Menéndez Pidal. The sense 'vow', favoured in my edition of the *Poema*, is to be discarded. In the *Poema* the gloss is a pious note probably introduced because of the lengthy description which the *Historia Roderici* gives of the dedication of the cathedral at 968.1–13.

7   The construction naturally abounds in the twelfth-century Hispano-Latin texts, especially the *Historia Seminensis*. Perhaps the poet's use of it in contexts of the mass and of prayer ('la missa dicha, . . .', ll. 320, 1703; 'La oraçion fecha, . . .', l. 366) was his original one, echoing e.g. 'Peracto sermone ab episcopo Ouetensi et peracta missa . . .' of the *Chronica Najerensis* (III.58), the extension into secular contexts such as line 147 being secondary. There was early vernacular use of it also in an important legal text of the poet's own day: '. . . fasta que la paz sea adubada. Et, la paz adubada, tornen todo aquel debdo que dicho es de suso' (Treaty of Cabreros, 26 March 1206, in González, 1960: III, 368).

8   Dutton (1973: 76–7) lists French and Provençal words in Berceo, the *Alexandre*, and the *Apolonio*, relating their adoption to the influence of settlers and the French *magistri* at Palencia, etc. Herslund (1974: 115–16) has a list of such words, with a brief discussion. Lapesa's 1948 Avilés study remains fundamental, and there is further material in his 1975 paper. The whole question demands renewed study on a large scale.

9   These studies are gathered into his books of 1954, 1970, etc.: 'Debiera estar fuera de duda que, dondequiera que el autor del *Cid* echa mano de artificios épicos, tenía presente como modelo la técnica de los autores épicos franceses' (1954: 284–5).

10   Herslund (1974: 70–1) quotes Laugesen (whose book in Danish I regret I do not know) in translation: 'La forme du poème [of the Cid] indique sans équivoque des modèles français et ne donne pas de base pour admettre une ancienne tradition épique en Espagne même.'

11   In the *chansons de geste*, such things, if mentioned at all, have a secondary role. 'La bataille "champel" est plus efficace, ou la faim. En réalité prouesse et aide divine sont suffisantes et confèrent à la bataille le caractère d'ordalie; "engins" et "engineors" sont méprisés' (Vallecalle, 1979, summarised: 65).

12   On the tradition of these, see Spitzer (1945); also Smith (1977*b*: 95–6). Herslund (1974: 113) relates the other type of city-epithet, 'Burgos la casa', to French usage, as Bello and others had done, but similar phraseology in twelfth-century Hispano-Latin texts may be relevant also (Smith, 1977*b*: 95), and to it is to be added at least one example from a legal text: 'Nos tot concilio de Livriellos la cibdad gracias et laudes damus domine nostro . . .' (*Fuero de Ibrillos*, undated, but of the reign of Alfonso VIII, in González, 1960: III, 651). In the matter of 'Valençia la mayor' (l. 2105, etc.) I doubt whether Ubieto (1973: 68) is right – following in part an observation of Menéndez Pidal – to see this as a designation to avoid confusion with Valencia de Don Juan (so named from 1189; earlier 'Coyanza'), for this possibility would hardly have bothered a Burgos poet and public. But the fact that in *Garin le Loheren* – a poem, as Hook has shown, which the Spanish poet probably knew – there is a line 'Et fiert Hugon de Valence la grant' (l. 1950) may be more than purely fortuitous, in view of 'Valençia la grand' in the *Poema* (l. 3316).

13   In 1971 I remarked that 'Epic epithets for persons are not found in the Latin texts' of twelfth-century Spain, but Martínez (1975: 258) correctly observes the precedent for 'ardida lança'. Already in 1908, s.v. *lança*, Pidal drew attention to *Almería*'s lines, naturally without suggesting an imitation by the vernacular poet.

14   This is studied from an oralist viewpoint by Schlyter (1974). The practice of the *Roland* was related to that of Carolingian Latin poets by Chiri (1936: 79–80).

15   West (1975: 447 ff.) reviews the possible origins of the poet's usage. Of the aesthetic function of such language he observes that it appears not to have a merely line-filling function: 'Indeed, it adds weight and emphasis to the line, e.g. 649. The language of Romance epic could be characterised by its use of seemingly tautologous and unnecessary phraseology, of physical and binary phrases in particular, and this contributes to the dignity of the epic recitation.'

16   1981. But not all Hook's citations are likely to be relevant, since it cannot be shown on other grounds that Per Abad knew the *Couronnement de Louis* or the *Enfances Guillaume* (whereas *Garin* and *Doon* are, with *Raoul*, plainly relevant).

17   Kay (1978). This is probably the spirit in which von Richthofen presented his various analyses of rhetorical features in Romance epic, mentioned above. One recalls Tristram Shandy's surprise that his father achieved such brilliance as rhetorician and orator without ever having made any formal study of rhetoric or oratory (I, 19).

7.   'El romanz es leido, dat nos del vino'

1   However, when the project was under discussion in the 1940s and some kind of group statuary was envisaged, 'Sugirióse también poner al pie del grupo una imagen de Per Abat, rindiendo en el copista un homenaje al anónimo autor y aun completarla con la figura simétrica de un juglar' (Gárate Córdoba, 1955: 174).

2   '... praecepit decem cofros exterius pretiosis depictos coloribus atque ferro deargentato ligatos cum bonis serraturis emere' (1948 edition, 39–40).

3   The 'existence' and name of the horse were taken from the *Poema*, but the idea of a cult of the hero's horse was taken by Cardeña from another monastery. In 'Leyendas de Cardeña' I mention two of these: that of Broiefort, retired war-horse of Ogier de Danemarche, at the abbey of Saint-Faron near Meaux, and of the horse of Waltharius at the monastery of La Novalesa near Turin. I have shown that Cardeña derived pseudo-historical and heroic materials from this Italian house.

4   This phrase 'cum uxore' may justify one in thinking that in the *Poema* the marriages are not consummated until the night before the Corpes outrage even though some of what the poet says might lead one to suppose that consummation had occurred immediately after the Valencian 'bodas' and nuptial mass (l. 2240), with episcopal blessing. When the Cid addresses the Infantes: '¡En braços tenedes mis fijas tan blancas commo el sol!' (l. 2333) during the period of non-consummation he is, on my terms, uttering what is merely a social formula, also occurring elsewhere; the 'cum uxore' phrase of Alfonso VIII's notaries during the period before his marriage was con-

summated is another such formula. The question would be well worth investigation by a historian of canon law.

5 Sandoval, Yepes, and others of the time had grave doubts about the historicity of the marriages of the Infantes to the Cid's daughters. For the honour of Carrión, its *regidor* Juan de Cisneros y Tagle denounced the tale as an unpleasant fiction in 1629, demonstrating how historical facts served to disprove it (*Recopilación de las grandezas y antigüedades de la muy noble Villa de Carrión . . .*, Códice 333B of the Archivo Histórico Nacional, Madrid, fols. 212v–218r). Berganza in 1719 tried, as was his wont, the impossible task of harmonising fiction and history.

6 I list here, for the convenience of others who may work in this field, the French epics from which Per Abad probably drew inspiration, suggestions, and materials. The list, containing only those poems mentioned in the present study, is naturally made in the present state of our very unsatisfactory knowledge, and in the full awareness that future work by others (in what is still a quite new field of inquiry in some ways, even though the first steps were made so long ago by Bello) may modify or extend it. The dating of these poems is a notoriously uncertain matter. I take refuge in the vague belief that most, apart from the *Roland*, were composed 'in the last decades of the twelfth century' but think that one or two poems may have become known to the Spanish poet only in the years about 1200 or even a short time before he finished his work in 1207; this might take account of the arguments of Deyermond and Hook (1981–2) about *Florence*, may be necessary in the case of *Parise* (composed 'aux environs de l'an 1200, plutôt en avant qu'en arrière', according to the editors in 1860), and may be helpful in the case of the *Prise de Cordres*, dated by its editor to about 1190–5, but by one more recent authority to as late as 1211. The thought indeed occurs to one that, if in the course of time Per Abad's knowledge of certain of these texts comes to be regarded as proven, help may come from this for the problem of dating the French texts. Meanwhile the reader should consult, apart from a few specialist studies, the introductions to the editions used (cited in Smith, 1977b: Chapter 6, and in Hook's various papers), together with the general works of Lévy (1957), Riquer (1962), and Fox (1974). The poems are: *Chanson de Roland* (version related to 'O' or 'V⁴'), *Amis et Amiles*, *Berte aus grans piés* (known only in Adenet's reworking of 1272–5), *La Chevalerie d'Ogier de Danemarche*, *Doon de la Roche*, *Fierabras*, *Florence de Rome*, *Garin le Loheren*, *Girart de Roussillon*, *Parise la duchesse*, *La Prise de Cordres et de Sebille*, *Raoul de Cambrai*.

List of works cited

Adams, K. J. 'The Metrical Irregularity of the *Cantar de mio Cid*', *Bulletin of Hispanic Studies*, 49 (1972), 109–19

'*Pensar de*: Another Old French Influence on the *Poema de mio Cid* and other Medieval Spanish Poems', *La Corónica*, 7 (1978–9), 8–12

'Possible French Influence on the Use of the Historic Present in the *Poema de mio Cid*', *Modern Language Review*, 75 (1980), 781–96 [= 1980*a*]

'Further Aspects of Sound-patterning in the *Poema de mio Cid*', *Hispanic Review*, 48 (1980), 449–67 [= 1980*b*]

Aebischer, P. *Préhistoire et protohistoire du 'Roland'*, Berne, 1972

Aguirre, J. M. 'El nombre propio como fórmula oral en el *Cantar de mio Cid*', *La Corónica*, 9 (1980–1), 107–19

Alamo, J. del. *Colección diplomática de San Salvador de Oña*, 2 vols., Madrid, 1950

Alonso, D. *Obras completas*, 5 vols. (in progress), Madrid, 1972–8

'El anuncio del estilo directo en el *Poema del Cid* y en la épica francesa', in *Mélanges ... R. Lejeune*, 2 vols., Gembloux, 1969, I, 379–93 (reprinted in *Obras completas*, II, 195–204)

Alvar, C. *La poesía trovadoresca en España y Portugal*, Madrid, 1977

Amador de los Ríos, J. *Historia crítica de la literatura española*, 7 vols., Madrid, 1861–5 (facsimile edition, Madrid, 1969)

Armistead, S. G. 'The *Mocedades de Rodrigo* and Neo-individualist Theory', *Hispanic Review*, 46 (1978), 313–27

Aubrun, C. V. 'La Métrique du *Mio Cid* est régulière', *Bulletin Hispanique*, 49 (1947), 332–72

'Le *Poema de mio Cid*, alors et à jamais', *Philological Quarterly*, 51 (1972), 12–22

Bandera Gómez, C. El '*Poema de mio Cid*': poesía, historia, mito, Madrid, 1969

Barceló, M. 'Sobre dos textos cidianos', *Boletín de la Real Academia de Buenas Letras de Barcelona*, 32 (1967–8), 15–25

Beltrán de Heredia, V. 'La formación intelectual del clero en España durante los siglos XII, XIII y XIV', *Revista Española de Teología*, 6 (1946), 315–57

Berganza, F. de. *Antigüedades de España ...*, 2 vols., Madrid, 1719–21

Bloch, R. H. *Medieval French Literature and Law*, Berkeley and London, 1977

Burt, J. R. 'Raquel and Vidas in Light of the Exodus Pattern', *Crítica Hispánica*, 1 (1979), 115–20

Bustos Tovar, J. J. *Contribución al estudio del cultismo léxico medieval*, Madrid, 1974

Cañas Murillo, J. (ed.) *Libro de Alexandre*, Madrid, 1978

Castro, A. 'Poesía y realidad en el *Poema del Cid*', *Tierra Firme*, 1 (1935), 7–30 (reprinted in *Atenea*, 121 (1955), 175–95; and in *Estudios de literatura española*, Princeton and New York, 1956)

Catalán, D. 'La *Estoria de los reyes de Africa* del maestro Gilberto o Sujulberto. Una obra del siglo XIII perdida', *Romance Philology*, 17 (1963–4), 346–53

Cázares, L. 'Dísticos en la épica castellana', *Nueva Revista de Filología Hispánica*, 22 (1973), 91–101

Chalon, L. *L'Histoire et l'épopée castillane du Moyen Age*, Paris, 1976
'La historicidad de la leyenda de la Condesa traidora', *Journal of Hispanic Philology*, 2 (1978), 153–63 [= 1978*a*]
'Le Poète du *Cantar de mio Cid* s'est-il inspiré de Salluste?', *Le Moyen Age*, 33 (1978), 479–90 [= 1978*b*]

Chasca, E. de. *El arte juglaresco en el 'Cantar de mio Cid'*, 2nd edn, Madrid, 1972
The Poem of the Cid, Boston, 1976

Chiri, G. *L'Epica latina medioevale e la 'Chanson de Roland'*, Genoa, 1936 (reprinted at Geneva, 1974)

Cirot, G. 'Une Chronique léonaise inédite', *Bulletin Hispanique*, 11 (1909), 259–82
'Sur le Fernán González', *Bulletin Hispanique*, 30 (1928), 130–41

Cotrait, R. *Histoire et poésie: le Comte Fernán González*, Grenoble, 1977

Criado de Val, M. 'Geografía, toponimia e itinerarios del *Cantar de mio Cid*', *Zeitschrift für Romanische Philologie*, 86 (1970), 83–107

Cummins, J. S. 'The Chronicle Texts of the Legend of the *Infantes de Lara*', *Bulletin of Hispanic Studies*, 53 (1976), 101–16

Curtius, E. R. *European Literature and the Latin Middle Ages*, translated by W. R. Trask, London, 1953

Defourneaux, M. *Les Français en Espagne aux XIe et XIIe siècles*, Paris, 1949

Delbouille, M. 'D'où venait la chanson de geste?', *Cahiers de Civilisation Médiévale*, 15 (1972), 205–21

Deyermond, A. D. *Epic Poetry and the Clergy: Studies on the 'Mocedades de Rodrigo'*, London, 1969
The Middle Ages, vol. 1 of *A Literary History of Spain*, London and New York, 1971
'Structural and Stylistic Patterns in the *Cantar de mio Cid*', in *Medieval Studies ... R. W. Linker*, Madrid, 1973, 55–71
Review of the 3rd edn of Menéndez Pidal's *La leyenda de los Infantes de Lara*, *Hispanic Review*, 42 (1974), 462–5
'The Lost Genre of Medieval Spanish Literature', *Hispanic Review*, 43 (1975), 231–59
'Medieval Spanish Epic Cycles: Observations on their Formation and Development', *Kentucky Romance Quarterly*, 23 (1976), 282–303
(ed.) *'Mio Cid' Studies*, London, 1977; including his introductory paper 'Tendencies in *Mio Cid* Scholarship, 1943–73', 13–47

Deyermond, A. D., and M. Chaplin. 'Folk-motifs in the Medieval Spanish Epic', *Philological Quarterly*, 51 (1972), 36–53

Deyermond, A. D., and D. Hook. 'Doors and Cloaks: Two Image-patterns in the *Cantar de mio Cid*', *Modern Language Notes*, 94 (1979), 366–77

'The *Afrenta de Corpes* and Other Stories', *La Corónica*, 10 (1981–2), 12–37

Dozy, R. P. A. *Recherches sur l'histoire et la littérature de l'Espagne pendant le Moyen Age*, 3rd edn, 2 vols., Leyden, 1881

Duggan, J. J. 'Formulaic Diction in the *Cantar de mio Cid* and the Old French Epic', *Forum for Modern Language Studies*, 10 (1974), 260–9

Dunn, P. N. 'Levels of Meaning in the *Poema de mio Cid*', *Modern Language Notes*, 85 (1970), 109–19

Dutton, B. 'French Influences in the Spanish *mester de clerecía*', in *Medieval Studies . . . R. W. Linker*, Madrid, 1973, 73–93

'The Popularization of Legal Formulae in Medieval Spanish Literature', *Studies . . . J. E. Keller*, Newark, 1980, 13–28

Edery, M. 'El fondo bíblico del *Mio Cid*', *Revista de Occidente*, 3rd series, nos. 20–21 (1977), 56–60

Entwistle, W. J. 'On the *Carmen de morte Sanctii regis*', *Bulletin Hispanique*, 30 (1928), 204–19

'My Cid – Legist', *Bulletin of Spanish Studies*, 6 (1929), 9–15

'Remarks concerning the Order of the Spanish *cantares de gesta*', *Romance Philology*, 1 (1947–8), 112–23

Fábrega Grau, A. *Pasionario hispánico*, 2 vols., Madrid and Barcelona, 1953–5

Faulhaber, C. B. 'Neo-traditionalism, Formulism, Individualism, and Recent Studies on the Spanish Epic', *Romance Philology*, 30 (1976–7), 83–101

Fletcher, R. 'Diplomatic and the Cid Revisited: The Seals and Mandates of Alfonso VII', *Journal of Medieval History*, 2 (1976), 305–37

Fox, J. *The Middle Ages*, vol. 1 of *A Literary History of France*, London and New York, 1974

Fradejas Lebrero, J. *Estudios épicos: el Cid*, Ceuta, 1962

Estudios épicos: el Cerco de Zamora, Ceuta, 1963

Fraker, C. F. 'Sancho II: Epic and Chronicle', *Romania*, 95 (1974), 467–507

Galmés de Fuentes, A. *Épica árabe y épica castellana*, Barcelona, 1978

Gárate Córdoba, J. M. *Las huellas del Cid*, Burgos, 1955

García Gallo, A. 'El carácter germánico de la épica y del derecho en la Edad Media española', *Anuario de Historia del Derecho Español*, 25 (1955), 583–679

García González, J. 'El matrimonio de las hijas del Cid', *Anuario de Historia del Derecho Español*, 31 (1961), 531–68

García-Villoslada, R. *La poesía rítmica de los goliardos medievales*, Madrid, 1975

Garci-Gómez, M. '*Mio Cid*': estudios de endocrítica*, Barcelona, 1975

(ed.) *Cantar de mio Cid*, Madrid, 1977

Gerli, E. M. 'The *Ordo Commendationis Animae* and the Cid Poet', *Modern Language Notes*, 95 (1980), 436–41

Gifford, D. J. 'European Folk-tradition and the "Afrenta de Corpes"', in '*Mio Cid*' *Studies*, ed. A. D. Deyermond, London, 1977, 49–62

'Un ratón en la cerveza', in *Actas del Sexto Congreso Internacional de Hispanistas* (1977), Toronto, 1980, 325–8

González, J. *Alfonso IX*, Madrid, 1944

El reino de Castilla en la época de Alfonso VIII, 3 vols., Madrid, 1960

Guerrieri Crocetti, C. 'Problemi di epica spagnola', in *Nel mondo neolatino*, Bari, 1969, 378–445 (an article first published in 1953–4)

Guglielmi, N. 'La curia regia en León y Castilla', *Cuadernos de Historia de España*, 23–4 (1955), 116–267, and 26–7 (1958), 43–100

'Cambio y movilidad social en el *Cantar de mio Cid*', *Anales de Historia Antigua y Medieval*, 12 (1963–5 [1967]), 43–65

Hackett, M. 'Le Climat moral de *Girart de Roussillon*', in *Etudes ... J. Horrent*, Liège, 1980, 165–74

Hall, R. A. 'Old Spanish Stress-timed Verse and Germanic Superstratum', *Romance Philology*, 19 (1965–6), 227–34

Hamilton, R. 'Epic Epithets in the *Poema de mio Cid*', *Revue de Littérature Comparée*, 36 (1962), 161–78

Hart, T. R. 'The Infantes de Carrión', *Bulletin of Hispanic Studies*, 33 (1956); 17–24

Hathaway, R. L. 'The Art of the Epic Epithets in the *Cantar de mio Cid*', *Hispanic Review*, 42 (1974), 311–21

Herslund, M. 'Le *Cantar de mio Cid* et la chanson de geste', *Revue Romane*, 9 (1974), 69–121

Hinojosa, E. de. 'El derecho en el *Poema del Cid*', in *Homenaje a Menéndez y Pelayo*, Madrid, 1899, I, 541–81 (reprinted in Hinojosa's *Obras completas*, Madrid, 1948, I, 183–215)

El elemento germánico en el derecho español, Madrid, 1915

Hitchcock, R. 'The *Kharjas* as Early Romance Lyrics', *Modern Language Review*, 75 (1980), 481–91

Hook, D. 'The Conquest of Valencia in the *Cantar de mio Cid*', *Bulletin of Hispanic Studies*, 50 (1973), 120–6

'Some Observations upon the Episode of the Cid's Lion', *Modern Language Review*, 71 (1976), 553–64

'Pedro Bermúdez and the Cid's Standard', *Neophilologus*, 63 (1979), 45–53 [= 1979a]

'The Opening Laisse of the *Poema de mio Cid*', *Revue de Littérature Comparée*, 53 (1979), 490–501 [= 1979b]

'On Certain Correspondences between the *Poema de mio Cid* and Contemporary Legal Instruments', *Iberoromania*, 11 (1980), 31–53 [= 1980a]

'The Legal Basis of the Cid's Agreement with Abbot Sancho', *Romania*, 101 (1980), 517–26 [= 1980b]

'The *Poema de mio Cid* and the Old French Epic: Some Reflections', in *The Medieval Alexander Legend and Romance Epic: Essays ... D. Ross*, New York, 1981

Horrent, J. Review of E. Kohler's translation of the *Poema*, in *Revue des Langues Vivantes*, 25 (1959), 449–50

'Tradition poétique du *Cantar de mio Cid* au XIIe siècle', *Cahiers de Civilisation Médiévale*, 7 (1964), 451–77 (reprinted in Horrent's 1973 book, 245–311)

Historia y poesía en torno al 'Cantar del Cid', Barcelona, 1973

'L'*Historia Silense* ou *Seminense*', *Marche Romane*, 23–4 (1973–4), 135–50

Jones, A. 'Sunbeams from Cucumbers: An Arabist's Assessment of the State of *Kharja* Studies', *La Corónica*, 10 (1981–2), 38–53

Kay, S. 'The Nature of Rhetoric in the *chanson de geste*', *Zeitschrift für Romanische Philologie*, 94 (1978), 305–20

Kirby, S. D. 'Legal Doctrine and Procedure as Approaches to Medieval Hispanic Literature', *La Corónica*, 8 (1979–80), 164–71

Kohler, E. *Le Poème de mon Cid*, Paris, 1955

Lacarra, M. E. 'El *Poema de mio Cid* y el monasterio de San Pedro de Cardeña', in *Homenaje a J. M. Lacarra*, 2 vols., Saragossa, 1977, II, 79–94

'El significado histórico del *Poema de Fernán González*', *Studi Ispanici*, 10 (1979), 9–41

El '*Poema de mio Cid': realidad histórica e ideología*, Madrid, 1980 [= 1980a]

'La utilización del Cid de Menéndez Pidal en la ideología militar franquista', *Ideologies and Literature*, 3 (1980), 95–127 [= 1980b]

Lapesa, R. *Asturiano y provenzal en el Fuero de Avilés*, Salamanca, 1948

'De nuevo sobre la apócope vocálica en castellano medieval', *Nueva Revista de Filología Hispánica*, 24 (1975), 13–23

Lecoy, F. Review of Menéndez Pidal's *Poesía juglaresca* (6th edn, 1957), in *Romania*, 80 (1959), 419–23

Leo, U. 'La "Afrenta de Corpes", novela psicológica', *Nueva Revista de Filología Hispánica*, 13 (1959), 291–304

Lévy, R. *Chronologie approximative de la littérature française au Moyen Age*, Tübingen, 1957

Linaje Conde, C. *Repertorio de historia de las ciencias eclesiásticas en España*, Salamanca, 1976

Lomax, D. W. 'The Lateran Reforms and Spanish Literature', *Iberoromania*, 1 (1969), 299–313

'La lengua oficial de Castilla', *Actele celui de-al XII-lea Congres Internacional de Lingvistica şi Filologie Romanica*, Bucharest, 1971, 411–17

'The Date of the *Poema de mio Cid*', in *'Mio Cid' Studies*, ed. A. D. Deyermond, London, 1977, 73–81

'La fecha de la *Crónica Najerense*', *Anuario de Estudios Medievales*, 9 (1974–9), 405–6

Magnotta, M. *Historia y bibliografía de la crítica sobre el 'Poema de mio Cid' (1750–1971)*, Chapel Hill, 1976

Maldonado de Guevara, F. '"Knittelvers", "verso nudoso"', *Revista de Filología Española*, 48 (1965), 39–59

Marcos Marín, F. *Poesía narrativa árabe y épica castellana*, Madrid, 1971

Martínez, S. 'Tres leyendas heroicas de la *Najerense*', *Anuario de Letras*, 9 (1971), 115–77

El '*Poema de Almería' y la épica románica*, Madrid, 1975

Menéndez Pidal, R. *Cantar de mio Cid*, 3 vols., Madrid, 1908–11

(ed.) *Poema de mio Cid*, Madrid, 1913 (Clásicos Castellanos, 24; often reprinted)

'Relatos poéticos en las crónicas medievales', *Revista de Filología Española*, 10 (1923), 329–72

La España del Cid, 2 vols., Madrid, 1929; 5th edn, Madrid, 1956

Castilla, la tradición, el idioma, Buenos Aires and Mexico, 1945 (Colección Austral, 501)

Reliquias de la poesía épica española, Madrid, 1951; new edn with a critical introduction by D. Catalán, Madrid, 1980

Poesía juglaresca y orígenes de las literaturas románicas, 6th edn, Madrid, 1957

'La Chanson de Roland' y el neotradicionalismo, Madrid, 1959

En torno al 'Poema del Cid', Barcelona, 1963

'Los cantores épicos yugoeslavos y los occidentales. El *Mio Cid* y dos refundidores primitivos', *Boletín de la Real Academia de Buenas Letras de Barcelona*, 31 (1965–6), 195–225

'Los *Infantes de Salas* y la epopeya francesa', in *Mélanges . . . R. Lejeune*, 2 vols., Gembloux, 1969, I, 485–501

Menéndez y Pelayo, M. *Antología de poetas líricos castellanos*, 14 vols., Madrid, 1903–28

Michael, I. 'Geographical Problems in the *Poema de mio Cid*. I. The Exile Route', in *Medieval Hispanic Studies . . . R. Hamilton*, London, 1976, 117–28

'Geographical Problems in the *Poema de mio Cid*. II. The Corpes Route', in *'Mio Cid' Studies*, ed. A. D. Deyermond, London, 1977, 83–9

(ed.) *Poema de mio Cid*, 2nd edn, Madrid, 1978

Milá y Fontanals, M. *De la poesía heroico-popular castellana* (1874), ed. M. de Riquer and J. Molas, Barcelona, 1959

Monteverdi, A. 'Il cantare degli Infanti di Salas', *Studi Medievali*, N.S. 7, (1934), 113–50

Myers, O. T. 'Multiple Authorship of the *Poema de mio Cid*: A Final Word?', in *'Mio Cid' Studies*, ed. A. D. Deyermond, London, 1977, 113–28

Nichols, S. G. 'The Interaction of Life and Literature in the *Peregrinationes ad loca sancta* and the *Chansons de Geste*', *Speculum*, 44 (1969), 51–77

Pattison, D. G. 'The Date of the *Cantar de mio Cid*: A Linguistic Approach', *Modern Language Review*, 62 (1967), 443–50

'Legendary Material and its Elaboration in an idiosyncratic Alphonsine Chronicle', *Belfast Spanish and Portuguese Papers*, Belfast, 1979, 173–81

Pavlović, M., and R. M. Walker. 'Roman Forensic Procedure in the *Cort* Scene in the *Poema de mio Cid*', *Bulletin of Hispanic Studies*, forthcoming

Powell, B. 'The *Poema de mio Cid* from the twelfth to the fourteenth century with particular reference to its prose redaction in the *Crónica de veinte reyes*', University of Cambridge Ph.D. dissertation, 1977 (to be published)

Procter, E. S. *Curia and Cortes in León and Castile, 1072–1295*, Cambridge, 1980

Reig, C. *El cantar de Sancho II y cerco de Zamora*, Madrid, 1947

Restori, A. 'Osservazioni sul metro, sulle assonanze e sul testo del *Poema del Cid*', *Il Propugnatore*, 20 (1887), (i) 97–158, (ii) 109–64, 408–37

Riaño Rodríguez, T. 'Del autor y fecha del *Poema de mio Cid*', *Prohemio*, 2 (1971), 467–500

Richthofen, E. von. *Estudios épicos medievales*, Madrid, 1954
    Nuevos estudios épicos medievales, Madrid, 1970
Rico, F. 'Las letras latinas del siglo XII en Galicia, León, y Castilla', *Abaco*,
    2 (1969), 9–91
    'Çorraquín Sancho, Roldán y Oliveros: un cantar paralelístico del siglo
    XII', in *Homenaje . . . Rodríguez-Moñino*, Madrid, 1975, 537–64
Riquer, M. de. 'Bavieca, caballo del Cid Campeador, y Bauçan, caballo de
    Guillaume d'Orange', *Boletín de la Real Academia de Buenas Letras de
    Barcelona*, 25 (1953), 127–44 (reprinted in his 1968 book, 227–47)
    Los cantares de gesta franceses, Madrid, 1962
    La leyenda del Graal y temas épicos medievales, Madrid, 1968
Rodríguez-Puértolas, J. 'El *Poema de mio Cid*': nueva épica y nueva
    propaganda', in *'Mio Cid' Studies*, ed. A. D. Deyermond, London,
    1977, 141–59
Rubio García, L. *Realidad y fantasía en el 'Poema de Mio Cid'*, Murcia, 1972
Russell, P. E. 'Some Problems of Diplomatic in the *Cantar de mio Cid* and
    their Implications', *Modern Language Review*, 47 (1952), 340–9 (trans-
    lated in his 1978 book, 15–33)
    'San Pedro de Cardeña and the Heroic History of the Cid', *Medium
    Aevum*, 27 (1958), 57–79 (translated in his 1978 book, 73–112)
    Temas de 'La Celestina' y otros estudios (del 'Cid' al 'Quijote'), Barcelona,
    1978
Rychner, J. *La Chanson de Geste. Essai sur l'art épique des jongleurs*, Geneva,
    1955
Salvador Miguel, N. 'Reflexiones sobre el episodio de Rachel y Vidas en
    el *Cantar de mio Cid'*, *Revista de Filología Española*, 59 (1977 [1979]),
    183–224
Sánchez-Albornoz, C. 'Sobre el autor de la llamada *Historia Silense'*,
    Cuadernos de Historia de España, 23–4 (1955), 307–16 (reprinted in his
    1967 book, 224–34)
    'El relato de Alfonso III sobre Covadonga' (first published 1957), in his
    1967 book, 161–202
    Investigaciones sobre historiografía hispana medieval, Buenos Aires, 1967
Sánchez Belda, L. (ed.) *Chronica Adefonsi Imperatoris*, Madrid, 1950
Sandoval, P. de. *Historia de los reyes . . .* , Pamplona, 1615
Schlyter, K. *Les Enumérations des personnages dans la 'Chanson de Roland'.
    Etude comparative*, Lund, 1974
Seniff, D. P. 'All the King's Men and All the King's Lands: The Nobility
    and Geography of the *Libro de la caza* and the *Libro de la montería'*, in
    La Chispa '81 (Selected Proceedings of the Second Louisiana Confer-
    ence on Hispanic Languages and Literatures), New Orleans, 1981,
    297–308
Serrano, L. *El obispado de Burgos y Castilla primitiva*, 3 vols., Madrid,
    1935–6
Serrano Castilla, F. 'El *Poema del Cid*, obra probable de algún monje
    benedictino', *Estudios*, 10 (1954), 67–71
Sholod, B. *Charlemagne in Spain: The Cultural Legacy of Roncesvalles*,
    Geneva, 1966

Siciliano, I. *Les Chansons de geste et l'épopée*, Turin, 1968
Smith, C. 'Sobre la musicalidad del *Polifemo*', *Revista de Filología Española*,
    44 (1961 [1963]), 139–66
Ramón Menéndez Pidal, 1869–1968, London, 1970 (Diamante, 19)
'The Personages of the *Poema de mio Cid* and the Date of the Poem',
    Modern Language Review, 66 (1971), 580–98 (translated as Chapter 2 of
    Estudios cidianos) [= 1971*a*]
'Latin Histories and Vernacular Epic in Twelfth-century Spain: Simi-
    larities of Spirit and Style', *Bulletin of Hispanic Studies*, 48 (1971), 1–19
    (translated as Chapter 4 of *Estudios cidianos*) [= 1971*b*]
(ed.) *Poema de mio Cid*, Oxford, 1972; Spanish version, Madrid, 1976
'Per Abbat and the *Poema de mio Cid*', *Medium Aevum*, 42 (1973), 1–17
    (translated as Chapter 1 of *Estudios cidianos*)
'Literary Sources of Two Episodes in the *Poema de mio Cid*', *Bulletin of
    Hispanic Studies*, 52 (1975), 109–22 (translated as Chapter 5 of *Estudios
    cidianos*)
'The Cid as Charlemagne in the **Leyenda de Cardeña*', *Romania*, 97
    (1976), 509–31 [= 1976*a*]
'On Sound-patterning in the *Poema de mio Cid*', *Hispanic Review*, 44
    (1976), 223–37 [= 1976*b*]
'On the Distinctiveness of the *Poema de mio Cid*', in *'Mio Cid' Studies*, ed.
    A. D. Deyermond, London, 1977, 161–94 (adapted and translated as
    Chapter 3 of *Estudios cidianos*) [= 1977*a*]
Estudios cidianos, Madrid, 1977 [= 1977*b*]
'Further French Analogues and Sources for the *Poema de mio Cid*', *La
    Corónica*, 6 (1977–8), 14–21
'La métrica del *Poema de mio Cid*: nuevas posibilidades', *Nueva Revista
    de Filología Hispánica*, 28 (1979), 30–56
'The Choice of the Infantes de Carrión as Villains in the *Poema de mio
    Cid*', *Journal of Hispanic Philology*, 4 (1980), 105–18 [= 1980*a*]
'Sobre la difusión del *Poema de mio Cid*', *Etudes . . . J. Horrent*, Liège,
    1980, 417–27 [= 1980*b*]
'The Diffusion of the Cid Cult: A Survey and a little-known Docu-
    ment', *Journal of Medieval History*, 6 (1980), 37–60 [= 1980*c*]
Review of Lacarra's 1980 book, in *Modern Language Review*, 76 (1981),
    716–19
'Epics and Chronicles: A Reply to Armistead', forthcoming in *Hispanic
    Review*
'Leyendas de Cardeña', forthcoming in *Boletín de la Real Academia de la
    Historia*
Spitzer, L. 'El sintagma *Valencia la bella*', *Revista de Filología Hispánica*, 7
    (1945), 259–76
'Sobre el carácter histórico del *Cantar de mio Cid*', *Nueva Revista de
    Filología Hispánica*, 2 (1948), 105–17 (reprinted in *Sobre antigua poesía
    española*, Buenos Aires, 1962, 9–25)
Strausser, M. J. 'Alliteration in the *Poema de mio Cid*', *Romance Notes*, 11
    (1969–70), 439–43
Such, P. T. 'The Origin and Use of School Rhetoric in the *Libro de
    Alexandre*', University of Cambridge Ph.D. dissertation, 1978

Ter Horst, R. 'The Meaning of Hypothesis in the *Poema de mio Cid'*, *Revista Hispánica Moderna*, 37 (1972–3), 217–28

Terlingen, J. 'Uso profano del lenguaje cultual cristiano en el *Poema de mio Cid'*, in *Estudios . . . Menéndez Pidal*, 7 vols., Madrid, 1950–62, IV, 265–94

Tilander, G. 'Fuentes jurídicas', in *Enciclopedia lingüística hispánica*, ed. M. Alvar and others, II, Madrid, 1967, 447–60

Ubieto Arteta, A. 'Observaciones al *Cantar de mio Cid'*, *Arbor*, 37 (1957), 145–70

(ed.) *Corónicas navarras*, Valencia, 1964

(ed.) *Crónica Najerense*, Valencia, 1966

'El *Cantar de mio Cid* y algunos problemas históricos', *Ligarzas*, 4 (1972), 5–192; also published as a book, Valencia, 1973

Vallecalle, J. C. 'Remarques sur l'emploi des machines dans quelques chansons de geste', in *Mélanges . . . P. Jonin*, Paris, 1979, 689–702; summarised in *Rencesvals*, 12 (1980), 65

Van Antwerp, M. '*Razón de amor* and the Popular Tradition', *Romance Philology*, 32 (1978–9), 1–17

Van Emden, W. 'Trial by Ordeal and Combat: The Deliquescence of a Motif', in *Essays for Peter Meyer*, Reading, 1980, 173–93

Vàrvaro, A. 'Dalla storia alla poesia epica: Alvar Fáñez', *Studi . . . S. Pellegrini*, Padua, 1971, 655–65

Walker, R. M. 'The Role of the King and the Poet's Intentions in the *Poema de mio Cid'*, *Medieval Hispanic Studies . . . R. Hamilton*, London, 1976, 257–66

'A Possible Source for the "Afrenta de Corpes" Episode in the *Poema de mio Cid'*, *Modern Language Review*, 72 (1977), 335–47

Walsh, J. K. 'Religious Motifs in the Early Spanish Epic', *Revista Hispánica Moderna*, 36 (1970–1), 165–72

'Epic Flaw and Final Combat in the *Poema de mio Cid'*, *La Corónica*, 5 (1976–7), 100–9

Waltman, F. M. 'Formulaic Expression and Unity of Authorship in the *Poema de mio Cid'*, *Hispania* (U.S.), 56 (1973), 569–78

West, G. R. 'History as Celebration: Castilian and Hispano-Latin Epics and Histories, 1080–1210 A.D.', University of London Ph.D. dissertation, 1975

Wilmotte, M. *L'Epopée française*, Paris, 1939

Windelberg, M. L. 'Theoretical Questions about Metrical Irregularities in the *Chanson de Roland'*, *Olifant*, 6 (1978–9), 6–19

Wright, R. 'The First Poem on the Cid – The *Carmen Campi Doctoris'*, *Arca*, 3 (1979), 213–48

'Spanish Verse, 600–1200', paper read to the Oxford Conference of the Association of Hispanists of Great Britain and Ireland, March 1981

Yepes, A. de. *Crónica general de la Orden de San Benito*, abridged in *Biblioteca de Autores Españoles*, vols. CXXIII–V (the original appeared in 7 vols., 1609–21)

Zahareas, A. 'The Cid's Legal Action at the Court of Toledo', *Romanic Review*, 55 (1964), 161–72

Index

255

Index